C000111723

THE CUNNING SECRET OF THE WISE

THE CUNNING SECRET OF THE WISE

A RESPONSE TO THE SPIRIT OF THE TIMES

FREDERICK BURNISTON

To order additional copies of this book, contact:
Xlibris
UK TFN: 0800 0148620 (Toll Free inside the UK)
UK Local: 02036 956328 (+44 20 3695 6328 from outside the UK)
www.Xlibrispublishing.co.uk
Orders@Xlibrispublishing.co.uk
819803

He is your mirror and you are His mirror in which He sees His Names and their determinations, which are none other than Himself.

(Ibn 'Arabi)

In individual emotional development the precursor of the mirror is the mother's face.

(D.W. Winnicott)

The Angel is the Face that our God takes for us, and each of us finds his God only when he recognizes that Face.

(Henry Corbin)

CONTENTS

PRIMA MATERIA

THEORIA

APPENDICES

ACKNOWLEDGEMENTS

This book has been a very long time in the making, and many of my formative influences have passed on in the meantime.

My first acknowledgement must go to Ninian Smart, the father of religious studies. Although I only studied under him for a year at the University of Lancaster, Ninian put me on the long road that led to this book. His amazing scholarship set the bar very high.

After Lancaster, I found my way by a circuitous route to the consulting room of Irene Champernowne. Mrs Champernowne had been part of the pre-war Jungian community in Zurich and had worked closely with C. G. Jung himself. Although I only had twelve extended analytic hours in 1975, they opened my eyes to the depths of the collective unconscious.

My second analyst was almost the antithesis of the first. Irene Champernowne was an ultraconservative Jungian; Giles Clark was iconoclastic by comparison. He led me up to the gates of the Underworld. Giles died in Australia in 2019, but the news of his death did not reach me until late 2020, when I had all but completed the last chapter of this book.

In 1984, I sent an essay I had written on Meister Eckhart to Kathleen Raine, a poet and Eranos scholar and the editor of an exciting new journal, *Temenos.* In her reply, Kathleen invited me to contribute a paper to the journal (now chapter 3 of this book). Her letter had the force of an enormous Yes that set the wheels in motion for *Cunning Secret of the Wise.*

It may seem strange that I should now pay tribute to a man who delivered a resounding No a few years later. He was a distinguished Islamic scholar and a practicing Sufi. But he regarded Jungian psychology as so much bogus spirituality. In the correspondence that followed our meeting in 1986, my adherence to Jung was put to a trial by fire. Martin Lings was unfailingly courteous even when dialogue became confrontation which it did very soon. (See: Ch.5: 3)

I have written this book without the benefit of a scholarly community. But "in the midst of the greatest obstructions, friends come." (Wilhelm I Ching, 39th hexagram, 9 at 5th) The friends who came were Andrew Rawlinson, whose support has been as rock solid as his criticism has been trenchant, and Gregory Lipton, whose book *Rethinking Ibn 'Arabi* resolved many of my impossible conflicting narratives about Frithjof Schuon. Friends also came from the Muslim community. My conversations with Samir Mahmoud, Abbas Zahedi, Rabia Malik and Sachi Arafat have contributed as much, if not more to this book than their distinguished predecessors.

Ann McCoy's painting *Hermaphroditus* is the very image of the cunning secret of the wise. My heartfelt thanks to her for permission to use it for the cover.

And heartfelt thanks go to Richard Webster who designed the cover and to Amrik Singh at Seaton Computers who came to my rescue more times than I can remember.

My wife Nada Kuzmanov has accompanied me through every twist and turn of this forty- year opus alchemicum. She's true like ice, like fire.

INTRODUCTION

In *Liber Novus* or *The Red Book*, Jung spoke of the conflict between the spirit of the times and the spirit of the depths. The first spirit is concerned exclusively with this quotidian world, and Jung confesses that he too thought in this way. But now he is impelled to give voice to the spirit of the depths "that from time immemorial and for all the future possesses a greater power than the spirit of this time." This spirit has taken away Jung's belief in science and placed him "at the service of the inexplicable and the paradoxical". (Jung 2009:119) Those who defy the spirit of the times and serve the spirit of the depths have submitted to a prophetic vocation.

Jung's descent into the Underworld after the break with Freud in 1912 was a dangerous venture. He risked ending up like his predecessor Nietzsche who had fallen into an irreversible psychosis. But how did he avoid this pitfall? How did he keep his balance on the tightrope? The alchemists, who had trodden this path long before him insisted on the necessity for a *theoria* or doctrine to provide a set of coordinates. Jung defined the alchemical *theoria* as "the quintessence of the symbolism of unconscious processes":

> It is the one solid possession from which the adept can proceed. He must find "the magnet of the wise" which will enable the adept to draw up the sparks of light (scintillae) embedded in the prima materia. For the prima materia always remains to be found, and the only thing that helps him is "the cunning secret of the wise," a theory that can be communicated. (CW. 9/2:219)

Without the doctrine it was impossible for the alchemist to proceed with the work in the laboratory, the *practica*. Jung formulated his own powerful *theoria* to bring order to the chaos that threatened to overwhelm him. In *Memories, Dreams, Reflections* he described the material that burst out from the unconscious psyche as "the prima materia for a lifetime's work". (MDR:225)

Morienus, who has provided the motto for this introduction, trod this path long before Jung. He was a Christian hermit and alchemist of the seventh century, who lived in the mountains near Jerusalem. Like Morienus, Jung knew that the prima materia is within ourselves.

In *Cunning Secret of the Wise,* I roam far and wide, from Nietzsche to Ibn 'Arabi. But I have one unifying objective, and this is to deepen the foundations and extend the range of Jung's *theoria* so to meet the challenges of the spirit of the times in its present manifestation. The theologian Langdon Gilkey characterized this spirit as "the secular mood." In *Naming the Whirlwind*, he unpacked this term:

> The modern spirit is thus radically this—worldly. We tend not to see our life and its meanings as stretching out towards an eternal order beyond our existence, or our fortunes as dependent on a transcendent ruler of time and history. We view our life as here, and our destiny as beginning with birth and ending with the grave, as confined in space and time to this world in nature and among men.

Nothing could be more contrary to the Christian doctrine of fallen man's total dependence on divine grace than the secular mood. In marked contrast to our forefathers, we pride ourselves on our self-reliance. Whatever meaning we can find in our short life depends entirely on our powers of intellect and will, "not on the grace and mercy of an ultimate heavenly sovereign." (Gilkey 1969:39) Such is the theoria of the spirit of the times.

In two books, *The Crisis of the Modern World* and *The Reign of Quantity and the Signs of the Times*, the metaphysician and esotericist Rene Guenon delivered an uncompromising critique of the secular mood. (Guenon 1962 and 1972) He rejected the very premises on which our post-Enlightenment culture is based and argued that only a civilization grounded in revealed truth was worthy of the name. Guenon and his successors (known as the Traditionalists) are implacably hostile to all forms of psychoanalysis. Their critique has served me well as a destruction test for Jung's *theoria*.

The order of the chapters is loosely chronological and the book can be read sequentially. But each chapter is self-contained which leaves the reader free to break into the text at any point. There are a few unavoidable repetitions and recurring quotations. *Cunning Secret* is divided into two parts and three sections: *Opus, Prima Materia,* and *Theoria.* In *Opus,* which takes up Part 1, I read and misread Jung from various perspectives (e.g., Platonist and Nietzschean). Part 2 consists of two chapters about the experiential background to this metaphysical odyssey (*Prima Materia*) followed by three on Ibn 'Arabi and Jung (*Theoria*). Ibn 'Arabi was a recondite thinker and, as I am not an Islamic scholar, I too found him exceptionally challenging. Why did I make the attempt? I believe that the visionary mysticism of Ibn 'Arabi is the bridge between Jung and the Islamic world. Someone had to do it.

Part 1

Opus

1. *How Deep Is the Ocean? A Brief Introduction to Jung's Theoria*

An introduction to some of Jung's key concepts: the collective unconscious, the archetypes, the conflict of opposites and its resolution, the compensatory function of dreams. This chapter has been written for readers who are new to Jung's psychology, but it might offer one or two insights to those who are not.

2. *Microcosmos: Mircea Eliade, Henry Corbin, and C.G. Jung at Eranos*

An exercise in contextualization: these three great Eranos scholars shared the same radical agenda: to reinstate the sense of cosmic sacrality that has all but disappeared from the modern world. Eliade did so through the phenomenology of archaic religions, Corbin through Sufism, and Jung through alchemy. All three swam against the current the secular mood.

3. *A Word Conceived in Intellect: Theoria and Practica in Sacred Art*

According to Philo of Alexandria, God is constantly creating and conferring being on the world through the divine Logos. The human artist does not merely mimic the external forms of nature but actively participates in the ever-creating Logos. Both the metaphysician Ananda

Coomaraswamy and the psychologist Jung view the creative process from this Platonic perspective.

4. *Pneuma and Psyche: Why Did Jung Offend the Gnostics?*

I am probably the only person in the Jungian community to engage in a dialogue with a leading Traditionalist. I met Islamic scholar Martin Lings face-to-face in 1986 and continued the conversation by letter. In this way, I could really engage with the Traditionalist narrative. Chapter 4 is a reply to a Traditionalist polemic against Jung by Dr. Ling's colleague Titus Burckhardt.

5. *The Guardians of Sacred Order*

Frithjof Schuon was the leading spokesman of the Traditionalist movement and Philip Rieff was one of the great Freud scholars. I must ask my Jungian friends to put aside all the beastly things they said about C.G. Jung and consider the work of each man on its own terms. Schuon, was implacably hostile to psychoanalysis in any form and Freud famously described himself as "a Godless Jew". But the extremes meet. The third section consists of an account of my meeting with Martin Lings. I was surprised to find myself talking face to face with Guenon's former secretary and he was dismayed to learn that I was a practicing Jungian.

6. *C.G. Jung, Rene Guenon and the Myth of the Primordial Tradition*

It is hardly surprising that Guenon was deeply hostile to Jung. Nothing could be more antithetical to his metaphysical perspective than Jung's Kant based empiricism. And yet on closer investigation the phenomenological correspondences between Guenon's myth of the Primordial State and Jung's myth of wholeness are undeniable. Needless to say, Martin Ling's response to this proposition was incredulous and scathing.

7. *Synchronicity: A Dionysian Perspective*

Nietzsche conceived his thought of eternal recurrence in a visionary experience "6,000 feet beyond man and time". Such experiences activate synchronistic events. In the preceding chapter, the idea of synchronicity is Platonic, Logo-centric, and Apollonian. This chapter is slightly different. Out goes Plato and in comes Nietzsche, Logos is dethroned for the anarchic rule of Eros, and synchronicity is the dancing star that comes out of the chaos. The shift of perspective has revealed a conceptual weakness in Jung's model of synchronicity. It lacks anything like Nietzsche's radical critique of causality.

8. *The Active Door: Nietzsche, Jung, and Suhravardi*

A comparison of two initiatory visions: One from Nietzsche's *Zarathustra: The Vision and the Riddle* and the other from the Sufi philosopher Suhravardi that is included in Henry Corbin's anthology *Spiritual Body and Celestial Earth*. (Corbin 1977) Nietzsche and Suhravardi passed through the Active Door, an opening into eternity that must be taken in the instant. I also give Nietzsche the opportunity to challenge Jung's questionable diagnosis of his condition.

9. *The Way Up and the Way Down Are One and the Same*

A quest for the stone that has spirit. I begin in the darkness of the somatic unconscious, work my way up through the instinctual level of the collective unconscious to the imaginal level and then to the spiritual unconscious. Jung's concept of synchronicity unifies all four levels.

Part 2

Prima Materia

10. *From Stanley Spencer's* Resurrection *to John Coltrane's* Ascension

Holy Trinity Church in the Berkshire village of Cookham is the setting of Spencer's visionary painting of the *Resurrection in Cookham Churchyard*. My connection to this church in my home village was severed when I was packed off to boarding school at fifteen. Before long my religious faith, such as it was, collapsed. A few years later I discovered John Coltrane's revelatory albums *A Love Supreme* and *Meditations*. His extraordinary music prepared the ground for an imaginal encounter with Sri Ramana Maharshi. This experience contained the seeds of my own *theoria*.

11. *Persona Non Grata*

After the truth of Yes, I reflect on the lie of No. In this chapter I delineate the archetype of the outcast. Can he ever extricate himself from his accursed fate?

Nietzsche and the 36ᵗʰ hexagram of the I Ching provide some useful strategies. In the second half I recount a dystopian dream journey that I once took to a world ruled by Nietzsche's last men. The news of the Death of God had not reached them or perhaps they just averted their gaze.

Theoria

12. *On Archetypes and Divine Names*

Metaphysical statements, according to Jung, arise out of numinous experiences and numinous experiences arise out of the collective unconscious. Ibn 'Arabi's Quranic metaphysics are overwhelming in their numinosity. This chapter explores three themes: the *imago Dei* as understood by Jung and Ibn 'Arabi, the Divine Names and the archetypes, and finally, a comparison between psychological individuation and Sufi spiritual practice.

13. *Opposition Is True Friendship: Jung, Ibn 'Arabi, and* Answer to Job

In a late letter to Erich Neumann, Jung wrote, "The question: *an creator sibi consciens est?* (Is the creator conscious?) is not a pet idea but an exceedingly painful experience with well-nigh incalculable consequences." (L2: 493) In *Answer to Job* Jung answered the question with an emphatic No. Ibn 'Arabi did so with an equally emphatic Yes. Neumann disagreed with Jung, and consequently, his model of the individuation process is much closer to the Shaykh. This chapter was inspired by Henry Corbin's long review of *Answer to Job, Eternal Sophia.*

14. *Respecting Confusing Treads*

In this final chapter, I will reflect on such themes as Unity of Being, Universal Man, and the distinction between spirit and soul from the standpoints of two great Ibn 'Arabi scholars: Titus Burckhardt and Toshihiko Izutsu. The book closes with a dialogue on Jung and Ibn 'Arabi between the author and Islamic scholar Samir Mahmoud.

OPUS

1

HOW DEEP IS THE OCEAN?

A brief introduction to Jung's theoria

Jung is the bridge between Darwin and God.
—Irene Champernowne

One autumn day, the French biologist Rene Quinton (1867–1925) discovered a hibernating snake and took it home. When it was in a warmer environment, the snake soon became lively and quite dangerous. Then Quinton came up with an intriguing hypothesis. Life, he conjectured, did not create the snake to be inert. So it must have appeared on earth at a time when the climate was much warmer, and it would have been active all year round. He went on to formulate a novel theory of evolution on the basis of this observation.

When life began in the oceans, the first species were in a state of total osmosis with their environment. As the earth cooled, the temperature of the ocean dropped, and the species had to adapt to the new conditions. Consequently, they lost some of their original vitality. But life refused this loss of vitality, and a new species evolved that was capable of maintaining its temperature at one degree above the temperature of the ocean. The ocean continued to cool down, and another species emerged that could maintain its temperature at two degrees above the ocean. And so it continued. As the ocean became colder and the salt levels increased, the new species maintained their temperature and salinity to the best level for life's optimal manifestation. The progressive development of the organism's inner environment compensated for what was lost in the outer. In this way, the species evolved. Darwin's model of evolution was based on mutation and adaptation, but Quinton proposed an evolutionary process based on dynamic equilibrium. (Network 1997:30-2)

The principle of evolutionary compensation informs Alfred Adler's theory of personality development. We all have our Achilles's heel, for example a weak, illness prone area of the body (organ inferiority), not to mention our weaknesses and vulnerabilities on the psychological level. Paradoxically, these weaknesses are a source of strength. Feelings of inferiority and the sense of disempowerment in relation to more powerful others are the spur to overcome or at least compensate for our deficiencies. Without these pressures, we would have no reason to get up in the morning.

Jung incorporated Adler's theory of compensation into his own model of psychospiritual development. The psyche is a self-regulating system, and consequently, any disturbance of its equilibrium calls forth a proportionate compensation. There is nothing mechanistic about this. "The psyche," says Jung, "does not merely react; it gives its own specific answer to the influences that work upon it." (CW4:665)

These answers are never definitive. The resolution of one conflict is the seed of another, a synthesis that in turn becomes the thesis for a new antithesis, which in turn generates a synthesis. Jung once illustrated this idea with a just-so story. A Stone Age man had a lovable but mischievous little boy. One day the child pushed his luck too far, and his impulsive father lashed out so hard that he killed the boy. In his grief-stricken remorse, the father was jolted out of his unconsciousness, and he took a small step towards self-awareness. The idea of dynamic equilibrium applies to the individual (ontogenesis) and to the species (phylogenesis).

Both Freud and Jung were the great exponents of a dynamic psychology. In psychoanalysis, vitality is libido or psychic energy. In Latin, libido means "I desire," and Freud famously equated libido with sexuality. As the word hunger denotes the drive behind the nutritional instinct, so does libido denote the dynamism behind our sexual instincts. But Jung found this definition restrictive and maintained that libido cannot be confined to sexuality alone. "We know far too little about the nature of human instincts and their psychic dynamism to risk giving priority to any one instinct," he argued. Much to Freud's dismay, Jung proposed that the libido concept should not be confined to sexuality. He redefined libido as an energy value that could find its outlet in any field of activity whatsoever: "hunger, hatred, sexuality or religion without itself being a specific instinct." (CW5:197)

This formulation, however, does not convey the dynamism of the libido. Here is a more evocative definition:

> The visible father of the world is, however, the sun, the heavenly fire; therefore Father, God, Sun, Fire are mythologically synonymous. The well-known fact that in the sun's strength the great generative power of nature is honoured shows plainly, very plainly . . . that in the Deity man honours his own libido . . . (Jung 1919:53-4)

Libido, in the Freudian sense, involves sexual fantasy as much as it involves sexual activity. Indeed, sexual activity without a background in fantasy is almost inconceivable. This universal truth is also applicable to all the other activities that are included in Jung's extended concept of libido: power, hunger, hatred, religion, etc. Everything we do has an imaginal background because "Fantasy as imaginative activity is identical with the flow of psychic energy." (Jung CW6: 722) Without libido, we would all be zombies. But even a zombie has a low level of libidinal life.

The libido is constantly producing fantasy images, and these images inform the unconscious background to everything we do, whether we are acting out our erotic fantasies or not. In sleep, the threshold of consciousness is lowered, and we engage in the flow of imaginative activity through our dreams. This dream process is going on all the time we are awake. But we are engaged in routine ego tasks and don't notice what is going on in the unconscious background. Without this constant flow of images, we would be at the mercy of raw libidinal drives—a truly terrifying prospect.

Our dreams and our fantasies may seem to be arbitrary, but as Freud discovered, they possess their own logic beneath the surface. This logic breaks down in psychosis, but mercifully, psychosis tends to be episodic, and eventually, order is restored. Jung postulated the archetype to account for the ordering principles behind the flow of fantasy images. Archetypes operate like instincts. Just as an instinct is a pattern of outer behaviour, so is an archetype a pattern of inner behaviour. In other words, an instinct is an innate disposition to act in a certain way, and the archetype is an innate disposition to form an image.

It is essential to keep in mind the distinction between an archetype as a disposition to form an image and the archetypal image thus formed. We only inherit the dispositions, not the images. Archetypal images are not pale shadows and carry a mighty libidinal charge. They have the potential to transform the conscious personality. We usually encounter these potencies in our dreams. For the most part, dreams are cluttered with fragments of the day's residues or more distant memories. This stuff is pretty banal and will have been conscious to the dreamer at some time if only fleetingly. By contrast, archetypal images do not originate in the day world. They are constituted in the deepest levels of the unconscious psyche *and, therefore, will not have been previously conscious to the dreamer.* Such an image is not the product of a waking experience but an autonomous creation of the archetype. In other words, it is the psyche's own specific response to whatever influence has worked upon it.

Dream events that are specific to the dreamer belong to *the personal unconscious.* This layer consists of everything that has been forgotten or repressed since early infancy. Archetypal images originate in the pre-infantile psyche, which is common to all mankind. Jung designated this layer as *the collective unconscious.* The contents of the collective unconscious have changed very little over time. An archetypal image dreamt by your ancestor a millennia ago could be structurally identical with such an image in one of your dreams or mine. Time, as we know it, does not exist in the realm of the archetypes.

The great Sufi shaykh Ibn 'Arabi (1165–1240) had the following dream:

> One night I saw myself united in marriage to all the stars of heaven, and I was married to each and every one with a most extraordinary spiritual joy. After I had been united to the stars, I was then given the letters of the alphabet and was united in marriage to all of them, as individual letters and as joined to others . . .

A friend of Ibn 'Arabi took the dream to an interpreter who declared,

> This is the limitless ocean—the one who has had this dream shall have revealed to him knowledge of the highest things, of the mysteries and special properties of the stars and the letters, which will be granted to no one else in this time. (Hirtenstein 1999:144)

The cosmic images in this dream came out of the limitless ocean of the collective unconscious. They have nothing to do with Ibn 'Arabi's personal situation at the time and cannot be understood in these terms. Indeed, the dream interpreter was not even told whose dream he was looking at.

Ibn 'Arabi dreamt he was married to the stars. The archetypal potential of the dream, its emotional power, is located in this motif rather than in the image of the night sky, sublime though it is. Archetypes do not only manifest themselves in isolated images but also in dynamic processes such as conjunction or conflict. (Freud's Oedipus complex was the first archetype.) Perhaps it would be more accurate to define as archetype a disposition to form an imaginal narrative. Of course, the richest source of such narratives is mythology. This is nothing less than the repository of all the archetypes.

The opposites are the ineradicable and indispensable preconditions for all psychic life. (CW14:206)

The principle of opposition informs almost everything Jung wrote from *Psychological Types* (1921) to *Mysterium Coniunctionis: An Inquiry into the Separation and Synthesis of Psychic Opposites* (1955/6). Without polarity, there would be no psychophysical development.

"Heaven lies about us in our infancy," says Wordsworth in his *Ode: Intimations of Immortality from Recollections of Early Childhood.* The newborn child has no centre of consciousness or ego and, consequently, no unconscious psyche as such; it is contained in the paradise of indivisible oneness. This condition is symbolized by the uroboros serpent with its tail in its mouth. In *The Origins and History of Consciousness*, Erich Neumann describes the inevitable splitting of the uroboros when the infant becomes aware of existing separately from its mother. The moment of division is the moment of creation that initiates all subsequent stages of psychogenesis:

> The world begins only with the coming of light which constellates the opposition between heaven and earth as the basic symbol of all opposites. Before that there reigns "the illimitable darkness . . . With the rising of the sun or—in the language of ancient Egypt—the creation of the firmament, which divides the upper from the lower, mankind's day begins and the universe becomes visible with all its content." (Neumann 1954:106-7)

Cosmogonic myths narrate the moment when our earliest ancestors emerged out of unconscious bondage to instinct and first saw the world as existing apart from themselves. Each one of us recapitulates this moment in our infancy. We emerge like Adam and Eve after they had eaten the forbidden fruit and discovered they were ashamed of their nakedness. In the Liturgy of Easter Eve, our fall from paradise is said to be the felix culpa, a happy Fall, because there would have been no redemption if our first parents had not sinned.

"Shades of the prison house begin to close upon the growing boy," says Wordsworth in the *Ode*. The ego is both our emancipation and our prison. But the fall is not irrevocable. In the Christian myth, Christ Jesus is the second Adam. St. Paul encapsulated this myth in two unforgettable sentences:

> For as by a man came death, by a man has come also the resurrection of the dead. For as in Adam all die, so also in Christ all shall be made alive. (1 Corinthians 15:21-2)

It has to be like this: Without the Fall, there would be no redemption; and without redemption, there would only be a regression to a pre-biographical paradise.

Jung entered upon his initiatory ordeal after his catastrophic break with Freud in 1913. His ego defenses collapsed, he dropped into the Underworld of the collective unconscious, and he only emerged around 1919. In that year, he dreamt he was in Liverpool. The city was dark, and of course, it was raining, but then he came upon a magnolia tree standing in an island of sunlight. He described this visionary dream as "an act of grace." (MDR:223-4)

The dream is a private myth, and the myth is a public dream.

A colleague who knew Jung well once remarked that during the confrontation with the unconscious, he was the asylum and the chief psychiatrist in one. So how did he come through in one piece? Why wasn't he torn apart by the conflict and thrown to the lions like his psychotic patients? And why do psychotic patients usually return to normal ego - consciousness?

The human psyche is protected by an inbuilt homeostasis or, as Jung puts it, *the unconscious psyche exists in a compensatory relationship to the conscious psyche.* Dreams, slips of the tongue, and accidents of fate are the agents of this compensatory mechanism. By these means, nature heals our divisions or restores lost equilibrium. There is something verging on the miraculous in the psyche's capacity to reconstitute itself. Contrary to Freud, Jung maintained that our dreams do not present a false facade but mean what they say. If we find a dream incomprehensible, it is because we do not understand the language that the unconscious psyche is using. There is no intention to deceive; the unconscious is simply compensating for the deviations of the ego through the medium of the dream. Here are two relatively uncomplicated examples:

- A young man dreams of jumping his horse over a ditch full of water, while the rest of the party fall into the ditch.
- An ambitious professor dreams that he has returned to his home village. His former classmates and the locals remark that he does not visit them anymore.

In the first case, the young man was lacking in confidence. He was capable of more than he believed he could achieve. The dream is encouraging him to be more ambitious. But the opposite applies to the professor who needs to be reminded of his humble origins.

In situations of crisis or at crucial points of psychological development, the unconscious will speak directly to consciousness. These are the big dreams, and they do not merely compensate for a one-off deviation on the part of the dreamer's ego. The imagery is always archetypal and consequently it can transform the entire personality. One of Jung's patients, a Protestant theologian, had a rather disconcerting dream:

> He stood on a mountain slope with deep valley below, and in it a dark lake. He knew in the dream that something had always prevented him from

approaching the lake. This time he resolved to go to the water. As he approached the shore everything, everything grew dark and uncanny and a gust of wind suddenly rushed over the face of the water. He was seized by a panic fear and awoke.

This dream is reminiscent of Genesis 1:2

And the earth was without form and void: and darkness was on the face of the deep. And the Spirit of God moved on the face of the waters.

Here is what Jung has to say about the Spirit:

The dreamer descends into his own depths, and the way leads him to the mysterious water. And now there occurs the miracle of the pool of Bethesda: an angel comes down and touches the water, endowing it with healing power. In the dream it is the wind, the pneuma that bloweth where it listeth. Man's descent to the water is needed in order to evoke the miracle of its coming to life. But the breath of the spirit rushing over the dark water is uncanny, like everything whose cause we do not know—since it is not ourselves. It hints at an unseen presence, a numen, to which neither human expectations nor the machinations of the will have given life. It lives of itself, and a shudder runs through the man who thought that the spirit is merely what he believes, what he makes himself, what is said in books or what people talk about. (CW9/1:34-5)

This is a numinous dream. The great theologian Rudolf Otto coined this term to denote the unique feeling tone of religious experience. Just as the omen can be used as an adjective (ominous), so can the numen be made into the adjective: numinous. The experience of the numen is an encounter with the Spirit, the "Wholly

Other," which we do not know because it is not of this world. Naturally, this experience gives rise to a deep and conflicted ambivalence—primal fear and primal fascination in equal measure. (Otto 1958) No wonder the theologian woke in terror: "He wanted nothing of it, for such things are met with only in the Bible, or at most on Sunday mornings as the subject of sermons, and have nothing to do with psychology. All very well to speak of the Holy Ghost on occasions—but it is not a phenomenon to be experienced!" (MDR:163- 4)

Jung once said that the experience of the numinous was the real therapy. Some people take this to mean that Jungian psychology is some kind of religion. Indeed, according to Richard Noll, Jung was a charismatic cult leader, an Aryan Christ, operating under a cloak of scientific neutrality. (See Noll 1994, 1997) But in a 1945 letter, Jung makes his position very clear:

> If you have formed the peculiar notion that I am proclaiming a religion, this is due to your ignorance of psychotherapeutic methods. When for instance, the heart no longer functions as it always functioned it is sick, and the same goes for the psyche, whose functioning depends on archetypes. The doctor sees to it that the heart gets into its old rhythm again and the psychotherapist must restore the "original pattern," the original way the psyche reacts. This is done today, as several thousands of years ago, through the "anamnesis" of the archetype. I can't help it if religions also work with archetypes. (L1:361)

A dream, said Joseph Campbell, is a private myth, and a myth is a public dream. Both dreams and myths have a common source in the collective unconscious. This is why the big dreams contain mythological motifs, which are often unknown to the dreamer. The material arises from the unconscious depths to compensate for any disruption of psychic equilibrium. Religious traditions are institutionalized forms of the public dream. But it looks like the era of the great religious traditions is over now. The wind no longer disturbs the waters. As Nietzsche said, "God is dead."

Or is something going on in the unconscious background that could compensate for our traumatic loss of religious certainty? I will conclude with two lengthy quotations from Jung; first, a prophetic utterance from *The Undiscovered Self*:

> We are living in what the Greeks called the kairos - the right moment for a "metamorphosis of the gods", of the fundamental principles and symbols. This peculiarity of our time, which is certainly not of our conscious choosing, is the expression of the unconscious man within us who is changing. Coming generations will have to take account of this momentous transformation if humanity is not to destroy itself through the might of its technology and science. (CW10:585)

Who is the unconscious man within us? This brings me to the second passage from Jung's essay *Analytical Psychology and Weltanschauung*[1]:

> The collective unconscious is in no sense an obscure corner of the mind, but the mighty deposit of ancestral experience accumulated over millions of years, the echo of prehistoric happenings to which each century adds an infinitesimally small amount of variation and differentiation. Because the collective unconscious is, in the last analysis, a deposit of world processes embedded

---

[1]   Weltanschaaung means world view.

in the structure of the brain and sympathetic nervous system, it constitutes in its totality a sort of timeless and eternal world image which counterbalances our conscious momentary picture of the world. It means nothing less than another world if you will. But unlike a mirror image, the unconscious image possesses an energy peculiar to itself, independent of consciousness. By virtue of this energy it can produce powerful effects which do not appear on the surface but influence us all the more powerfully from within. (CW8:729)

We should not get too carried away by Jung's prophetic rhetoric in the previous passage from *The Undiscovered Self.* If our momentary picture of the world is so unbalanced as to be leading us to the point of mass self-destruction, is it any wonder that the million-year-old man within us is having his reaction?

2

MICROCOSMOS

Mircea Eliade, Henry Corbin and C.G. Jung at Eranos

In *The Quest, History and Meaning in Religion* Mircea Eliade proposed that the phenomenology of religious symbolism could be pursued as a kind of spiritual discipline in its own right:

> A considerable enrichment of consciousness results from the hermeneutical effort of deciphering the meaning of myths, symbols and other traditional religious structures; in a certain sense one can even speak of the inner transformation of the researcher and hopefully of the sympathetic reader. What is called the phenomenology and history of religions can be considered among the very few humanistic disciplines that are at the same time propaedeutic and spiritual technique. (Eliade 1969 - cited in the Preface)

The Conferences at Casa Eranos in Ascona (1933-1987) were established to promote this enriched consciousness. They were aptly described as "a gigantic symposium on symbolism." (Wasserstrom 1999:85) Eliade was a key participant as was Henry Corbin and C. G. Jung. To illustrate how these three scholars deciphered the symbols and transformed the consciousness of their readers, I will focus on one particularly potent archetypal motif: the image of man as a microcosm. Eliade approached this symbol through the religious experience of archaic man, Corbin through Iranian Islam, and Jung through alchemy. Each of them conveys a vivid impression of what it is like to be a microcosm or second little world contained in the vastness of the macrocosm. All three believed that it is possible to regain the sense of cosmic sacrality through a spiritual discipline of the imagination or "active imagination." The implications of this proposal are little short of revolutionary.

The Sense of Cosmic Sacrality

There is only one way to understand the symbolic universe of archaic man, and that is "to place oneself inside it, at its very centre, in order to progress from there to all the values that it possesses." (Eliade 1959:165) Eliade's phenomenology gives us the view from the centre. Archaic man's world is "not an opaque mass of objects arbitrarily thrown together but "a living cosmos, articulated and meaningful." (Eliade1963:141) It exists because it was created by the gods, and consequently, every aspect of this totality is an epiphany. As Eliade puts it, the world reveals itself or rather speaks to religious man:

> For religious man the cosmos lives and speaks.
> The mere life of the cosmos is proof of its sanctity,

since the cosmos was created by the gods and the
gods show themselves to man through cosmic life.
(Eliade 1959:143)

When the world speaks to man "through its heavenly
bodies, its plants and animals, its rivers and rocks, its
seasons and nights, he answers it by his dreams and
imaginative life." His myths and symbols enable him
to respond in a coherent way and to participate in the
sanctity of the cosmos. He is at the centre of creation, a
microcosm "who finds in himself the same sanctity he
recognizes in the cosmos." (Eliade 1959:165)

According to Eliade, archaic man is an instinctive
Platonist, and conversely, Plato was the outstanding
philosopher of primitive mentality. Objects and actions
are real for him insofar as they participate in their
celestial archetypes. (Eliade 1971:34) This Platonic
continuity was ruptured during the late Middle Ages,
when the unity of man, cosmos, and transcendence
broke down. According to the historian of religion Louis
Dupre, Nominalist philosophers in the fourteenth and
fifteenth centuries placed so much emphasis on divine
omnipotence that they removed God from creation
and left a rift between the realms of grace and nature.
As the sense of cosmic sacrality receded, nature was
reduced to an object, and gradually, the human subject
became the sole source of meaning. (Dupre 1993:3)
Although these developments brought an unprecedented
increase of self-consciousness and self-determination,
man was thrown back on himself, and he became
confined to the immanence of the historical moment.

Western theology never found a way to regain a
unified world picture, and by the seventeenth century,
the rise of the mechanistic perspective set the seal

on the process of disenchantment. Yet Eliade, ever the optimist, maintains these developments are not necessarily irreversible. The history of religions demonstrates how all religious values are continually lost and regained throughout the millennia. Nothing is ever irrevocable. (Eliade 1958:464-5) According to Eliade, the phenomenology of religion has a major role to play in the restoration of the sacred in our secular, post-Renaissance culture. How does this approach work in practice? Eliade asks us to consider the correspondences between "house-body-cosmos" that is common to many archaic cultures:

> Man inhabits the body in the same way that he inhabits a house or the cosmos that he himself created. Every lawful and permanent situation implies a location in a cosmos, in a universe perfectly organized and hence imitated from the paradigmatic model, the Creation. Inhabited territory, temple, house, body are all . . . cosmoses. (Eliade 1959:176-7)

By stark contrast, "modern man's habitation has lost its cosmological values and his body is without religious or spiritual significance." But what would happen if he were to regain an understanding of the body/cosmos correspondences with the aid of a transformative phenomenology of religion? The consequences would be incalculable:

> By regaining awareness of his anthropocosmic symbolism . . . modern man will obtain a new existential dimension totally unknown to present day existentialism and historicism: this is an authentic and major mode of being, which defends man from nihilism and historical relativism without thereby taking him out of history. (Eliade 1961:36)

This passage comes from an important essay on *The Symbolism of the Centre.* In anticipation of those who regard such assertions as utopian and naïve, Eliade points out that authentic existence cannot be confined to the consciousness of its own historicity. The universal experiences of love, anxiety, joy, melancholy, etc. each have their own specific temporal rhythm "and all combine to constitute what might be called the integral man, who neither denies himself his historic moment, nor consents to be identified with it." (Eliade 1961:171-2, n.13) In other words, the rediscovery of the body as microcosm is not a retrograde step into magical thinking. The new existential dimension is the place of the integral man who regains the sense of cosmic centrality without renouncing his consciousness of or responsibility towards his situation in history.

A World in Which Spirits Are Corporealized and Bodies Spiritualized

Henry Corbin has some interesting things to say about the breakdown of the axis between man, cosmos, and transcendence from his vantage point as an Islamic scholar. The Neoplatonist cosmology of Avicenna (Ibn Sina, d. 1037) is based upon a hierarchy of ten Archangels or separate Intelligences that proceed from the One Necessary Being. With the exception of the tenth and last Intelligence, each one of the other nine emanates a celestial soul and a corresponding celestial sphere. These spheres are suprasensible and correspond to the nine heavens of traditional Islamic astronomy:

> Each heaven and its Soul both emanate from the thought of their Angel; the heaven is thus interior, immanent to the Soul that moves it by its ardent desire; rather than the Soul being in the heaven,

> it is the heaven that is in the Soul, as it can be in
> an Angel brought into being by another Angel.
> While the terrestrial clime is external to the human
> soul and common to the multitude of souls, each
> heaven is proper to each celestial Soul and perfectly
> individuated to it. (Corbin 1988: 335, n.11)

Every celestial Soul yearns for the Intelligence from which it proceeds, and in doing so moves its sphere in its orbit: "The cosmic revolutions, in which all motion originates, are thus the aspiration of love that remains forever unassuaged." (Corbin 1993:171)

Avicenna's cosmological vision was demythologized by Averroes (Ibn Rushd, d. 1198) who rejected the doctrine of a successive emanation of the Intelligences from the One and the subsequent emanation of the celestial Souls from the Intelligences. There was neither creation nor emanation, only simultaneity in the eternal beginning. Although the hierarchy of the Intelligences and the spheres is left intact, the celestial Souls that move the spheres have been eliminated. Averroes regarded the notion that the Soul moves its sphere through its perpetual yearning for the Intelligence that generated it as a mere metaphor. It was no metaphor for Avicenna. The Souls are a reality and, being free from the infirmities of the sensory faculties, possess imagination in its purest form. They are, says Corbin, "the Angels of the intermediate world where prophetic inspiration and theophanic visions have their place." (Corbin 1969:11). When the Western scholastic establishment endorsed Averroe's Aristotlelian cosmology, they severed the continuity between the celestial soul and its Angel. This, Corbin maintained, was a metaphysical catastrophe. All mediation between the human soul and its Angel was abolished and the angelic hierarchy became impersonal and remote. "The

twofold notion of celestial Angel Souls and terrestrial—
that is virtual—angel-souls establishes, as its absence
invalidates, the idea of angel pedagogy." (Corbin 1988:
68) The individual soul was deprived of its guardian
Angel and thrown back on itself.

Like Eliade, Corbin believed passionately in the
transformative power of religious hermeneutics. His
approach is based on two complementary terms,
derived from Shi'ite Islam: t'awil, which means to cause
to return, and t'anzil, which means to cause to descend.
Whereas t'anzil applies to the descent of the Quranic
revelation to the Prophet, t'awil proceeds in the reverse
direction, from the manifest to the hidden reality,
from the symbol to its archetype. It penetrates beneath
the literal content of a sacred text to the underlying
spiritual sense. T'awil is not a disembodied intellectual
exercise because "it brings to play the Soul's most secret
sources of energy." (Corbin 1988:28) These sources
of energy will only become operative if salvation is
at stake. The work of t'awil delivers the soul from its
exile in the quotidian world and makes an exegesis an
exodus, a return to the perfection of origins. The t'awil
of a sacred text is the t'awil of the soul.

Corbin's scholarship covered a vast field: Sufism,
Shi'ism, Ishmailism, and also Iran's pre-Islamic
traditions. The ancient Zoroastrian myth was based on
a division of the cosmic totality into "an infinite height
of Light which dwells for all eternity, Ohrmazd, the Lord
of Wisdom, and an unfathomable abyss of Darkness that
conceals the counterpart of negation, disintegration and
death, Ahriman." (Corbin 1977:6) These two powers are
utterly irreconcilable, and the battle between them will
continue until the close of the aeon, when the demonic
counter-powers will be cast into the abyss. However,

Mazdaism is not Platonism. The domain of light is not equated with the spiritual world, nor is the world of darkness equated with a separate material world. There is subtle matter (*menok*), and there is dense matter (*getik*). This ancient tradition does not recognise a distinction between ideas and matter.

Iranian Islamic cosmology takes a Platonist turn: There is now the sensory world, an intermediate world of the celestial angels that move the spheres; and there is the intelligible world, which is the realm of the Cherubic Intelligences. Each of these three levels is apprehended through a distinctive mode of knowing:

> 1.The sensory world is apprehended by the hylic or material intellect whose operation requires a sharp polarization between subject and object. The world is experienced as being external to consciousness on this level.

> 2. In the intermediate world the subject-object relation has a paradoxical form. The Active Imagination is independent of the physiological faculties and belongs to the subtle body. Objects are constituted in consciousness as they are on the level of ordinary imagination but are also autonomous as they are on the level of sensory perception

> 3. Knowledge of the intelligible world is attained by the perfect Sage. On this level, the subject-object relationship is transcended, and the adept "becomes a copy, an exemplar in which all the universes of being are inscribed; he becomes an intelligible universe in himself." (Corbin 1988:252)

The theosophists of Islam call this intermediate world *alam al mithal*, a term that presents a dilemma to the translator. If he uses the word "imaginary" for this world, it implies fantasy or make-believe. Corbin coined the word "imaginal" to avoid this unfortunate connotation. The *mundus imaginalis* is the place where visionary experiences occur:

> We are not dealing here with irreality. The *mundus imaginalis* is a world of autonomous forms and images. It is a perfectly real world preserving all the richness and diversity of the sensible world but in a spiritual state. (Corbin 1966:406-7)

Unlike the sensory world, where subject and object are split in two, "consciousness and its object are ontologically inseparable" in the *mundus imaginalis* (Corbin 1995:15). Whereas acts of imagination in the sensory world are private and subjective, imaginal consciousness is not "in me," and it has cognitive value within its own world.

Corbin has uncovered many correspondences between Iranian Sufism and the visionary theology of Emanuel Swedenborg (1688-1772): "One cannot but be struck," he remarked, "by the concordance or convergence of statements by the great Swedish visionary with those of Sohravardi, Ibn Arabi or Sadra Shirazi." (Corbin 1995:13) These affinities extend to Zen Buddhism. D.T. Suzuki, the spokesman for Zen in the West, was an Eranos scholar and he had translated four works of Swedenborg into Japanese. In a Round table discussion Henry Corbin asked him how he understood the teachings of the Buddha of the North. The Zen master picked up a spoon and said, "This spoon now exists in Paradise . . . We are now in Paradise." (Corbin 1969:354-5, n.41)

Muhsin Fayz was a seventeenth-century Iranian theosophist and poet who had studied under Mulla Sadra. He would have understood Suzuki's demonstration immediately. In his *Sayings Kept Secret*, he wrote,

> There is no existent thing, whether in the intelligible world or in the sensory world, whose image is not recorded in the intermediate universe. This universe in the macrocosm is homologous to the active Imagination in the human microcosm. (cited in Corbin 1977:176)

The starry heavens of the sensory world have a corresponding heaven in the *mundus imaginalis*. This is *Hurqalya*. According to the Iranian theosophists, *Hurqalya* possesses its own earth. The celestial earth of *Hurqalya* is constituted by the Active Imagination of the adept and also provides the adept with the subtle element he needs for his own body of resurrection. As Muhsin Fayz puts it, "This is a world in which Spirits are corporealized and bodies are spiritualized." The Active Imagination is an alchemical opus that participates in the creation of a new heaven and a new earth.

Understand You are a Second Little World

In his path breaking essay *Towards an Archetypal Imagination*, Edward Casey makes a distinction between active imagination and archetypal or visionary imagination. (Casey 1991:3-28). Active imagination is a highly effective technique of therapy devised by C.G. Jung. Archetypal imagination is a spiritual discipline in its own right. The voluminous writings of Ibn 'Arabi are, for example a sustained work of visionary imagination. But this is not a hard and fast distinction. Active imagination can result in an experience of transcendence and archetypal imagination can have therapeutic benefits.

While he was a medical student in the 1890s, Jung read all the books he could lay his hands on about Spiritualism and the paranormal, including seven volumes of Swedenborg. These works would serve him well after the catastrophic break with Freud in 1913. It was then that he followed in Swedenborg's footsteps and ventured into the intermediate world. He has left an account of his journey in chapter 6 of *Memories, Dreams, Reflections: Confrontation with the Unconscious.* His entry into this world was by way of a descent rather than an ascent:

> In order to seize hold of these fantasies, I frequently imagined a steep descent. I even made several attempts to get to the very bottom. The first time I reached, as it were, a depth of about a thousand feet; the next time I felt myself at the edge of a cosmic abyss . . . I had the feeling I was in the land of the dead. The atmosphere was that of another world. Near a steep slope of rock I caught sight of two figures, an old man with a white beard and a beautiful young girl. I summoned up my courage and approached them as though they were real people and listened attentively to what they told me. The old man explained he was Elijah and that gave me a shock. But the girl staggered me even more, for she called herself Salome! She was blind. What a strange couple Elijah and Salome. But Elijah assured me that he and Salome had belonged together from all eternity, which completely astounded me . . . Of Salome I was distinctly suspicious. Elijah and I had a long conversation which, however, I did not understand. (MDR:205-6)

When Jung entered into dialogue with Elijah, he was following Swedenborg's example. The volumes he read as a student may well have taught him the protocols of the *mundus imaginalis.*

Origen's proposition that man is a second little world containing the sun, moon, and the stars within himself anticipates Swedenborg's doctrine of correspondences. This mythopoetic idea expresses a profound psychological truth. The microcosm was once projected onto the body just as the alchemists projected their own unconscious contents onto chemical substances. But said Jung, "It is altogether different when the microcosm is understood as that interior world whose inward nature is fleetingly glimpsed in the unconscious." He continues,

> And just as the cosmos is not a dissolving mass of particles but rests in the unity of God's embrace, so man must not dissolve into a whirl of warring possibilities and tendencies imposed on him by the unconscious but must become a unity embracing them all. (CW16: 397)

The individual who becomes an all-embracing unity is the integral man that Eliade speaks of in connection with the new existential dimension. His mode of being is characterized by openness to the world, not solipsism. In a short essay, "On Resurrection," Jung spelt out exactly what this openness to the world meant:

> The realization of the self means a re-establishment of Man as microcosm, i.e., man's cosmic relatedness. Such experiences are frequently accompanied by synchronistic events.

(The prophetic experience of vocation belongs to this category. (CW18:1573)

In Jung's psychology, the term "self" always denotes the totality of psychic processes, unconscious and conscious, and the term "ego" refers exclusively to the conscious personality. The self is a supraordinate numinous totality that transcends and includes the ego.

The self, said Jung, "as its symbolism proves, embraces the bodily sphere as well as the psychic." (CW14: 717) In his essay on *The Psychology of the Child Archetype*, Jung describes the interrelatedness of the psyche, the body, and the world like this:

> The deeper "layers" of the psyche lose their individual uniqueness as they retreat farther and farther into darkness. "Lower down" that is to say as they approach the autonomous functional systems they become increasingly collective until they are universalized and extinguished in the body's materiality, i.e. in chemical substances. The body's carbon is simply carbon. Hence at bottom the psyche is simply world. (CW9/1:291)

As the layers of the psyche recede towards the nadir and merge with matter, space and time become increasingly relativized. Jung designates this intermediate zone as quasi-psychic or psychoid. If we look towards the apex, the *mundus imaginalis* opens out as a hierarchy of lights. Time and space are relativized in the opposite direction.

There is, according to Jung, a paradoxical relationship between the lowest degree of darkness and the highest degree of light. For example, the serpent is chthonic and at the same time the most spiritual of creatures. In the symbolism of the alchemical vessel or rotundum, the Original Man and the atom are identical:

> The round Hermetic vessel in which the mysterious transformation is accomplished is God himself, the Platonic world soul and man's own wholeness. It is therefore another counterpart of the Anthropos and at the same time the universe in its smallest most material form. (CW9/2:380)

This paradoxical relationship between the heavy darkness of the earth and the Platonic World Soul converts the vertical hierarchy into a circle—a uroboric serpent with its tail in its mouth.

The *coincidentia oppositorum* is also central to Eliade's interpretation of archaic mythologies, shamanic, and yogic practices:

> From a certain point of view one may say that many beliefs implying a coincidentia oppositorum reveal a nostalgia for Paradise, a nostalgia for a paradoxical state in which the contraries exist side by side without conflict and the multiplications form aspects of a mysterious unity. (Eliade 1962:122)

Corbin seems to be a dissenting voice. While he has no problem with a *coincidentia oppositorum* between matter and spirit (after all, the *mundus imaginalis* is the realm of spiritual matter), he rejects a *coincidentia* between light and darkness or good and evil:

> To deplore that Christianity is centered on a figure of goodness and light and entirely overlooks the

dark side of the soul would be no less valid an evaluation if applied to Zoroastrianism. But how could reintegration consist in a complicity between a "totalization" of Christ and Satan, Ohrmazd and Ahriman? (Corbin 1978:47)

These figures, Corbin maintains, are not complementary but contradictory opposites: "Complementary elements can be integrated but not contradictory ones." In Corbin's myth of ascent, the Gnostic does not carry his shadow into *Hurqalya*; he discards it.

For Eliade, the image of man as the microcosm points back to our primordial wholeness and forward to our eschatological perfection. It is the door to the new existential dimension "which defends man from nihilism and historical relativism without thereby taking him out of history." But what does this mean? Eliade does not hide his light under a bushel:

For history will one day be able to find its true meaning: that of the epiphany of a glorious and absolute human condition. We have only to recall the value attached to history by Judaeo-Christianity to realize how and in what sense history might become "glorious" and even "absolute." (Eliade 1961:36)

According to Jung, wholeness is not perfection because it must necessarily include imperfection. Light and shadow paradoxically coexist in the wholeness of man and cannot be split apart:

The Christ image is as good as perfect (at least it was meant to be so), while the archetype (so far as known) denotes completeness but is far from being perfect. It is a paradox, a statement about something indescribable and transcendental. Accordingly the realization of the self, which would logically follow from the recognition of its supremacy, leads to a fundamental conflict, to a suspension between opposites (reminiscent of the crucified Christ between two thieves), and to an approximate state of wholeness that lacks perfection. (CW9/2:123)

Unlike Corbin and Eliade, Jung viewed eschatologies of perfection with suspicion. I will return to this divergence in chapter 8.

3

A WORD CONCEIVED IN INTELLECT

Theoria and Practica in Sacred Art

The Ever-Creating Logos

In his revelatory essay, "Consequences Flowing from the Mystery of Our Subjectivity," Frithjof Schuon suggested that if we could only awaken to "the miracle that is intelligence," we would see that we are, indeed, made in the image of God. (Schuon 1982: 5-12) At the core of our subjectivity, there is a faculty that allows us to participate directly in divine knowledge; this is the Intellect. Human reason, which is wholly valid on its level, is a distant reflection of the Universal Intellect. According to Meister Eckhart, this faculty is "uncreated and uncreatable":

> There is a power in the soul that touches neither time nor flesh, flowing from the spirit, remaining in the spirit, altogether spiritual. In this power God

> is ever verdant and flowering in all the joy and all
> the glory that he is in himself. (Eckhart 1979:74)

This power in the soul finds creative expression in the Practical Intellect, which, says Ananda Coomaraswamy[2], is "an extension of the Universal Intellect by which all natural things are made." As Aquinas succinctly put it, "The artist works by a word conceived in Intellect and through the direction of his will towards the object to be made." (*Summa Theologica* - cited in Coomaraswamy 1977: 228). This proposition encapsulates Coomaraswamy's entire philosophy of art. This philosophy in turn had its source in Philo of Alexandria (20BC-40AD).

Philo read the Bible from a Platonist perspective. For example, he thought that the passage in Genesis: "Let us make Man in our image" applied to the human mind rather than the body. In other words, the human mind is made after the pattern of the divine mind. Thanks to the miracle of our intelligence, we have the capacity to conceive of the absolute and transcend the world of the senses:

> And so, carrying its gaze beyond the confines of all
> substance discernible by sense, the mind comes to
> a point at which it reaches out after the intelligible
> world, and on descrying in that world sights of
> surpassing loveliness, even the patterns and the
> originals of the things of sense which it saw there,
> it is seized by sober intoxication. (Philo 1929:70-1)

---

[2]   Ananda Coomaraswamy (1877-1947) was largely responsible for introducing ancient Indian art to the West. Along with Rene Guenon and Frithjof Schuon he was a leading exponent of the Perennial Philosophy or Traditionalist school. The range and depth of his scholarship encompasses them both.

In this ecstatic state "the mind longs to pass beyond the world of forms to the great King himself; but amid its longing to see Him, pure and untempered rays of concentrated light stream forth like a torrent, so that by its gleams the eye of understanding is dazzled." Just as Moses could not look at God directly and live, so must our longing to apprehend the divine essence remain perpetually unfulfilled. But the soul is granted a mediated vision of the great king through the Logos. According to Philo, the Logos is the active principle of God's thought and also the intelligible world, the world of the ideas. In *De Opificio Mundi*, he describes the way in which this suprasensible world was made to serve as the archetype of the creation:

> So when he willed to create this visible world, he first formed the intelligible world, so that he might employ a pattern completely God like and incorporeal for the production of the corporeal world, a more recent image of the one that was older, which was to comprise as many sensible kinds as there are intelligible ones in the other. (Philo 1981:99)

The intelligible world is comparable to the blueprint for a city drawn up by an architect. Just as the architect puts his plan into action to construct the city, so does God set the intelligible world into motion to create the sensible world. According to Philo, the intelligible world in the act of creation is the Logos:

> If one should wish to express it more baldly he would say that the Intelligible world is nothing else than the Divine Logos already in the act of building the cosmos, for the intelligible city is nothing else than the reasoning of the architect already intent on founding a city. (Philo 1981:100)

As the active cause of the world, the Logos requires a passive cause to work on. This, said Philo, "is in itself lifeless and motionless, but when moved, shaped and quickened by the Mind, it is transformed into a perfect master work, this world." But Philo had to avoid the suggestion that this passive cause is any kind of pre-existent matter coeternal with God because that would contradict Jewish monotheism. To circumvent this problem, he defined matter as a reflection or shadow of the intelligible world and, therefore, indirectly created by God. However, the procession of the passive cause from the active cause is not chronological, "for time there was not before there was a world." Whereas the architect plans and builds his city, in temporal stages, "God's conceiving and creating the world is simultaneous and timeless". (Philo 1981:106) His thinking was not anterior to his creating and, therefore, unformed matter does not exist:

> So it is that He, always thinking, creates and gives beginning of being to sense perceptible things, so that both could exist together: the ever-creating divine mind and the sense perceptible things to which beginning of being is given. (Philo1981:109)

Human intelligence is formed in the image of the ever-creating Logos. As a portion of the divine mind, the mind of man participates in God's continuous act of thought, and conversely, God is ever verdant and flowering in the soul. This correspondence applies to the practical intellect, and in the next section, I will amplify Coomaraswamy's proposition that "the human artist in possession of his art is such by participation in the master Architect's creative power." (Coomaraswamy 1977/a: 21).

Beauty is truth

In a neglected essay, *A Psychological View of Conscience*, Jung says that from a theological point of view, conscience is the voice of God and, therefore, cannot be understood by means of rational psychology:

> This view is not a contrivance of the intellect, it is a primary assertion of the phenomenon itself; a numinous imperative which from ancient times has been accorded far higher authority than the human intellect. (CW10: 853)

Both Jung and Philo maintained that true conscience is not a matter of conforming to an external code of conduct; it derives from the Logos of the soul. When the Logos is hidden or absent, we seem to be free of any sense of guilt:

> But when the Scrutinizer, the true priest, enters us like a beam of light utterly pure, we then discover the tainted intentions stored up in our soul and the guilty and censurable actions to which we put our hand in ignorance of what is to our benefit. (Philo 1981: 202-3)

Coomaraswamy, who was a Platonist first and foremost, extends this insight into the domain of art:

> Just as there is a conscience about doing, so is there a conscience about making, and these two consciences operate independently, notwithstanding that both are referable to one common principle, that of the spark of Divine Awareness, to which the Middle Ages referred by the name "Synteresis." (Coomaraswamy 1977: 46)

The synteresis or inward controller operates in the field of art or craft as the Practical Intellect. The artist who works in conformity with this principle is said to be "in possession of his art." The archetype of the work of art is conceived in the Practical Intellect. It is "the art in the artist." This archetype corresponds to the created artefact in exactly the same way that an object in the sensory world corresponds to its counterpart in the intelligible world:

> The art of God is the Son "through whom all things were made"; in the same way the art of the human artist is his child through which some one thing is made. The intuition-expression of an imitable form is an intellectual conception born of the artist's wisdom, just as eternal reasons are born of the Eternal Wisdom. (Coomaraswamy 1959: 34)

The artist does not mimic the divine act of creation; he or she participates in God's creative Logos. "Art," said Aquinas "is an imitation of nature in her manner of operation." By "nature," he means the intelligible world, not the sensory world. An artist in possession of his or her art does not copy an external object but creates an image that reflects a suprasensible form. He or she proceeds by a word conceived in intellect. (Coomaraswamy 1977: 34) To do this, the artist must become one with the latent form:

> The artist is first of all required to remove himself from human to celestial levels of apperception; at this level and in this state of unification, no longer having anything external to himself, he sees and realizes, that is to say becomes what he is afterwards to represent in wrought material. (Coomaraswamy 1977:165)

The freedom of the artist derives from this realization. An artist who blindly copies an external object is no free agent. Of course, the act of conception must be followed by the production of the artefact in whatever medium the artist has chosen. In the medieval philosophy of art, the first act is called the free act, and the second, the servile act. Philo illustrates this distinction by way of Yahweh's instruction to Moses that he appoint Bezalel as the craftsman of the sanctuary. (Exodus 31) But says Philo,

> Bezalel will bear away the secondary honours . . . whereas Moses will carry off the primary ones. For the former fashions the shadows as painters do, for whom there is no divine licence to create anything animate. Bezalel in effect means "making in the shadows." Moses on the other hand, was assigned the task of producing not shadows but the very archetypes of things. (Philo 1981: 166-7)

In a true artist, the free and the servile acts are combined. The images that arise in his spirit are not the property of the artist as a private individual. Invention or intuition is the application of first principles contained in the Universal Intellect: "The Synteresis . . . and not the individual as such is the ground of inventive power." (Coomaraswamy 1977:49)

If art imitates nature in her mode of operation and not in her visible manifestation, the artefact must be assessed in accordance with its similarity to the formal cause rather than its resemblance to perceptible objects. "It is not by the looks of things," said Augustine, "but by their ideas, that we know what we proposed to make should be like." (cited in Coomaraswamy 1959: 35) Accordingly, the artist does not self-consciously aim to create beauty, but his creation will be beautiful to the extent it conforms to its archetype. Similarly, the spectator should not seek merely to derive pleasure from the artefact but will be delighted to the extent he has understood what it signifies. The pleasure of comprehension does not exclude the pleasure of the senses, but it transcends "what is enjoyed by the eye's intrinsic faculty." (Coomaraswamy 1977: 62)

The Light of Nature

Ananda Coomaraswamy was a metaphysician who spoke directly from the Intellect or Synteresis. C G Jung was an empirical psychologist who observed the limits of knowledge established by Kant. But his extraordinary intuition often broke out of the Kantian prison. In this section, I will suggest that Jung's theory of the instincts and Coomaraswamy's model of the creative process have a common source in the Philonic Logos.

In his essay *Instinct and the Unconscious*, Jung says that "only those unconscious processes which are inherited and occur uniformly and regularly can be called instinctive." Such processes must show the mark of compelling necessity and have the uniformity and regularity of reflexes. But while instincts have certain properties in common with reflexes, they cannot be reduced to this level. Whereas reflexes are mechanical, instincts are purposive patterns of behaviour. In *On the Nature of the Psyche*, Jung reflects on the teleology of instinct:

> There are in fact no amorphous instincts, as every instinct bears with in itself the pattern of its situation. Always it fulfils an image, and the image has fixed qualities. The instinct of the leaf cutting ant fulfils the image of ant, leaf, cutting, transport

and the little garden of fungi. If any one of these
conditions is lacking, the instinct does not function
because it cannot exist without its total pattern,
without its image. Such an image is an a priori
type. It is inborn in the ant prior to any activity,
for there can be no activity at all unless an instinct
of corresponding pattern initiates and makes it
possible. (CW8: 398)

The last sentence suggests that the image is inborn
in the ant, which makes no sense. If Jung had made it
clear that the disposition to fulfil the image was inborn
in the ant rather than the image itself, there would not
have been any confusion. Images cannot be inherited,
only the archetypes, as dispositions to form images are
inherited. Jung made this crucial distinction on many
occasions, but he let it lapse in this passage.

The living creature is a psychophysical totality. Whereas
the instinct, as an observable pattern of behaviour, is
physiologically based, its corresponding archetype,
which confers meaning on the instinct, is located in the
psyche:

> The archetypal image might suitably be described
> as the instinct's perception of itself, or as the self
> portrait of the instinct, in exactly the same way
> as consciousness is an inward perception of the
> objective life process.

Without its corresponding archetype, an instinct is a
mere reflex:

> Just as conscious apprehension gives our
> actions form and direction so does unconscious
> apprehension through the archetype determine the
> form and direction of the instinct. (Jung CW8: 277)

The term "archetype" can be traced all the way back to Philo, who used it to denote the Ideas in the intelligible world. Jung's transposition of this term into the psychology of instinct has provoked furious accusations of reductionism. Frithjof Schuon declared that Jung had destroyed the intellectual intuition, and his close colleague Titus Burckhardt tells us why this is the case:

> For Jung the collective unconscious is situated below, at the level of physiological instincts. It is important to bear this in mind, since the term collective unconscious, in itself, could carry a wider and in some sort more spiritual meaning as certain assimilations made by Jung seem to suggest, especially his utilizing–or rather in point of fact usurping–of the term "archetype" in order to indicate the latent, and as such, inaccessible contents of the "collective unconscious." (Burckhardt 1974:169)

If Burckhardt had read Jung's long essay on *Paracelsus as a Spiritual Phenomenon* he would have discovered an inconvenient truth. In the essay Jung endorsed Paracelsus's teaching that man, at his birth, is endowed with the perfect light of nature. This light is an inborn spirit and also dwells in animals. (CW13: 390 and n.78) His theory of the instincts is wholly in accord with Philo's doctrine of the Divine Logos. The complex behaviour of the leaf-cutting ant is an instance of this participation. It is a manifestation of God's ever-creative thought actualised in his creature. If instinct viewed from within is a numinous factor, so too is the archetype when it transgresses the psychic domain and manifests itself externally as a synchronistic event. According to Von Franz, a synchronistic incident is "the meaningful coincidence of an external material event with an inner symbol or psychic event, without these two events having a causal relationship . . . The two events are linked only by their common meaning." (Von Franz 1992: 248) I will have more to say about this key Jungian concept in chapters 6, 7, and 9.

Jung formulated the synchronicity hypothesis through his dialogue with the physicist Wolfgang Pauli (Jung and Pauli 1955). If matter and the psyche are two sides of the same coin it is logical to posit a common substratum, a neutral psycho- physical background to the world. In *Mysterium Coniunctionis* he described the substratum like this:

> The background of our empirical world . . . appears to be in fact a unus mundus. This leads to the probable hypothesis which satisfies the fundamental tenet of scientific theory: "Explanatory principles are not to be multiplied beyond the necessary." The transcendental psychophysical background corresponds to a potential world in so far as all the conditions which determine the form of empirical phenomena are inherent in it. (CW14: 769)

Jung derived the idea of the *unus mundus* from the Paracelsian alchemist Gerhard Dorn. And he suggested that Dorn, in turn, probably found this idea in Philo's *De Opificio Mundi*:

> Philo Judaeus . . . says that the creator made in the intelligible world an incorporeal heaven, an invisible earth and the idea of air and void. Last of all he created man, a "little heaven" that bears in itself the reflections of many natures similar to the stars. (CW14: 761)

Clearly, Philo is referring to the microcosm, the psychic unity of man and cosmos, i.e., the *unus mundus*. For Philo, "the relation of the Creator to the mundus intelligibilis is the imago or archetypus of the relation of mind to body."

The Laws of Instinct and the Spirit

In his commentary on *The Secret of the Golden Flower*, a Chinese alchemical text that had been translated by Richard Wilhelm, Jung reflected on the psychology of the authors. They were not world-denying Gnostics and had fulfilled the instinctive side of human nature before becoming detached from the world. Jung could find no signs of premature or guilt-ridden repression, and he was moved to ask, "Are our eyes opened to the spirit only when the laws of the earth are obeyed?" (CW13: 6)

The laws of the earth and the imperatives of the spirit are complementary opposites. For this reason, Jung sees no contradiction in speaking of a creative instinct. In his essay *Psychological Factors Determining Human Behaviour,* he writes,

> We use the term creative instinct because this factor behaves at least dynamically like an instinct. Like instinct it is compulsive, but it is not common and it is not a fixed and invariably inherited organization. (CW8: 245)

For Coomaraswamy, this notion is simply a contradiction in terms. Plato maintained that any art produced under the compulsion of instinct is not worthy of free men. It looks like Jung has fallen into a category error and blurred the distinction between the free and the servile acts. Or was he compelled to postulate a creative instinct on account of the empirical facts? How would Coomaraswamy account for the Dionysian side of the creative process? If an artist or musician has surrendered voluntarily to the dynamism of instinct, has he ceased to be in possession of his art?

Jung's hypothesis of a creative instinct was based on years of careful observation of patients engaged in active imagination:

> And so it is with the hand that guides the crayon or brush, the foot that executes the dance step, with the eye and the ear, with the word and the thought: a dark impulse is the ultimate arbiter of the pattern, an unconscious a priori precipitates itself into plastic form, and one has no inkling that another person's consciousness is being guided by these same principles at the very point where one feels utterly exposed to the boundless subjective vagaries of chance. Over the whole procedure there seems to reign a dim foreknowledge not only of the pattern but of its meaning. (CW8: 402)

The creative instinct manifested itself with compelling force whenever his patients spontaneously produced mandalas. This activity was not an aesthetic diversion but a means of finding ontological security in a borderline state:

> (The mandalas) serve to produce an inner order— which is why—when they appear in series they follow chaotic, disordered states marked by conflict and anxiety. They express the idea of inner reconciliation and wholeness. (CW9/1: 710)

Of course, these spontaneous productions of the unconscious are not works of art. But as Coomaraswamy himself acknowledges in his essay *The Intellectual Operation in Indian Art*, they are a valid means of reintegration (*samskarana*). (Coomaraswamy 1977)

Although therapeutic mandalas emerge out of chaotic states, they express the fundamental orderliness of the psyche. For Jung, the unconscious was not a seething chaotic Freudian id. The human psyche is a microcosm, and its structure is mirrored in the fourfold symmetry of the mandala. Jung's therapeutic methods derive their efficacy from the healing power of the Logos. According to Philo, this power manifests itself as an angel. In his comments on Jacob's words, "The God who nourishes me from my youth to this day, the Angel who redeemed me from all ills heal these boys," (Genesis 48:15–16), Philo wrote:

> How appropriate is his mode of expression! He considers God as the one who nourishes him, not his Logos but the Angel, who is the Logos, as healer of ills. These words are fully in accord with reality. (Philo 1981: 178)

Because the mandala is a replica of the intelligible world, it serves to bring the soul back into harmony with the rhythms of the cosmos. Philo describes the realization of the microcosm like this:

> For he wishes to represent the sage's soul as a replica of heaven, or if one may speak hyperbolically, a heaven on earth, containing within itself, as does the ether, pure forms of being, ordered movements, harmonious circuits, divine revolutions, beams of virtue utterly star like and dazzling.

In such a soul, the miracle that is intelligence becomes conscious of itself. "The eyes of the body," Philo concludes, "are but the smallest part of the eye of the soul. That is like the sun; the others are like candles, accustomed to be lighted and extinguished." (Philo 1981: 244)

This essay was first published in Temenos 6 (London, 1985) under my former name, Andrew Mouldey. It was commissioned by the editor Kathleen Raine. I have made numerous improvements to the presentation and style, but the argument remains essentially the same. My thanks to the present editor John Carey for permission to publish the essay in this book.

4

PNEUMA AND PSYCHE

What Did Jung Do to offend the Gnostics?

For Giles Clark in Memoriam

Since the Stars Have Fallen from the Sky

When Martin Buber wrote his critique of Jung's psychology, he accused him of promoting Gnosticism and cited *The Seven Sermons to the Dead* as Exhibit A. (Buber 1953) This was acutely embarrassing for Jung who characterized this piece of writing as a sin of his youth. (CW18:1501) (Actually, he was forty years old when he wrote, or rather channeled, the text under the pseudonym of Basilides.) Thirty-five years after *The Seven Sermons*, Jung wrote *Aion*. In the last two chapters of this work, he distanced himself from the world-denying spirituality of the Gnostics. The pneumatic man of the early Christian era "was separated from evil by an abyss," and he would have found modern psychology's emphasis on the instinctual shadow "an obnoxious anachronism." (CW9/2:255-6) Jung had brought the ancient Gnostic myth down to earth. Now spirit and instinct, light and shadow coexisted in a paradoxical union.[3]

It would be incorrect to assume that Jung's position is no longer a source of offence to Gnostic sensibilities. In *The Reign of Quantity and the Signs of the Times*, the twentieth-century French esotericist Rene Guenon expressed his distaste for modern psychology and its preoccupation with the shadow:

> There is certainly something more than a mere question of vocabulary in the fact, very significant in itself, that present day psychology considers nothing but the "subconscious" and never the "super conscious" which ought logically to be its correlative; there is no doubt that this usage expresses the idea of an extension operating only in a downward direction, that is, towards aspects of things that corresponds both here in the human being and elsewhere in the cosmic environment to the "fissures" through which the most malefic influences in the subtle world penetrate, influences having a character that can truthfully be described as "infernal". (Guenon 1972:274)

Guenon, who came from a conservative Catholic background, believed that psychoanalysis was a Satanic masterstroke. No doubt Jung would have regarded this as an "obnoxious anachronism." But it would

---

[3]   These two chapters in Aion are a psychological commentary on a Gnostic text, the Naassene Sermon. Mark Gaffney's book Gnostic Secrets of the Naassenes (Gaffney 2004) makes it much easier to negotiate Jung's densely packed argument.

be an injustice to casually dismiss a metaphysician of such rare genius. His writings on Hinduism inspired Heinrich Zimmer and Mircea Eliade. Ananda Coomaraswamy, who corresponded extensively with Guenon, declared that he was the most significant thinker in contemporary Europe.

Guenon died in 1951, and his legacy has been carried forward by a religious movement known as Traditionalism or Perennialism. Traditionalists regard the world's religious traditions, indigenous and revealed as so many expressions of a unanimous perennial philosophy. But this reservoir of wisdom is off limits to those outside orthodox tradition and the notion of a secular spirituality is a contradiction in terms. Most of the Traditionalists are, as was Guenon himself, Muslims or Muslim converts. The leading figures are Frithjof Schuon, Titus Burckhardt, Martin Lings, and S H Nasr. Their scholarship is profound, and it opens one's inner eye to the grandeur and beauty of Islam. But they are implacably hostile to Jung. The purpose of this essay is twofold: to give a long-overdue answer to their refutation of Jungian psychology and to uncover the psychological attitude behind this rather unconvincing critique.

Guenon and his disciples argue that the priori limits of knowledge are not absolute. They maintain that it is possible to have access to "things in themselves" (the noumena) at the deepest cognitive level of the soul. But Guenon did not claim such knowledge for himself as a private individual. Gnosis, said Frithjof Schuon, "is not possessed by the individual as he is an individual but insofar as in his innermost essence, he is not distinct from the divine principle." (Schuon 1984:xxx) Meister Eckhart said it even more eloquently, "The eye through which I see God is the same eye with which God sees me: one seeing, one knowing and one love." (Eckhart 1981:87)

This mode of knowing is not confined to the Gnostic elite. It is mediated to everyone through myth and symbol, through sacraments and in sacred art. It can also manifest itself in dreams as the authoritative voice. This phenomenon is an instance of the absolute knowledge of the unconscious. (CW8:912) But whereas Jung locates the source of absolute knowledge in the unconscious psyche below, Guenon and the Traditionalists insist that it can only come from the spirit above. Jung is regarded as the arch-reductionist, and his psychology can only "ruin insidiously all transcendence and all intellection." (Schuon 1968:71-2)

The pneumatic man and the psychological man are separated from each other by an abyss. In his essay *The Archetypes of the Collective Unconscious,* Jung gives us a measure of the distance. He is talking about the unprecedented impoverishment of symbolism in contemporary culture and its psychological consequences:

> Since the stars have fallen from heaven and our highest symbols have paled, a secret life holds sway in the unconscious. That is why we have a psychology today and why we speak of the unconscious. All this would be quite superfluous in any age or culture which possessed symbols. Symbols are spirit from above and under those conditions spirit is above too. Therefore it is a senseless undertaking to wish to experience or investigate an unconscious that contains nothing but the silent undisturbed sway of nature. Our unconscious on the other hand hides living water, spirit that has become nature and that is why it is disturbed. (CW9/1:50)

Guenon and the Traditionalists would agree with Jung's diagnosis of the modern world, which has all but banished the sacred. But they would regard the cure Jung proposes as worse than the disease. The unconscious psyche is labyrinthine, and I was warned that if I entered it, I would never return.

Titus Burckhardt has led the campaign against Jung. In a long essay, *Cosmology and Modern Science*, he challenges the very premises upon which the modern scientific world view depends. His critique takes in Einstein, Darwin, and Jung. As the argument contra-Darwin provides the premise for Burckhardt's devastating critique of Jung, I must give a brief account of the Traditionalists' version of Intelligent Design.

Whereas the modern account of the origins of life is evolutionary and horizontal, the Traditionalists have a devolutionary and vertical perspective. This narrative is Platonist rather than creationist. Each life form participates in the archetype of its species, which are in no way subject to transformative evolution:

> A species (is) in itself an immutable "form," it could not evolve and become transformed into another species, although it can include variants, all these being diverse projections of a single essential form from which they will never become detached, just as the branches of a tree never become detached from their trunk. (Burckhardt 1986:141)

The living creature is a "crystallization" of an archetype that is immutable and suprasensible; it is not the product of natural selection and random mutation. According to Burckhardt, transformist evolution makes no distinction between species and simple variation.

Resemblances that undoubtedly exist between different species are taken as indications of genetic descent. But the attempt on the part of Darwinians to read a continuous line of development into the fossil record runs into too many lacunae. At first, "missing links" were postulated to rescue the theory, and later this notion was replaced by an evolution through abrupt mutations. But these explanations derive from an inability "to conceive of dimensions of reality other than purely physical sequences." (Burckhardt 1986:147)

If transformist evolution is an untenable hypothesis, then the argument for the infra-human origins of man is equally untenable. So how do Traditionalists account for the evidence of the fossil record? The answer is pure Blavatsky. Evolutionary scientists have misconstrued the fossil remains of anthropoid apes. These are not the remains of our ancestors but degenerate survivors of a cataclysm at the end of a terrestrial epoch. But if that is the case, why are there no traces of our true ancestors in the fossil record? Here is the explanation:

> The bodies of the most ancient men have not necessarily left solid traces, either because their bodies were not yet materialized or "solidified" to that point, or else because the spiritual state of those men, conjointly with the cosmic conditions of their time, rendered possible a reabsorption of the physical "body" into the subtle "body" at the moment of death. (Burckhardt 1986:150)

There is no denying it—this argument can never be falsified.

Burckhardt opens his attack on Jung by pointing out that modern psychology is afflicted by a paralyzing relativism. Indeed, Jung himself conceded this point when he said that "the psyche is the object of psychology and—fatally enough—also its subject." (CW11: 87) How can he escape this vicious circle without an Archimedean point? This problem is inherent in any psychology based on evolutionary premises. But Traditional science provides an alternative with a vision that is both static and vertical:

> It is static because it refers to constant and universal qualities and it is vertical in the sense that it attaches the inferior to the superior, the ephemeral to the imperishable. The modern vision on the contrary is basically "dynamic" and "horizontal"; it is not the symbolism of things that interest it but their material and historical connections. (Burckhardt 1986: 131)

In this world view, there can be no individuation as Jung understood that term, only eternal rest in the eternal "I am." Man is conceived as a microcosm, and he occupies the central state in the greater macrocosm. This cosmological doctrine is, according to Burckhardt, based on principles that are "inherent in human intelligence at its most profound." (Burckhardt 1986: 122) Modern science as represented by Jung, and Einstein is divorced from these principles. Its methods lead to a false objectivity, and its abstract mathematical models bear no relation to the concrete intuition of things. Such an approach "empties the world of its qualitative sap." (Burckhardt 1986:131) These quantitative theories possess immense practical efficacy, but Burckhardt maintains that a false theory can still work. It is this very applicability that enables modern science to dominate the popular imagination. Burckhardt's critique sets out to expose the alleged lacunae of modern science and show how they arise out of an ignorance of suprasensible realities. It is difficult to see how Burckhardt can go on to "refute" Jung or, indeed, Darwin and Einstein. All he can do is point out that their theories are based on premises that do not conform to the devolutionary axioms of the perennial philosophy.

Jung's Heresies

I only know of one face-to-face dialogue between a Traditionalist and a Jungian. This was the one that took place between Martin Lings and me in 1986.[4] I found him very approachable, and he listened courteously to me when I explained my position. Then some amiable argument about the subject and object of psychology being one and the same ended in goalless draw. It would be too much of a digression to go into the full discussion or the subsequent correspondence between us. But one remark he made is relevant to the argument here. As I was about to take my leave, I said to him that Jung's path of individuation is not risk free and that the outcome is not guaranteed. Martin Lings responded by telling me that he could never pursue a spiritual path that was not absolutely certain. This would explain the powerful appeal of a world view that is static and vertical. It satisfies the deep need we all have for certainty. No one understood this fundamental human need better than Sigmund Freud.

Jung is regarded as a much greater threat to the Traditionalists than Freud. Whereas Freud was an out and out atheist, Jung sympathized with the religious traditions and subverted them at the same time. But

---

[4]   I have given an account of this meeting in Chapter 5:3.

even Titus Burckhardt had to concede that Jung got it right some of the time. For example, his observations on the logic of dreams are accurate "despite the radically false theses of that author." These theses are, of course, evolutionary.

There are deeper affinities that Burckhardt has conveniently overlooked. For instance, they are as one when it comes to "esse in anima." First two quotes from Jung:

> It seems to me that certain psychic contents or images are derived from a material environment, while others, which are in no way less real, seem to come from a "spiritual" source which appears very different from the physical environment. (CW8:681)

> As a matter of fact, the only form of existence of which we have immediate knowledge is psychic. We might well say, on the contrary, that physical existence is a mere inference, since we know matter only insofar as we perceive psychic images mediated by the senses. (CW11:16)

According to Titus Burckhardt:

> A self-same psychic "event" can simultaneously occur in answer to a sensory impulsion, to the manifestation of a wish, as a consequence of an interior action, or it can appear as a trace of the typical ancestral form of the individual, as the expression of his genius, or again as the reflection of a supra-individual reality. (Burckhardt 1986: 161)

The theory of the collective unconscious in a nutshell! We are, indeed, as Burckhardt puts it so concisely, "steeped in the ocean of the subtle world as fishes are in water." (Burckhardt 1986:161)

Burckhardt seems to be unaware that Jung's theory of the instincts is almost indistinguishable from his own account in *Cosmology and Modern Science*. Both would agree that instinct has "nothing of automation about it." To account for the purposiveness of instinct, Jung argued that there must be an instinctive act of comprehension or an intuition in the Bergsonian sense of the word. The form of this intuition is determined by the archetype and, conversely, an instinctual pattern of behaviour "fulfils an image." "Just as conscious apprehension gives our actions form and direction," so does the archetype regulate instinctual behaviour. (CW8:277)

Burckhardt says more or less the same thing in a different form of words:

> Instinct is a non-reflective modality of intelligence . . . determined not by a series of automatic reflexes but by the form- the qualitative determination of the species. This form is like a filter through which the universal intelligence is manifested. (Burckhardt 1986:171)

Surprisingly, Burckhardt does not reject the idea of the collective unconscious. The idea is not unacceptable in itself, but Jung understands it reductively as "ancestral structures having their root in the physical order." To prove his case, Burckhardt cites the following passage from Jung's *Commentary on The Secret of the Golden Flower*:

> The fact that the collective unconscious exists is
> simply the psychic expression of the identity of
> cerebral structures beyond all racial differences ...
> The different lines of psychic evolution start
> out from one and the same trunk of which the
> roots plunge through the ages. It is here that the
> psychic parallelism with the animal is situated.
> (Burckhardt 1986:168/CW13:11)

For Burckhardt, the roots of the tree are located in the sky above, not in the earth below:

> For Jung, "the collective unconscious" is situated
> "below" at the level of physiological instincts. It
> is important to bear this in mind since the term
> "collective unconscious" in itself could carry a
> wider and in some sense, more spiritual meaning.
> (Burckhardt 1986:169)

There is, as Burckhardt correctly discerns, a plainly Darwinian turn in this thesis. But he is preaching to the converted. The evolutionary basis of Jung's psychology can only be objectionable to the Traditionalists who adhere to a static and vertical view of life.

The sources Burckhardt deploys to prove that Jung's model of individuation is based on "an inferior psychism" are very meagre. He quotes a few passages from the *Two Essays on Analytical Psychology* and the commentary to *The Secret of the Golden Flower.* There are some cursory references to five other pieces, and he dips into *Memories, Dreams, Reflections.* Did Burckhardt actually study these texts? His treatment of the archetypes of the individuation process displays some inexplicable lacunae. The shadow archetype, that is so deeply offensive to the pneumatic man, is not even mentioned. He does mention the anima and alleges that Jung was seduced by her. In fact, Jung resisted her insinuations on the first encounter. (MDR:211-3). The self, however, does receive some attention. Burckhardt begins well enough with a well- chosen passage from The *Relations between the Ego and the Unconscious*:

> With the sensation of the self as an irrational and indefinable entity, to which the "I" is neither opposed nor subordinated, but to which it adheres and round which it revolves in some sort like the earth going round the sun, the aim of individuation is attained. I use the term "sensation" to express the empirical character of the relation between I and self. In this relation there is nothing intelligible, for one can say nothing about the contents of the self. The "I" is the only content of the self we can know. The individualized I feels itself to be the object of another subject, unknown and superior to itself. (Cited in Burckhardt 1986:175)

Burckhardt gives this passage a cautious welcome: "Despite a terminology too much bound up with the current scientism one might be tempted to grant full credit to the presentiments expressed in the above passage and find in it an approach to the traditional metaphysical doctrines . . ." But he withdraws this small concession immediately. Jung, he alleges, "relativizes the notion of the self by treating it this time not as a transcendental principle but as the outcome of psychological process." (Burckhardt 1986:176) Had Burckhardt conducted his research less selectively, he would have been faced with a very inconvenient proposition. In *Aion*, Jung wrote that "although the self can become a symbolic content of consciousness it is, as a supraordinate totality, necessarily transcendental as well." (CW9/2:264) Burckhardt concludes his argument by saying, "There are some realms in which dilettantism is unforgivable." But to whom does this apply?

Jung receives a schoolmasterly rebuke for "avoiding" Sri Ramana Maharshi when he was on a tour in India in 1938: "He did not wish to see Sri Ramana Maharshi—alleging a motive of insolent frivolity—doubtless because he feared instinctively and 'unconsciously' . . . a contact with a reality that would disprove his own theories." (Burckhardt 1986:177-8) Burckhardt does not bother to explain exactly how Sri Ramana's teachings would have falsified Jung's psychology. As far as I can see, there is no contradiction on an empirical level between the passage he cited at length from "The Relations between the Ego and the Unconscious" and Sri Ramana's doctrine of the "I" thought. (See *Cunning Secret* ch.10, pp. 129-30)

Burckhardt does not cite the passage in Jung's essay *The Holy Men of India* that has offended him. I suspect it was this:

> The man who is only wise and only holy interests me about as much as the skeleton of a rare saurian, which would not move me to tears. The insane contradiction, on the other hand, between existence beyond Maya in the cosmic Self, and that amiable human weakness which fruitfully sinks many roots into the black earth, repeating for all eternity the weaving and rending of the veil as the ageless melody of India—this contradiction fascinates me; for how else can one perceive the light without the shadow, hear the silence without the noise, attain wisdom without foolishness? (CW11:953)

I too find the first sentence objectionable and, for this reason, will let the rebuke stand. But Titus Burckhardt's psychoanalytic conjecture is hopelessly skewed. There is a much simpler explanation why Jung did not visit Sri Ramana. His time in India was limited, and a hasty one-off meeting would have amounted to spiritual tourism.

Living in the Last Days

In 1945, Rene Guenon declared that the modern world was entering the last days of the Iron Age or the Kali Yuga. While the initial stages of degeneration have manifested themselves in the "anti-tradition," we are now entering the "counter tradition." The former term refers to all the forces that simply eliminate *Sophia Perennis*, e.g., materialism, the dissolution of social caste, secularization, etc. But at least you know where you are with the anti-tradition; the counter tradition is another matter. The second phase mimics and subverts traditional forms often in very plausible ways. Like Freud, Guenon also wanted a bulwark against the black tide of mud that was occultism. This counter tradition will, he prophesied, culminate in the Grand Parody, a non-stop Fellini-esque carnival that marks the last gasp of this aeon. Time itself will accelerate until the Kali Yuga comes to an abrupt end and a new golden age is inaugurated. *The Reign of Quantity and the Signs of the Times* has a compelling force that overrides the reader's incredulity. (Guenon 1972)

Guenon singled out psychoanalysis as one of the worst signs of the times, resembling "the sacraments of the devil." Schuon went one step further and maintained that while Freud represented the anti-tradition, Jung was the prophet of the counter tradition:

> People generally see in Jungism, as compared to Freudism, a step towards reconciliation with the traditional spiritualities, but this is in no wise the

> case. From this point of view the only difference is
> that where Freud boasted of being an irreconcilable
> enemy of religion, Jung sympathizes with it while
> emptying it of its contents which he replaces by the
> collective psychism, that is to say by something
> infra-intellectual and therefore anti-spiritual.
> (Burckhardt 1982:177, note 65)

In other words, Freud is Satan and Jung is the
Antichrist! This diatribe confirms Jung's analysis
of the psychological attitude of the pneumatic man.
Schuon exhibits the mentality of a Gnostic in the early
Christian era:

> (His) original dependence on a pneumatic sphere
> to which he clung like a child to its mother, was
> threatened by the Kingdom of Satan. From him the
> pneumatic man was delivered by the Redeemer,
> who broke the gates of Hell and deceived the
> archons; but he was bound to the Kingdom
> of Heaven in exactly the same degree. He was
> separated from evil by an abyss. This attitude
> was powerfully reinforced by the immediate
> expectation of the Second Coming. (CW9/2:403)

The Traditionalists live in exactly the same state of
expectation but do not say publicly exactly when
the eschaton will arrive. They will probably be
disappointed like the early Gnostic pneumatic man.
When the Second Coming failed to materialize, all the
hope invested in it flowed back into man, severed the
umbilical cord, and heightened his consciousness of
himself. In this way, the pneumatic man came into the
knowledge of the shadow.

The Reign of Quantity is a blend of the myth of the
Antichrist and the myth of the four Yugas of Hinduism.

It mixes together two incompatible eschatological myths: New Testament apocalypse, which is based on linear time, and the doctrine of the Yugas, which presupposes cyclical time and is not strictly speaking an eschatology. It's a bit rich for Guenon to vehemently condemn the syncretism of H. P. Blavatsky or Rudolf Steiner.

Jung kept his feet firmly in the Christian tradition and preferred the eschatology of Joachim of Fiore. In his essay *A Psychological Approach to the Trinity*, he gives a psychologist's view of the three ages of the Father, Son, and Holy Ghost according to Joachim. At the Father stage, consciousness is childlike, "still dependent on a definite ready-made pattern of existence which is habitual and has the character of law." (CW11:270) This is a passive, unreflective mode of being. The situation changes at the Son stage. Reflective consciousness begins to emerge, and the increased discrimination begets conflict: "Freedom from the Law brings a sharpening of opposites, in particular moral opposites. Christ crucified between two thieves is an eloquent symbol of this fact." At the third stage, the initial Father stage is recovered. But the values of the second stage must be held fast to prevent a regression:

> Though the new level of consciousness acquired through the emancipation of the son continues in the third stage, it must recognize that it is not the source of the ultimate decisions and flashes of insight which rightly go by the name of "gnosis," but that these are inspired by a higher authority which, in projected form, is known as the Holy Ghost. Psychologically speaking inspiration comes from an unconscious function. (CW11:272)

Inspiration from the Holy Ghost or gnosis is very dangerous and can lead to the insidious pitfall of inflation. Only an individual who knows that "we are no more than the stable in which the Lord is born" (Jung 1969:267) can safely enter this new dispensation. In the Paraclete, the pneumatic man and the carnal man are one and the same.

End Note

An earlier version of this chapter was published under the title *Pneuma and Psyche: A Reply to a Gnostic Critique of Jung in Spring Journal 54*, Putnam, Connecticut, 1993. Since then, attitudes towards Jung have shifted in the Traditionalist community. For example, in chapter 5 of his book *The Science of the Greater Jihad* Charles Upton gives an even- handed critique of Analytical Psychology. (Upton 2011) His essay is titled, somewhat tendentiously, *Can Jung be Saved? A Sufic Revisioning of the Jungian Archetypes.* This critique has none of Burckhardt's rhetorical hostility and it contains some thoughtful and sometimes challenging criticisms of Jung's psychology. Unfortunately, Upton does not cite a single passage from the Collected Works in support of his arguments! It will take more than an unsourced 20 -page essay to revision Jung's psychology from a Sufic perspective.

5

THE GUARDIANS OF
SACRED ORDER

Late in 1974, the library angel led me to a book with a rather striking title: *The Transcendent Unity of Religions.* The author, Frithjof Schuon, was unknown to me, but he had merited a glowing recommendation from T S Eliot. There was, in his opinion, "no more impressive work on the comparative study of Oriental and Occidental religion." (Schuon 1984) I read the opening pages while waiting for my train home. It was a moment of unveiling.

In the preface, Schuon explained the distinction between gnosis and faith. He defined gnosis as "the direct and active participation in divine knowledge and not a passive participation as is faith." (Schuon 1984:xxx) A Gnostic has access to the direct intuition of the Absolute through gnosis, but a man of faith is dependent on revelation, "the word of God spoken to his creatures." From the standpoint of faith, the truth claims of the major religions are, indeed, mutually exclusive. But from a Gnostic perspective, supreme truth is one. The contradictions amongst the faiths arise because this truth is providentially adapted to the endless diversity of collective humanity. Schuon's book raised the reader above the seemingly irreconcilable differences amongst the faiths and presented each religious tradition as an expression of a unanimous perennial philosophy. He was not just talking *about* the perennial philosophy. He was speaking directly *from* the vantage point of gnosis or Intellectual intuition. In *The Transcendent Unity*, he showed me how Hinduism, Islam, Christianity, and Buddhism each participated in *Sophia Perennis* in their own distinctive way. Everything that I had read at university was pedestrian by comparison.

But who was Frithjof Schuon? I soon discovered that he was the leading spokesman of the Traditionalist or perennial philosophy movement, and before long, I was reading whatever I could lay my hands on: Rene Guenon, Titus Burckhardt, Martin Lings, S H Nasr. No wonder T.S Eliot found this material compelling. So did the great Islamic scholar S.H. Nasr. Here is his assessment of Schuon's opus in his book *Knowledge and the Sacred*:

> Schuon has written of not only traditional doctrines but also of practical and operative aspects of spiritual life. He has written of rites, prayer, love, faith, the spiritual virtues, and the moral life from a sapiental point of view. Moreover, he has expanded the horizon of traditional expositions to include certain aspects of the spiritual life to include certain aspects of the Christian tradition, especially Orthodoxy which was passed over by Guenon, as well as American Indian tradition and Shintoism. He has expounded

in all its grandeur the metaphysics of virgin nature and, being himself an outstanding poet and painter in addition to a metaphysician, has written some remarkable pages on the metaphysics of traditional art and the spiritual significance of beauty.

After a survey of Schuon's writings, Nasr concludes,

With Schuon's writings the full-fledged revival as related to the rediscovery of the sacred in the heart of all traditions . . . has taken place, making it possible amidst a world suffocating from the poisonous atmosphere of nihilism and doubt for those who "are called" to gain access to knowledge of the highest order rooted in the sacred and therefore inseparable from the joy of light and certitude. (Nasr 1981:107- 9)

It will come as no surprise that at the time of writing these words, Schuon was Nasr's shaykh. My survey of the master's thought will be somewhat prosaic in comparison.

I

To be orthodox is to participate, by way of a doctrine that can properly be called "traditional", in the immutability of the principles that govern the Universe and fashion our intelligence. (Schuon 1999:1)

Freud gave short shrift to the notion that man occupied a privileged position in the order of nature. Science, he suggested, had dealt three blows to our self-esteem. Firstly, the Copernican revolution demonstrated that the earth was not the centre of the cosmos. Then

Darwin provided compelling evidence that man was descended from the animal kingdom and that we could no longer deny our ineradicable animal nature. Finally, psychoanalysis dealt a third blow by revealing that the ego was not the master of its own house but subordinate to the irrational forces of the unconscious psyche. Frithjof Schuon's philosophy, on the other hand, can be summed up in one proposition: that man is made for transcendence. There is no place for psychoanalysis and its Darwinian premises in his majestically hierarchical world picture. According to Schuon, the living creature did not emerge out of inorganic matter, "the origin of a creature is a non-material substance, it is a perfect and non-material archetype: perfect and consequently without need of transforming evolution, non-material and consequently having its origin in spirit and not in matter." (Schuon 1982:16)

Schuon did not reject the empirical fact of natural selection, nor did he deny that variations occur within a given species. But he maintained that each species is the manifestation of an immutable archetype or divine idea. Consequently, it is inconceivable that one species could undergo a metamorphosis into another. Man retains his privileged position at the centre of the creation. If he is the microcosm and the vessel of a divine incarnation, he cannot be "subject to any essential and transforming evolution." This, Schuon insisted, "is quite impossible for the infinite does not incarnate in the finite except by virtue of an absolute character that can indeed disappear, but cannot change in its essence and archetype." (Schuon 1978:90-1)

This absolute character of the human state seems to have disappeared in the modern age. Man is now a protean being who no longer rests in the permanence of the divine image. His loss of ontological security is compensated by the unconditional freedom that comes from being void of essence. He is no longer torn between the kingdom of heaven and the allurements of this world, nor is he inconvenienced by any vestiges of transcendental nostalgia. He lives in a post- Freudian world:

> With Freud Western man has learned the technical complexity of externalizing his inwardness, and has been able at last to usher out that crowd of shadows urging him to turn inward, so as to live in the bright sober light of the present, where ideally the moment is always high noon. (Rieff 1966/87:60)

Modern psychology has abolished any hierarchical ordering of the personality into higher/lower or spirit/ flesh. Each opposing tendency is granted equal rights. In his essay "The Psychological Imposture," Schuon wrote that psychoanalysis, "instead of allowing man to make use of his natural and in a sense providential disequilibrium . . . tends on the other hand to bring him to an amorphous equilibrium, rather as if one wished to spare a young bird the agonies of its apprenticeship by clipping its wings." (Schuon 1986:196) But man is a divine and a fallen being in one, and even the most sophisticated psychotherapy cannot abolish the disequilibrium that constitutes him. "The ambiguity of the human state," said Schuon in *Stations of Wisdom*, "is that we are as it were suspended between divinity and dust." (Schuon 1978:92-3)

Allah commanded the angels to bow down to Adam in recognition of man's central position in the order of creation. (Quran XV:29-30) His position as God's vicegerent derives from his intelligence that the Lord has breathed into him. "Human intelligence," said Schuon, "is characterized by its capacity to conceive of the Absolute." (Schuon 1984a:260) Those who repudiate this innate capacity fall below the level of human intelligence and are in danger of forfeiting the centrality of the human state.

Human intelligence consists of two faculties: Intellectual intuition and reason. The faculties of reason enable us to organize the data of sensory perception and to make logical inferences. This mode of knowing is confined to the world of appearances, the phenomenal world. But intellectual intuition is not confined by the a priori limits of knowledge and sees directly into the noumenal world. According to Guenon, it is not an individual faculty because it is not within the power of the individual to go beyond his own limits. Intellectual intuition, said Schuon, "is not possessed by the individual insofar as he is an individual, but insofar as he is not distinct from his Divine Principle." Whereas ordinary cognition is relative and, therefore, uncertain, gnosis is absolute "because of the identity between the knower and the known in the Intellect." (Schuon 1984:xxx) In Sufism, this faculty is called the eye of the heart. Every function of our intelligence has its root in the transpersonal intellect, and "there is no integral consciousness that does not prolong absolute consciousness." (Schuon 1982:7) Schuon expresses the matter in first-person terms in his essay *Aspects of the Theophanic Phenomenon of Consciousness*: "The Intellect, the mental faculties and the sensorial faculties, including sexual sensibility are so many aspects of this naturally supernatural prodigy that is subjectivity." (Schuon 1982:13)

"The conscious subject", Schuon declared, "is too vast and too profound or too real to be at the mercy of a fact so contingent and accidental as death." (Schuon 1984a:261) This proposition is the antithesis of Freud's death wish, the desire to return to the inertia of inorganic matter. Whereas religious man lives with the three traditional eschatological certainties of death, judgement, and eternity, modern psychological man only recognises the first. By rejecting the idea of judgement, he is not answerable to the sanctions of religious authority. Having dispensed with the sense of eternity, he is no longer suspended between divinity and dust. He has need neither of redemption from sin nor the institutions that mediate it. Schuon regarded this thanatology as indigent: "The human condition is . . . a door towards Paradise," or it is "a door towards hell for those who neglect the responsibility of human centrality". (Schuon 1986:78)

In Buddhism, this eschatological imperative is expressed as the human life hard to attain. Those who forfeit it will wander indefinitely in the vastness of Samsara. Christianity and Islam have the doctrine of the eternity of hell, which amounts to the definitive exclusion from the human state. In *Understanding Islam*, Schuon evocatively describes our central state as being surrounded by a ring of fire in which "there is only one choice, either to escape from the current of forms upwards towards God or to leave humanity downwards towards the fire, the fire which is like the sanction of betrayal on the part of those who have not realized the divine meaning of the human condition." These words raise the existential tension between our theomorphic and our fallen natures to the highest level of intensity: "From the gravity of hell we must infer the grandeur of man, we must not infer from the seeming innocence of man, the supposed injustice of hell." (Schuon 1998:82) This statement should not be taken literally, but it is meant to be taken seriously. In an earlier essay, *Understanding Esoterism*, Schuon declared that "the human individual has one great concern that exceeds all others: to save his soul." To this end, "he must adhere to a religion and to be able to adhere to it he must believe in it, but with the best will in the world one can only believe what is credible . . ." (Schuon 1981: 35)

The credibility of religious axioms has been subjected to death by a thousand cuts in the modern world. However, the Traditionalists argue that this situation is not irreversible. If, in an earlier age, gnosis was regarded as subversive of true faith, it must now come to its rescue. As Schuon put it succinctly, "Just as rationalism can remove faith so can esoterism restore it." (Schuon 1981:8) His hermeneutic of restoration is based on the distinction between esoteric and exoteric religious forms. In Sufism, every teaching has an inner esoteric meaning (*batin*) and an outer exoteric meaning (*zahir*). For the devout believer, the *zahir* is absolute, but for the Sufi, it is an imperfect reflection of a higher truth (*batin*). Paradoxically, it is the relativity of exoterism that provides the means by which it can be rescued. From the vantage point of sapiental esoterism, any exoteric doctrine is a partial adaptation of integral truth to the needs of a particular religious collectivity. Inevitably, this transposition will result in some degree of distortion. Whereas exoteric teachings of the religious traditions tend to be mutually exclusive, the esoteric traditions are so many branches of a unanimous perennial wisdom. If modern scepticism is a critique of the religious traditions from below, sapiental esoterism is a critique from above. Its intention is not to destroy but to fulfil.

This is an elitist solution to the crisis of faith in the modern world. While the spiritual proletariat are abandoned to their fate, those who are "in Tradition" are saved. But what exactly does it mean to be "in Tradition"? I combed the writings of Schuon and his circle (the Traditionalists) for an answer to this question and eventually found one in a little-known book by Lord Northbourne, modestly titled *Religion in the Modern World:*

> Tradition, in the rightful sense of the word, is the chain that joins civilization to revelation. It comprises all the distinctive characteristics that make any given civilization what it is including those that can be specifically called religion. (Northbourne 1963:34)

Northbourne goes on to distinguish between the horizontal and the vertical aspects of tradition. By the former term, he means the initiatic transmission of revealed truths through such channels as the priesthood, contemplative communities, or craft guilds. The vertical aspect is the social hierarchy within which each individual has his or her place and function. In the modern/postmodern world, however, both axes have entirely collapsed. The Traditionalists deplore this state of affairs and are implacably opposed to secular modernity. At the same time, they see the abolition of sacred order as a sign of the times, proof positive that we are living in the last days. Behind their denunciatory rhetoric, there is a quietism. All one can do is cling to the last vestiges of Tradition and seek one's own salvation.

Frithjof Schuon relocated to the USA in 1980, the last place one would expect a Traditionalist to choose. It was an ill-fated move, and the last decade of his life was marred by scandal. Sacred order in the tariqa he set up in Bloomington, Indiana, broke down. Eventually, he was brought before a grand jury on charges of cultic abuse. This chapter is not the place to address this ignominious end to a life of contemplative scholarship[5].

II

Therapies, however well they work, cannot transfer to themselves, democratic and mortal as they are, the immortality of revealed and aristocratic, even monarchical truth. (Rieff 1990: 352)

Philip Reiff was a great Freud scholar, and Schuon made no secret of his detestation of psychoanalysis. But there are some striking correspondences between Rieff's idea of sacred order and Schuon's notion of Tradition.

Rieff developed a compelling theory of culture from the concept of repression. Culture is the moral demand system that underpins civilisation and its discontents. If there were no distance between desire and its object, Rieff argues, then "everything thought or felt would be done on the instant." (Rieff 1979: 367) A society that abolished this distance would be cultureless:

> Culture, our ingeniously developed limitations is constituted by two motifs, which are dialectically related. These two motifs, which have shifting contents, I call interdicts and remissions from interdicts. Every culture is so constituted that there are actions one cannot perform, more accurately would dread to perform. (Rieff 1990:323)

---

[5]   See Appendix 1: The Other Frithjof Schuon.

Twenty years ago, I had an unforgettable insight into how the interdicts worked. I had taken a temporary post in an outer London junior school. To my dismay, the kids sabotaged every lesson with a never- ending series of minor and sometimes major disruptions. Consequently, they were not learning anything. The headmaster was remote and the school lacked any proper ethos. I decided that enough was enough and I gave in my notice at the end of the term. But when I told the class that I was not coming back a riot broke out. Many of the children wept, some grabbed computer paper and wrote out their protests in block capitals. One of these messages read: MR. BURNISTON OUR GOD. Such was this boy's craving for authority, such was the children's longing for sacred order.

Rieff's *Epilogue* to *Freud: The Mind of the Moralist* amounts to a refutation of Schuon's notion that psychoanalysts are in the business of abolishing the sense of guilt. (Schuon 1986:195) The object of Freudian therapy is not to turn the patient into a psychopath but to lift the repressions that are such a constant source of misery to all concerned. The removal of surplus repression is not a simple catharsis. Freud was surprised to discover that, at the critical point of an analysis, something independent of the patient's will would assert itself and defiantly resist the release of an emergent repression into consciousness. He deduced that this resistance could not have come from the unconscious, i.e., the repressed, but "from the same higher strata and systems of the mind which originally carried out the repression." (Freud 1964:289) Although the resistance originated in the ego, it remained unconscious to the patient. "We have come across something in the ego itself," Freud wrote in *The Ego and the Id*, "which is also unconscious, which behaves exactly like the repressed—which produces powerful effects without itself being conscious and which requires special work before it can be made conscious." (Freud 1964:356)

The initial act of repression and the repressed content split the unconscious into two, but then a third unconscious comes into the picture. Rieff designates this paradoxical factor as *the repressive imperative*, the intra-psychic authority behind every repression:

> By repressive imperative, I mean that authority external to all negational recognitions of it, which splits evil and good. Authority is vested in the unalterable craving of the mind for connecting oppositions—known and unknown, conscious and unconscious, rejections and acceptances. The sharp division of things into dark and light characteristics of human vision gives us our first impression of authority. (Rieff 1979:367)

The repressive imperative, which cannot be repressed itself, cuts into the continuum of sheer possibility that would render the personality meaningless. As the source of authority, it determines the boundaries within which each individual can actualise himself or herself. Anyone who acknowledges the authority of the repressive imperative lives a life in sacred order. Rieff introduced this concept in *The Triumph of the Therapeutic*, in which he defined sacred order as "the vertical in authority, those interdictory heights and transgressive depths between which mortals perform their remissive sidlings and shufflings." (Rieff 1967: xii)

Individual character, the inability to do otherwise, is sacred order internalised. This developmental process is regulated by "the secret intelligence of the repressive imperative." With this intelligence, said Reiff in the *Epilogue* "what is repressive directs conscious will and moral choice to function as agent, in character, in sacred order. From hidden existence derives every known existence." (Rieff 1979: 381) Those who trust in this hidden existence have faith, the evidence of things unseen. Conversely, an individual who defies the repressive imperative rejects life in sacred order and puts himself or herself on the road to psychosis. (Rieff 1979: 388) Whereas psychosis exposes the self to the demonic as sheer contingent possibility, faith accepts the constraints of a life in sacred order: "In the reserve, even the incommunicability of every response to sacred order personality is forged; there is no other way of becoming oneself except alone in this response." (Rieff 1979:386-7)

Without effective interdicts, this dialogue between self and authority cannot take place, and the personality is denied the means of integration. Rieff made no secret of his grave doubts as to the viability of the present social order in this respect, and he foresaw a cultureless society as the final triumph of the therapeutic:

> By psychologizing about themselves interminably Western men are learning to use their internality against the primacy of any particular organization of the personality. If this restructuring of the Western imagination succeeds in establishing itself, complete with institutional regimens, the human autonomy from the compulsions of culture may follow freedom already won from the compulsions of nature. (Rieff 1967:21)

Perhaps this new type of human, discharged from any obligation to the sacred, will find a way to establish an enduring social order. If so, what revolution has ever been so seemingly benign? Nietzsche had already anticipated this development in the last human: "One has one's little pleasure for the day and one's little pleasure for the night and one honours good health. We have invented happiness say the last humans and they blink." (Nietzsche 2005:16)

In a posthumously published work *Charisma: The Gift of Grace and How It Has Been Taken Away from Us*, Rieff examines the role of the charismatic prophet in the creation of sacred order. The true charismatic creates new interdicts. He taps into the repressive imperative and, by demanding new forms of renunciation, satisfies our innate craving for authority. He overturns the tables of the law, abolishes the old order of interdicts and remissions, and inaugurates a new one: "For through the Law I died to the Law, that I might live in God." (Galatians 2:19)

For Guenon and the Traditionalists who follow in his wake, the old order is modernity; the reign of quantity and the new order is the Primordial Tradition in which sacred order is fully reinstated. In his apocalyptic book *The Reign of Quantity and the Signs of the Times*, Guenon prophesied the end of "what may rightly be called a humanity." (Guenon 1972:330-1) But this, Guenon declared, in no way implied the end of the terrestrial world. When the present cycle of dissolution (the Kali Yuga) has exhausted every last possibility, a new cycle will begin immediately after the old one has expired: "But we shall be changed, in a moment, in the twinkling of an eye, at the last trumpet." (1 Corinthians 15: 51-52)

III

A few weeks after I discovered Schuon's *Transcendent Unity of Religions*, I found my way to my first Jungian analyst, Irene Champernowne. She told me that she had gone out to meet Jung in the 1930s and had entered into analysis with him. She returned to England before the war and established a residential therapeutic community on the outskirts of Exeter in 1942. (See Stevens 1986) In twelve analytic hours, she transmitted Jung's wisdom to me.

Throughout the '70s, I immersed myself in Jung's collected works while also exploring Schuon and the perennial philosophers. I found numerous points of contact and thought that I was working on complementary texts. My ecumenical daydream was shattered when I came across a scathing condemnation of Jung in one of Schuon's books, *In Tracks of Buddhism*. Jung, he declared, had reduced the spiritual to the psychic and, thereby, "insidiously ruined all transcendence and intellection." (Schuon 1968) This was not an isolated outburst, and it represented the consensus amongst all the Traditionalists. Titus Burckhardt had written an extended refutation of Jung in his long essay *Cosmology and Modern Science*. (in Needleman 1977) I read this carefully and found the case he made unconvincing. But I was up against a consensus, and that is infinitely more difficult to challenge than a set of arguments. It would be another ten years and considerably more analytical hours before I was ready to make a move.

Towards the end of 1985, I could see the way forward. I decided to write directly to Schuon through his

English publishers Perennial Books. Of course, if I declared my Jungian affiliation, my letter would end up in the shredder. But if I did not raise the point at issue, the entire exercise would be pointless. After much drafting and redrafting, this is what I sent out on 1 January 1986:

Dear Mr Schuon,

I am writing to express my deep appreciation of your books. Not only have they opened my eyes to the possibility of Intellectual Intuition, they have also had a lasting transformative influence on me. At the same time they present me with an intractable dilemma. Stated briefly: how are individuals such as myself to appropriate the experience of Gnosis in a society that can offer no meaningful context for this? Although there is now an unprecedented access to esoteric texts there is no way of grounding this essential knowledge in exotericism.

Without this access to the literature of religious esotericism my sense of the sacred would have been overwhelmed by the secular ideologies of the modern world. Having grown up in post war Europe I am constituted by large, depersonalized institutions. It is necessary to make an adaptation to them while preserving the integrity of one's inner life as best one can. In the absence of any kind of collective myth or ritual pattern, the longing for transcendence is confined to a private symbolic universe.

The light of Sophis Perennis has penetrated the darkness of modern consumer society but it can find no receptacle. Instead, the sparks are dispersed among numerous individuals or groups. It may be possible for privileged few to take refuge in a traditional community but the conditions of modern urban life preclude this option for the majority. If I have understood you correctly you maintain that only a life in Tradition can guarantee personal authenticity. And that is my dilemma.

I hope that in the process of explaining the problem, I have not obscured my original intention of conveying the profound impression your books have made on me.

Frithjof Schuon did not reply to me directly but forwarded my letter to Martin Lings who sent me an invitation to visit him at his home in Westerham, Kent.

Martin Lings (1919-2005), a.k.a. Abu Bakr Siraj Ad Din, was a major figure in the Traditionalist movement. He was also a poet, Shakespeare scholar, and one of the finest Islamic scholars of the twentieth century. For a full account of this remarkable man, go to www. martinlings.org.

We sat facing each other across a table. Some of Schuon's Native American icons were on the walls. I sensed that he had been looking forward to the meeting, but how would he react when he learnt where I was coming from? He told me that he could best answer the questions I had raised in my letter by telling me about his own background. He had studied under C S Lewis at Oxford and spoke highly of him. While he was teaching in Lithuania, he discovered Guenon's *Man and His Becoming According to the Vedanta*, a book that hit him with the force of revelation. It is difficult to recall his reception of Guenon from the rapid and condensed account that followed. He told me that once he had read Guenon, he was convinced of the necessity to enter Tradition without delay. He converted to Catholicism without telling his father confessor that this move was only a stepping stone to Islam. The fact that he now belonged to the Tariqa Maryimiah was, he claimed, a sign that providence had been guiding him from the outset.

He told me that he went on to secure a teaching post in Cairo. He found Guenon and acted as his unpaid secretary. Martin Lings was the first to proofread the master's apocalyptic text, *The Reign of Quantity and Signs of the Times*. I listened with fascination but could not see how any of this was meant to address the issues I had put to Schuon in my letter.

He invited me to give an account of my background. I told him about my Anglican childhood and how my faith, such as it was, collapsed under the pressure of peer group atheism when I was fifteen. I would have remained like this if Sri Ramana Maharshi had not come into my life like a flash of lightning four years later. But I soon realised that I could neither go back to the church nor forward to Sri Ramana Maharshi's Vedanta Advaita. Then I explained that I would have remained in limbo had I not entered a Jungian analysis. I added that I knew Titus Burckhardt's critique of Jung and was not convinced by his arguments.

Martin Lings was somewhat bemused and no doubt dismayed by my Jungian affiliation. After an inconclusive diversion on Jung's proposition, that the subject of psychology was also its object, he came to the point. The idea of pursuing an individual spiritual path on the basis of psychology rather than Tradition was a hiding to nothing. Psychology could not provide the three conditions necessary for spiritual development:

initiation, doctrine, and method. He had explained this point very clearly in his book *The Eleventh Hour*:

> All traditional forms of mysticism are known to insist on the three conditions as indispensable so that there is good reason to fear that if anyone of the three is not fulfilled, the whole endeavour "can only end up as a psychological exploit without any relation to the development of our higher states." (Lings 1987:99. The quotation is from Schuon's essay "The Nature and Function of a Spiritual Master.")

By now, it was time to bring the meeting to an end, so I suggested that we might continue this conversation by way of correspondence.

In his first letter, he told me bluntly what he thought of my Jungian position. Providence has been holding cards up her sleeve for the present state of spiritual emergency. But I was refusing to take one and using cards of my own fabrication instead. Jungian therapy is no avail in the eleventh hour and *what orthodox tradition has to offer is unobtainable elsewhere*. In my reply, I did not challenge this proposition and chose a card. I suggested that the best way forward would be for me to investigate the Christian way and to talk to someone in this tradition who understood the esoteric dimensions of the faith. In his reply, I was told that "it is almost out of the question that you would find a Spiritual Master in Anglicanism or for that matter in Catholicism. The fact that my Shaykh has one or two Roman Catholic priests as his disciples is significant. They wish to remain Christian but are convinced that they would never find his counterpart in Christianity today." He was referring to Shaykh Isa Nur ad Din (a.k.a. Frithjof Schuon). Martin Lings seemed to be offering me a way into the Tariqa Maryimiah by the back door.

But if I had followed up the hint in his letter and had taken a plane to Bloomington, Indiana, I would have encountered a very strange sort of "orthodoxy" indeed. (see Appendix 1)

In my next letter I played my strongest card. I sent Martin Lings my essay *A Word Conceived in Intellect* (chapter 4) and drew his attention to some of the anomalies in Titus Burckhardt's critique of Jung. His reply struck me as beside the point:

> What Titus Burckhardt is saying in the passage you quote (Burckhardt 1986:169) is that Jung uses terms below their normal level. The Ideas in the Platonic sense are supra- psychic and therefore supra-mental, belonging to the domain of the Spirit. The word "archetype" is normally reserved for spiritual reality, as is the word "transcendent."

> This abnormal use of terms is insidious and quite literally labyrinthine. Their traditional use has not only a doctrinal but also a methodic value; for the esoterist is centred a priori on the difference between soul and spirit, and he needs to keep pure and uncontaminated such words as "archetype" and "transcendent." For him this psycho-physical world is the world of symbols whose transcendent archetypes are no less than the spiritual and intellectual realities of the hereafter. Titus Burckhardt is warning us against what is in fact, a great danger. In other words, he is saying: "Beware that you do not stop short at the Jungian "archetype," but fly direct to the spiritual reality itself." (Handwritten letter dated 22/2/1986)

It is even more dangerous to disregard the unconscious psyche in this way and "fly direct to the spiritual reality". That is a recipe for a particularly insidious inflation.

I had no desire to become embroiled in an interminable defence of Jung. Was there any way of establishing some common ground between us? In a later letter suggested that Henry Corbin could be the mediating figure. Dr Lings was not enthusiastic, and in his reply, he told me that he did not believe Corbin could be of any help to me. When I pressed him on the matter, his reply was rather cryptic:

> I really have no right to speak about Corbin because I have not read enough of his writing. But, in what little I have read, I have been conscious of what I can only describe as a certain lack of essentiality. (10/10/1986)

Corbin chose not to embrace Islam, hence "the certain lack of essentiality." Just as Jung had his invisible guide in Elijah/Philemon (Jung/Jaffe: 207-9), so did Corbin follow an Uwaysi shaykh[6]. This was al Suhravardi who had died a martyr in 1191. As far as Martin Lings and the Traditionalists are concerned, only a flesh and blood spiritual master can confer an authentic initiation.

Rather than quote more passages from our correspondence, I have boiled down Martin Ling's theological position to four propositions:

1. That man was made for transcendence.
2. That access to transcendence was only possible within an orthodox religious tradition.

---

6   Uways al Qurani was a mystic and contemporary of the Prophet. They knew of each other's existence but never met. Instead, they communicated through dreams and visions. An Uwaysian transmission involves a connection with a spiritual figure with whom physical contact would have been impossible.

3. That the traditions may well be in a parlous state, but God, in his mercy, will always hold the doors to salvation open. One should simply "pray without ceasing."
4. That Guenon's prophecies of the imminent end of an entire Manvantara were true. All one can do is seek one's own salvation as a matter of urgency.

On the assumption that these four propositions are an accurate summary of his theological position, I will comment briefly on each one in turn:

The first proposition is the least problematic. The yearning for transcendence in some form is what makes us human. And it is also true that the religious traditions provide the best possible means of attaining this goal (second proposition). However, according to the Traditionalists, only an "orthodox" religious tradition can provide the path to authentic transcendence. Jung's idea of wholeness was, in Martin Ling's judgement, "pitifully relative." My reaction to this was visceral.

The third proposition is theologically sound: God's mercy is, indeed, infinite. But it sits uncomfortably with the fourth proposition. In his book, *The Reign of Quantity and the Signs of the Times*, Guenon declared that we are living in the last days of the Kali Yuga. Malice is prowling the world. (1 Peter 5:8) It is a heady brew of Hindu mythology and New Testament eschatology. Martin Lings believed it and repeatedly urged me to flee from the impending catastrophe. He spoke of "compensations" in this age of darkness and insisted that God, in his infinite mercy, would not abandon anyone who sought the means of salvation in earnest. He told me sternly that I lacked a sense of urgency. I had some difficulty in seeing how this scheme of salvation could actually work. The divine mercy, or so he told me, could only be mediated through one of the orthodox religious traditions. But these traditions were on the verge of extinction as the Kali Yuga accelerated towards its apocalyptic climax. Where was I meant to turn?

There is, however, an element of truth behind Guenon's colourful eschatology. The American theologian Langdon Gilkey coined the term "secularist mood" to define contemporary Western culture. The secularist mood consists of "the visceral sense that reality lies nowhere but amidst the visible and tangible, that all causes are physical, that all events begin and end here and all interests lie solely in this world." (cited in Dorrien,1997:152-3) In a word, the secularist mood is "a radically this-worldly mindset," i.e., the reign of quantity. The Traditionalists are implacably opposed to the secularist mood. (See for example Lings 1987) Jung, in marked contrast, preferred to engage with the spirit of the times.

I did not formulate this critique very clearly in 1986. But I found his arguments counterintuitive, and I suspected that he had trapped me in a double-bind situation. A few weeks after the correspondence was terminated, I was overtaken by drowsiness in mid-afternoon. I fell into a light sleep on the bed but retained a diffuse level of consciousness. A battle between two mighty protagonists was taking place above my head. They were landing heavy blows on each other. Then Jung's imaginal presence entered the arena, and the battle stopped immediately.

6

C G JUNG, RENE GUENON, AND THE MYTH OF THE PRIMORDIAL TRADITION

The Myth Science

C G Jung (1875–1961) and Rene Guenon (1886–1951) both came out of late nineteenth- to early twentieth-century occultism and spiritualism. But from this point on, their destinies sharply polarize. Jung enthusiastically embraced the modern scientific ideal and collaborated with Freud in the first decade of twentieth century. Guenon regarded modern science as the second fall and psychoanalysis as an Ahrimanic masterstroke. While Jung lived in the centre of Europe and helped shape its cultural identity, Guenon embraced Islam, vehemently denounced Theosophy, and retreated to Cairo. From his modest apartment above a sweet- shop, he wrote books that challenged the very premises upon which modern European culture is based.

No thinker has rejected modernity more radically than Rene Guenon. But to accuse him of turning the clock back to the Middle Ages is to fall into lazy thinking, something that both Guenon and Jung deplored. Guenon's writings are lucid and grounded in a coherent metaphysical perspective. He holds the mirror up to modern European culture dispassionately, and many people avert their gaze. His critique of secular humanism often provokes visceral reactions. But if you can overcome this reaction and hear him out, his arguments are both compelling and disturbing in equal measure.

Jung was at the centre of the Eranos conferences, one of the major currents in the contemporary Western esotericism. Guenon was the founding father of a rival esotericism that goes by the name of Traditionalism. The leading figures of this movement are certainly a match for their Eranos counterparts: Frithjof Schuon, Titus Burckhardt, Martin Lings, and S H Nasr are all distinguished scholars, not closet esotericists. If I attempt to describe the full range and cultural impact of this movement, I will never get beyond the starting point of my essay. Mark Sedgwick, in his book *Against the Modern World* (Sedgwick 2004), has given a far more comprehensive account than I could offer.

In 1986, I had the rare opportunity to meet to Martin Lings, who, it transpired, had been Guenon's secretary in Cairo. Our meeting constellated a positive transference between two introverted intuitive types, but as soon as I disclosed my loyalty to Jung, the portcullis came down. Some correspondence took place, but nothing was resolved. Martin Lings, if anything, became more entrenched in his hostility to Jung. I internalized the split and have worked on it and through it ever since. (For an account of my dialogue with Martin Lings, see Ch.5:3)

There was, however, one point of agreement between me and Martin Lings: that the modern West is in a prolonged spiritual crisis. In this essay, I will show how Guenon and Jung adopted antithetical strategies in response to this situation. I will begin with Jung's own crisis in 1913 after the break with Freud, which occurred on the eve of the First World War. In *Memories, Dreams, Reflections*, Jung recalled his predicament like this:

> Promptly the question arose of what, after all, I had accomplished. I had explained the myths of people of the past, I had written a book about the hero, the myth in which man has always lived. But in what myth does man live nowadays? In the Christian myth the answer might be. "Do you live in it?" I asked myself. To be honest the answer was no. For me it is not the myth I live by. "Then do we no longer have any myth. No, evidently we no longer have any myth. But then what is your myth—the myth by which you live?" At this point the dialogue with myself became uncomfortable and I stopped thinking. I had reached a dead end. (MDR:194 - 5)

As far as Guenon is concerned, Jung's existential dilemma amounts to a diversion or rather a flight from Tradition. All myths and sacred symbols are the expression of one unanimous perennial philosophy that is accessible to all through the religious traditions. There is no other way—you have only to decide on your point of entry. But what if all the doors are locked? I put this question to Martin Lings, and it made no sense to him. He told me that God, in his infinite mercy, would never withhold the means of salvation from anyone who sought them in earnest. "Then what should

I do?" I asked him. The answer was that I should pray without ceasing.

Guenon and Lings saw Jung as a man wandering around in the endless labyrinth of the unconscious psyche. I was strongly advised not to make the same catastrophic mistake. With respect, I see the matter very differently. Jung took a journey back or down to the source of all mythologies in the depths of the unconscious psyche. His itinerary took him beyond the personal unconscious which "ends at the earliest memories of infancy" to the transpersonal or collective unconscious that is universal to the human species:

> When psychic energy regresses, going beyond the period of early infancy, and breaks into the legacy of ancestral life, the mythological images are awakened: these are the archetypes. An interior world whose existence we never suspected opens out and displays contents which seem to stand in sharpest contrast to all our former ideas. (CW7:118)

A controlled descent to this level of the psyche does not lead to chaos and psychosis but to a coherent spiritual world. This world is ruled by the archetypes, the ordering principles of the collective unconscious.

If Jung is correct in his claim that archetypal images coincide with myth motifs, then it is the task of psychology to articulate these correspondences. Jung's psychology is itself a kind of myth as he explained in his piece on the child archetype:

> Psychology as one of the many expressions of psychic life operates with ideas which in their turn are derived from archetypal structures and

> thus generates a somewhat abstract kind of myth.
> Psychology therefore translates the archaic speech
> of myth into a modern mythologem—not yet
> recognized as such—which constitutes one element
> of the myth "science."

Jung does not say anything more about the provocative notion of the myth science. (It would be anathema both to Guenon and to Richard Dawkins for different reasons.) However, he does indicate the kind of myth he has in mind. It is not merely a product of the intellect:

> This seemingly hopeless undertaking is a lived and
> living myth, satisfying to persons of corresponding
> temperament, indeed beneficial insofar as they
> have been cut off from their psychic origins by
> neurotic dissociation. (CW9/1: 302 or Jung and
> Kerenyi 1969:98-9)

Jung's psychology is a "lived and living myth," and like all myths, it takes us back to primordial times. In his *Prolegomena to the Essays on a Science of Mythology,* Karl Kerenyi explains how myths are grounded in the *archai,* that is in primary substances or states "that never age, can never be surpassed, and produce everything always." Whereas the philosopher treats these states of being as concepts, "the teller of myths without any digression or searching on his part, without any studious investigation or effort . . . finds himself . . . in the midst of the *archai* of which he is speaking." The philosopher tries to tell us what "really is," but the teller of myths steps back into primordiality to tell us what "originally was." (Jung and Kerenyi 1969:7-8)

S H Nasr tells us the myth of the primordial tradition like this:

> From a certain point of view there is but one
> Tradition the Primordial Tradition, which always
> is. It is the single truth, which is at once the
> heart and origin of all truths. All traditions are
> earthly manifestations of celestial archetypes
> related ultimately to the immutable archetype of
> the Primordial Tradition in the same way that all
> revelations are related to the Logos or Word which
> was in the beginning. (Nasr 1981:74)

Guenon himself is wonderfully concise: He declared
that all the religions are "so many heresies" compared
with "the primordial and unanimous tradition." (cited
in an undated *Note on Rene Guenon* by Schuon in
Studies in Comparative Religion 17:1, pg.5).

Whereas Jung's psychological myth takes us back to the
foundations of psychic life, the myth of the perennial
philosophy returns to the origins of all religions in
the primordial tradition. But the two myths are based
on radically different premises. Nasr understands
archetypes in the Platonic sense as immutable ideas in
the mind of God. For Jung, the archetypes are located
in the collective unconscious. They are the product of
millions of years of evolution, not static immutable
entities. This was the rock upon which my dialogue
with Martin Lings crashed.

Guenon has shown that the archetype of the primordial
tradition is symbolized by the Holy Grail. In *The Lord
of the World*, he tells us that the Grail was originally
entrusted to Adam in the terrestrial paradise, only to
be lost when he was banished from Eden. Later Seth
obtained permission to return and recover the Grail
so as to restore the primordial order that had been
destroyed by the fall. There are no narratives to tell
us who kept the Grail until the time of Christ. Guenon

mentions Celtic sources of the myth and suggests that "the Druids had a part of it and should be counted amongst the regular guardians of the Primordial Tradition." (Guenon 1983: ch.5)

The terrestrial paradise is the true centre of the world, and it is traditionally represented as a mandala with the tree of life at the central point and the four rivers flowing towards the cardinal points. In the human microcosm, the corresponding centre is the heart, a symbolic equivalent to the grail. Both the heart and the Grail signify the true centre in man, namely the sense of eternity that was disrupted by the fall:

> The terrestrial Paradise was in fact the true "Centre of the World," which is everywhere Assimilated to the Divine Heart. Can one not say that Adam, by the fact that he was in Eden, truly lives in the Heart of God? (Guenon 1995:18)

Whoever regains this centre and lives in the heart of God reverses the fall and regains the primordial tradition. Such a person can be said to own the primordial state. For Jung, the quest for the centre is the individuation process. This is the inner work of restoring the wholeness of the psyche that is lost as a consequence of the fall into ego consciousness:

> To arrive at a primordial religious phenomenon, man must return to a condition where that functioning is absolutely unprejudiced, where one cannot say that is good or that is evil, where one has to give up all bias as to the nature of religion; for as long as there is any kind of bias, there is no submission. (DA:513)

Although this wholeness is inexpressible in discursive language, it can be intuited through a multiplicity of symbols: the mandala, quaternity, sphere, lapis, microcosm, etc. Guenon and Jung use the same symbolic language, but Jung had no time for metaphysics, and Guenon was implacably hostile to psychoanalysis. However, he was by no means dismissive of modern psychology:

> By definition psychology can only be concerned with human states, and further, what it stands for today is only a very limited part of the potentialities of the individual, who includes far more than specialists in this science are able to imagine. (Guenon 1986:52)

Jung would have had no objections to this, and he could have told Guenon that he had almost singlehandedly expanded the field of psychology to include the full range of human potentialities. In his paper on the Kore for *Essays on a Science of Mythology*, he says,

> The indefinite extent of the unconscious component makes a comprehensive definition of the human personality impossible. Accordingly, the unconscious supplements the picture with living figures ranging from the animal to the divine, as the two extremes outside man, and rounds out the animal extreme, through the addition of vegetable and inorganic abstractions, into a microcosm. (CW9/1:315 or Jung and Kerenyi 1969:161-2)

Needless to say, Martin Lings was not impressed. He complained to me that Jung had hijacked the key words of *Sophia Perennis* for his own ends and he had not properly understood them. His use of the word "archetype" is a case in point as was "transcendent/ immanent," which he did not begin to understand:

> Esotericism jealously reserves the word, "immanent" to express all that goes beyond the psyche in terms of subjective depth. Ultimately when we speak of the "immanent self", the word is used on the Divine Level. (Martin Lings – private letter: 13/3/86)

Jung's psychology encompasses the full range of our subjective depths whether they are defined as immanent or transcendent. His model of the psyche is grounded in the transpersonal self, a totality that includes all conscious and unconscious processes from the divine to the animal. An existence bound to ego consciousness can only actualize a limited range of an individual's potentialities. Jung's individuation process is a psychospiritual method of realizing this wholeness. In his short essay "On Resurrection," he explains what he means by this term:

> Through the progressive integration of the unconscious, we have a reasonable chance to make experiences of an archetypal nature providing us with the feeling of continuity before and after our existence. The better we understand the archetype the more we participate in its life and the more we realize its eternity or timelessness. (CW18:1572)

Jung goes on to quote from the *Mithraic Liturgy*: "I am a Star following its way like you." Wholeness and the sense of eternity are fused in this evocative image. The star is an exemplary image of the self, and Jung tells us that "the realization of the self means a re-establishment of Man as the microcosm, i.e., man's cosmic relatedness." (CW18:1573)

However, unlike Guenon, Jung doubted that the self could ever be comprehended in its totality. In the *Two Essays on Analytical Psychology*, he explained why:

> It is easy enough to think of ourselves as possessing part souls. Thus we can, for instance, see ourselves as a persona without too much difficulty. But it transcends the powers of imagination to form a clear picture of what we are as a self, for in this operation the part would have to comprehend the whole. There is little hope of our ever being able to reach even an approximate consciousness of the self, since however much we may make conscious there will always exist an indeterminate and indeterminable amount of unconscious material which belongs to the totality of the self. Hence the self will always remain a supraordinate quantity. (CW7:274)

As a psychiatrist, Jung could not have endorsed Guenon's proposal that it was possible to reverse the fall. Therein lays the road to an inflation of the ego:

> The ego fancies itself magnified and exalted, whereas in reality it is thrust into the background, so much so that the ego almost needs an inflation (the feeling of being one of the elect, for instance) in order not to lose the ground from under its feet, although it is precisely the inflation that lifts it off its foundations. It is not the ego that is exalted; rather, something greater than it makes its appearance: the self, a symbol that expresses the whole man. But the ego loves to think itself the whole man and therefore has the greatest difficulty in avoiding the danger of inflation. (CW10:721)

At the end of *Answer to Job*, Jung argued that the realization of our divine humanity does not cancel out our creaturely nature:

> Even the enlightened person remains what he is,
> and is never more than his own limited ego before
> the One who dwells within him, whose form has no
> knowable boundaries, who encompasses him on all
> sides, fathomless as the abysms of the ocean and as
> vast as the sky. (CW11:758)

Jung is much closer to St. Paul than Guenon who was closer to the Sufism of Ibn 'Arabi.

A Window into Eternity

Now I want to venture more deeply into alchemical territory. By way of road map, I have compressed the development of Jung's concept of the archetype over thirty years into three stages:

- The archetypes manifest themselves in one dimension. Initially, Jung defined archetypes as innate dispositions in the unconscious psyche to form images. Archetypes are analogous to instincts, i.e., to innate dispositions to behave in a certain way. Archetypes and instincts are universal in the human species and are the building blocks of the collective unconscious.
- The archetypes manifest themselves in two dimensions. Jung's observations of his own experiences and those of his patients suggested that an archetype could manifest itself both as an image in psyche and as an event in the external world. The most famous example of this was the rationalistic patient who took a dream of a scarab beetle to Jung. As she was reading it out, a rose chafer beetle landed on the window ledge, and Jung handed it to her. This had the immediate effect of breaching her rationalistic defenses

and removing a blockage in the therapeutic process. The theory of synchronicity was based on such observations and has been confirmed by countless Jungian analysts; it's routine now. If an archetype "transgresses" the boundary line between inner and outer, it is not exclusively psychic, but quasi-psychic or "psychoid."

· The archetypes transcend both dimensions. Synchronistic events point towards a unitary level of reality that is neither inner nor outer. Psyche and matter are just two sides of the same coin. The sixteenth-century alchemist Gerhard Dorn designated this unitary dimension of reality the *unus mundus*. Jung describes the *unus mundus* as "the transcendental psychophysical background [that] corresponds to a potential world insofar as all the conditions which determine the form of empirical phenomena are inherent in it." (CW14:769) This metaphysical perspective is known as dual-aspect monism.

In 1938, Jung took the alchemical writings of Dorn to study on his voyage to India. His final major piece of writing, chapter 6 of *Mysterium Coniunctionis*, is a meditation on these texts. There are three stages in Dorn's model of the alchemical opus. The first stage of conjunction is the unio mentalis and it consists in overcoming the body and its compulsive drives. This is a voluntary death for the natural man:

> The aim of this separation was to free the mind from the influence of "the bodily appetites and the heart's affections" and to establish a spiritual position which is supraordinate to the turbulent sphere of the body. This leads to a dissociation of the personality and the violation of the merely natural man. (CW14:671)

The unio mentalis enables the soul to disengage from the body and its impulses. It is released to unite with the spirit and create what Dorn called a spiraculum, an airhole or window into eternity.

Dorn regarded the mental union in the overcoming of the body as only the first stage of the alchemical *coniunctio*. The second stage was the unio corporalis; that is the reunion of the combined soul and spirit with the body. This second stage, says Jung, "consists in making a reality of the man who has acquired some self- knowledge of his paradoxical wholeness." (CW14: 679)

The unio corporalis is preparatory to the final stage, the union of the whole man with the *unus mundus*; that is with the intelligible world as it is conceived in the mind of God. Just as the primordial state is a return to the condition of man before the fall, so is the union with the *unus mundus* a return to the first day of the creation. At this point, the gap between Jung and Guenon narrows significantly.

In 1925, Guenon gave his only public lecture on "Oriental Metaphysics." He formulated a model of metaphysical realization that is applicable across a wide range of traditional spiritual disciplines, e.g., Yoga, Sufi, and Taoist meditation. There are three stages of realization:

· The first is the attainment of integral individuality, which Guenon defines as the "realization or the development of all the potentialities in the human individuality that . . . reach out in diverse directions beyond the realm of the corporeal and sensible." Whoever realizes this state escapes the inexorable flow of time so that "the apparent succession of events is transformed into simultaneity." (Guenon 1986: 49-50) In other words, the sense of eternity associated with the primordial tradition has been regained. This is the primordial state, the reestablishment of man's condition before the Fall. "He who fully owns the primordial tradition," says Guenon, "who has reached the degree of effective knowledge implied by this possession is . . . effectively reintegrated in the fullness of the primordial state." (Guenon 1983:28)

· At the second stage, the human condition is fully transcended. Guenon denotes this level as "the supra-individual state," which he describes like this:

> Here the world of man . . . is completely and definitely exceeded. It must also must be said that what is exceeded is the world of forms in its widest meaning comprising of all individual states; it is that which determines individuality as such. The being which can no longer be called human has henceforth left "the flow of forms" to use a Far Eastern expression. (Guenon 1986:50-1)

· Even though the supra-individual state transcends the flow of forms, it is still a conditioned mode of being and, therefore, transitory. Beyond this level, there is "the absolutely unconditioned stage free of all limitation." This third stage is the supreme identity, and only at this stage is final deliverance attained.

There are some intriguing correspondences between Guenon's stages of psychospiritual development and Dorn's three stages of the *coniunctio*:

Stage one of Guenon's model, the attainment of integral individuality or the primordial state, correlates with Dorn's second *coniunctio*, the unio corporalis. Stage two of Guenon's model, the supra-formal state, in which the being has left the flow of forms, correlates with the third *coniunctio*, namely the *unus mundus*. However, Dorn maintained that this stage was only attainable after death. Alchemy and, indeed, psychology are confined to conditioned states of being and cannot encompass the third and final stage of metaphysical realization, the supreme identity:

> The highest objective is the absolutely unconditioned state, free from all limitation; for this reason it is completely inexpressible, and all one can say of it must be conveyed in negative terms by the divestment of the limits that determine all existence in its relativity. (Guenon 1986:51)

In the first half of the twentieth century, Shaikh Ahmad Al Alawi in North Africa and Sri Ramana Maharshi in Southern India attained this level of realization. According to Martin Lings, their teachings are essentially the same. (Lings 1971:80, see also Osborne:1970) But the secular mood has gained such ascendency that it is difficult to see an Al Alawi or Sri Ramana Maharshi in the twenty-first century. My impression of Martin Lings when I met him at his home and from our subsequent correspondence was that he belonged to an age that was slipping away.

Above Us Only Sky

The post-religious world we live in now was anticipated by the Gnostic magus Basilides. He lived in Alexandria

in the second half of the second century. Only
fragments of his writings survive in the works of
Clement of Alexandria. His teachings were continued
by his son Isidore, and his school continued in Egypt
and Southern Europe until the fifth century. There
are two accounts of his doctrine, one in Irenaeus and
the other in Hippolytus. According to Gilles Quispel,
the one given by Hippolytus "is authentic and reflects
the original doctrine of Basilides." (Quispel 1968:212)
Jung would have known both accounts from his study
of ancient Gnosticism. Incidentally, he took the name
Basilides as a pseudonym for *The Seven Sermons of the
Dead*, a Gnostic text that he wrote, or rather channeled,
in 1916. I will conclude this chapter with an account of
the extraordinary eschatological vision of the historical
Basilides preserved in Hippolytus.

In his Eranos lecture, *Gnostic Man: The Doctrine of
Basilides*, Quispel contrasts the eschatology of primitive
Christianity, which paints the end of the world in garish
colours, with Basilides's Gnostic eschatology. According
to Basilides, at the end of the historical process,
"everything will be in its place, imbalance has been
done away with, disorder has ceased." There has been
no apocalypse; rather, the world has been painlessly
delivered of all conflict and strife. The pneumatics
will have returned to the Pleroma, while the hylics and
psychics remain below. They will be perfectly content
with their lot and know nothing of the beyond. The
great ignorance will spread through the universe,
and nothing will desire to be contrary to its nature.
There will be no distress, no more desire, and there
will not be any spirit either. "These are words," says
Quispel, "of infinite melancholy; imagine if you will,
this great merciful oblivion descending on the earth
and covering all things like snow." Which scenario is
more disturbing, Quispel asks, "the destruction of the

universe announced by primitive Christianity, or the heretic's vision of a world of eternal repose, without nostalgia"? (Quispel 1968:234-35)

The myth of the primordial tradition is based on a different premise. In his original Adamic perfection, man embodied the totality of the divine attributes. He ceased to do so after the fall, but the loss of the primordial state can never be final, and it can be regained at any point in the historical cycle. But how can this be possible today when the secular mood is all in all? In Patmos, Holderlin said,

> Near is God
> And hard to apprehend.
> But where the danger is, there
> Arises salvation also.
> (cited in CW6:446)

Is the secular mood the danger from which our salvation arises? If so it would be a catastrophic mistake to denounce it.

*

This essay was first delivered as a lecture for a conference on Jung and the perennial philosophy at the Canonbury Academy, London, in 1994 and published in Alexandria (Phanes Press, Grand Rapids, 1997). I have woven some of my correspondence with Martin Lings into the revised text. But I have given a one-sided impression of the man and his writings. His profound little book What Is Sufism? (George Allen & Unwin, London 1975) can be recommended as a corrective.

7

SYNCHRONICITY:
A DIONYSIAN PERSPECTIVE

The Archetype of Indestructible Life

The great Eranos classicist Walter Otto did not believe that the gods had evolved from primitive conditions but that they revealed themselves all at once in a mystical revelation. (Hakl 2013:113) The only other instance of a plenary theophany that I know of occurred in the youth of the Iranian Sufi master Suhravardi. In medieval Islamic cosmology there are only ten celestial intelligences. According to Henry Corbin Suhravardi "saw this closed spiritual universe explode and he was shown the multitude of those beings of light whom Hermes and Plato contemplated and the celestial beams which are the sources of the light of glory heralded by Zarathustra."[7] (Corbin 1993:208)

Otto's famous book *Dionysus: Myth and Cult* (Otto 1981) evokes the great god as a theophany:

> In the myth and in the experience of those who have been affected by the event, the appearance of Dionysus brings with it nourishing, intoxicating waters that bubble up from the earth. Rocks split open and streams of water gush forth. Everything that has been locked up is released. The alien and the hostile unite in miraculous harmony. Age old laws have suddenly lost their power and even the dimensions of time and space are no longer valid. (Otto 1981:95-6)

When the laws of time and space are suspended, causality recedes and synchronicity takes over. Nietzsche knew this. Although he did not have the term synchronicity in his vocabulary, he anticipated Jung by half a century. In what follows, I will show how Nietzsche's vision of acausal connectedness was centered on Dionysus just as Jung's was centered on Hermes. Hillman's provocative paper "On Psychological Femininity" (Hillman 1978: 215-298) was the catalyst. However, I have strong reservations about the way he polarizes Dionysus and Apollo much to the detriment of the latter. This reductionist tendency mars a very thought-provoking essay.

---

[7]   Shihab al - Din al - Suravardi (1155-1191) died a martyr at the age of 36. For an account of his philosophy of light see Corbin 1993: chapter VII.

Hillman's essay opens with some critical reflections on Jung's response to the papal declaration of the Assumption of the Virgin Mary. Pius XII had declared a new dogma in 1950: Mary was united with God the Son in the heavenly bridal chamber. To the bemusement of theologians in both denominations, Jung hailed this event as the most significant development since the Reformation. Mary, as *Sophia*, is united in body and soul with the Godhead. This marked a decisive break with the dualism that had underpinned Christianity thus far. It was a step in the direction of a unified world picture in which spirit and matter were one reality, an *unus mundus*. But the spectre of dualism had not gone away, and Jung raised the question, "What has become of the characteristic relation of the mother image to the earth, darkness, the abysmal side of bodily man with his animal passions and instinctual nature, and to 'matter' in general?" (CW9/1:195)

Hillman is with Jung on this point. The Virgin Mary represents only the light side of the mother archetype, and consequently, the dark side is excluded from the *imago Dei*. The difficulties of bringing matter and spirit into conjunction "reflect from the psychological point of view, prior difficulties in the harmonies of those opposites we call mind and body or even deeper male and female." He goes on to spell out the consequences of our failure to address the gender problem:

> It is all very well to talk of new theories of the relativity of matter and spirit, the end of materialism, of synchronicity and the unus mundus and of the possibility of a universal science, where matter and spirit lose their hostile polarity, but these are all projections of the intellect unless there is a corresponding change of attitude in regard to the material part of man himself which has, as Jung says, always been

associated in our tradition with the feminine. The
transformation of our world-view necessitates
the transformation of our view of the feminine.
(Hillman 1978:216)

A unified world image is meaningless without a
unified self-image. But such a conjunction can never
take place if we cling to the deep-rooted notion of
feminine inferiority. Hillman designated this attitude
as "Apollonic consciousness," which, "like its namesake,
kills from a distance (its distance kills) and keeping
with the scientific cut of its objectivity it never merges
with or 'marries' its material." (Hillman 1978:250)
As a corrective to this tendency, Hillman proposed a
consciousness ruled by the bisexual god, Dionysus.
Only by entering into Dionysian consciousness can we
redeem the feminine principle and reclaim the abysmal
side of bodily man with his animal passions and
instinctual nature.

It is true that Apollo is characterized by his distance,
but Hillman has forgotten that Walter Otto described
this attribute of the great god in a more nuanced way:

> In Apollo there greets us the spirit of clear eyed
> cognition which confronts existence and the world
> with unparalleled freedom- the truly Greek spirit
> which was destined to produce not only the arts
> but eventually even science. It was capable of
> looking on the world and existence as form, with
> a glance free alike from greed and of yearning for
> redemption. In form the elemental, momentary,
> and individual aspects of the world are cancelled,
> but its essence is acknowledged and confirmed. To
> attain it requires distance, of which no denial of
> the world is capable. (Otto 1955/79:79)

In his monumental study of Dionysus, Kerenyi traced
the origins of the myth and cult to Minoan Crete and
then described how it travelled north with the spread
of viticulture. (Kerenyi 1976) He rejected the theory that
Dionysian worship derived from spontaneous outbursts
of collective hysteria. (Dodds 1951: Appendix 1) The
religion of Dionysus arose from visionary experiences
of the divine life force (*zoe*). He also distanced himself
from Otto's depiction of Dionysus as the mad god.
(Otto 1981:136) Otto, Kerenyi argued, was too much
bound to Nietzsche. Consequently, he gave a one-
sided emphasis to the eruptive aspect of the great
god and dehumanized him. The life force (*zoe*) does
sometimes erupt violently, but this is not its only mode
of manifestation. Kerenyi was far more interested in the
erotic side of Dionysus.

The Greek word *zoe* denotes "life" in general, while
bios refers to specific life forms (hence, biology or
biography). Life as *bios* implies death, but *zoe* is infinite,
indestructible life and, therefore, the antithesis of
thanatos. *Zoe* is, as Kerenyi puts it, "the thread upon
which every individual bios is strung like a bead and
which in contrast to bios can be conceived of only as
endless." (Kerenyi 1976: xxxv) Immortal *zoe*, however,
requires soul to become incarnate in mortal *bios*.
This principle is personified in Dionysus's consort
Ariadne. She is the great goddess of the Aegean world.
Kerenyi understands her as the archetypal image
of the bestowal of soul that makes each and every
living creature a unique individual. The *coniunctio* of
Dionysus and Ariadne represents "the eternal passage
of zoe into and through the genesis of living creatures.
This occurs over and over again and is always
uninterruptedly present." (Kerenyi 1976:124-5)

To speak of a synchronistic relationship between body and soul seems rather prosaic after Kerenyi's eloquent and profound interpretation of the Dionysus-Ariadne *coniunctio*. In his essay on *Psychosomatic Medicine from the Jungian Point of View,* C A Meier speaks of the subtle body without which it is impossible to explain the reciprocal influence between psyche and soma. (Meier 1986:168 – 89) Kerenyi too had the subtle body in mind when he said that soul "is an essential element of zoe which needs it to transcend the seminal stage" and that "every conception of life is psychogony." (Kerenyi 1976:124) Mythological truth mirrors empirical observation.

Whereas Apollo and Dionysus are a distinct pair of opposites, Hermes and Dionysus overlap and merge. When Pausanias visited Thebes in the second century AD, he saw an ancient wooden statue preserved in bronze beside a bronze statue of Dionysus. This first statue was looked upon as a phallus idol and called Dionysus Kadmios, i.e., Dionysus-Hermes. (Kerenyi: 1976:194-5) On a number of Attic amphora, the two Gods are inextricably linked. For example, one depicts a couple who receives Dionysus in the presence of Silenus and with Hermes as guide. (Kerenyi 1976: 148, Plate 40) In a fifth-century vase painting, there is a troop of frisky silenoi led by one bearing the emblems of Hermes or Hermes takes over the role of Silenus as the teacher of Dionysus. He is shown carrying the child god on his arms. Another fifth-century vase shows Silenus and Hermes standing together with a deer between them. Silenus holds the lyre of Hermes, and Hermes holds the vessel of Dionysus. The complementarity extends beyond their common phallic natures and shows the friendly union of the Hermetic-spiritual and divine-animal aspects of the psyche. (See Kerenyi 1986: Part2:5)

In fifth-century Athens, Dionysus was honoured at his festival by a masked satyr chorus. Nietzsche, in *The Birth of Tragedy*, vividly described how each member of the chorus shed his social persona and became "the timeless servant of the God":

> In this magic transformation the Dionysian reveler sees himself as a satyr and as a satyr in turn he sees the God, which means that in his metamorphosis he beholds another vision outside himself, as the Apollonian complement of his own state. With this new vision the drama is complete. (Nietzsche 1967:64)

When the dithyramb was chanted, the Dionysian archetype manifested itself to the chorus and to the mass of the spectators. Nietzsche discovered the primal ground of tragedy in a synchronistic event, the shared vision of Dionysus. This experience resulted in "the shattering of the individual and his fusion with primal being."

The Birth of Tragedy, written when Nietzsche was twenty-seven, had a revolutionary impact comparable to Stravinsky's *Rite of Spring*. It dealt an iconoclastic blow to the prevalent notion of "Greek serenity" and uncovered the tragic, Dionysian side of Greek character and culture. *The Birth* prepared the ground for the emergence of psychoanalysis. In *Nietzsche: Disciple of Dionysus*, Rose Pfeffer suggests that it was "Nietzsche's re-interpretation of the Greek spirit that contributed to Freud's fascination with the figures of Greek mythology." (Pfeffer 1972:217) His influence on Jung was incalculable, but he has not, to the best of my knowledge, been recognized as one of the forerunners of the idea of synchronicity.

Regaining the Innocence of Becoming

It is customary to regard Nietzsche as a speculative and imaginative thinker with little interest in natural science. In fact, he was very well informed about the scientific developments of his time, and in the field of atomic theory, he anticipated some of the discoveries of the century he did not live to see. Pfeffer, who has studied Nietzsche's posthumously published notes, has argued that his outlook was closer to the dynamism of the twentieth century than it was to the mechanism of the nineteenth:

> Nietzsche's concept of "Kraft" (power) is, in its dynamic qualities, close to the energy theories of contemporary physics. He breaks with the materialistic and mechanistic explanation of the world that reduces all phenomena to a change in position of intrinsically immutable particles . . . His universe is close to that of Bergson, James and Whitehead in which atoms are not immutable bits of matter, but centers of energy whose essence is fluid and whose function it is to organize its own incessant activity. (Pfeffer 1972:139-40)

Jung's theory of synchronicity is based on the dynamic perspective of modern physics, "which shattered the absolute validity of natural law and made it relative." (Jung 1969: 818-9) Causality is not an iron law, but we tend to be misled by its immense practical efficacy. Neither is it the only way of making connections between events. According to the synchronicity principle, two events that are not causally connected are related to one another through a common core of meaning. For example, a friend of mine once had a blazing row with her lover near a car park. When they turned round and looked behind them, they saw two cars parked together. One had her initials on the number plate and her lover's initials were on the other.

Nietzsche's arrived at his critique of causality long before quantum physics:

> *Life not argument*—We have arranged for ourselves a world in which we are able to live—by positing bodies, lines, planes, causes and effects, motion and rest, form and content; without these articles of faith no one could endure living! But that does not prove them. Life is not an argument; the conditions of life might include error. (Nietzsche 2001: Aphorism 121)

Causality is one of the life-preserving errors. In reasoning that one thing must be the antecedent of another, we have not really explained anything:

> Cause and effect: there is probably never such a duality; in truth a continuum faces us, from which we isolate a few pieces, just as we always perceive a movement only as isolated points, i.e., do not really see, but infer . . . An intellect that saw cause and effect as a continuum, not, as we do, as arbitrary division and dismemberment—that saw the stream of the event—would reject the concept of cause and effect and deny all determinedness. (Nietzsche 2001: Aphorism 112)

Joan Stambaugh has shown how Nietzsche located our adherence to the notion of causality in the instinct for revenge. (Stambaugh 1972: 8-13) Whenever misfortune or tragedy strikes, we are compelled to find a culprit. But revenge is not simply an emotional reflex; it is an orientation towards time and its irreversibility. A vengeful person is constantly looking back to the past for the real or imagined cause of his affliction. When he realizes that he cannot will backwards and alter the past, he is reduced to impotence and teeth-gnashing:

> That time does not run backwards, this arouses the will's fury; "That which was"—that is the stone which it cannot roll away.

> And so it rolls stones away in fury and ill humour and takes revenge on whatever does not, like itself, feel fury and ill humour . . .

> This, yes, this alone, is what revenge itself is: the will's ill will towards time and it's "It was." (Nietzsche 2005:121)

Such an attitude prevents the present moment from being fully present and reduces it to a consequence of the preceding moment. As a result, one does not live fully in any moment.

Zarathustra teaches deliverance from the fiction of the efficient cause and of the final cause or purpose, from revenge and its counterpart, wishful thinking. Just as the habit of retrospection rigidifies the moment and binds it to the past, so does expectancy prevent the moment from existing in and for itself. It exists only for the moment that comes after it. Either way, the immediacy of the present moment is lost. His teaching releases the individual from this restrictive frame of reference. The world is not ordered according to a divine master plan—it is subject only to the eternal play of the gods. Nietzsche is going back to Heraclitus: "As children and artists play, so plays the ever-living fire. It constructs and destroys, in all innocence. Such is the game the Aeon plays with itself." (Nietzsche 1962:62)

By releasing events from the straitjacket of causality and purpose, Nietzsche restores the innocence of becoming. This liberation is possible only if one is free of resentment and can accept the present moment in all its *contingency.* Zarathustra makes this point eloquently in his discourse *Before the Sunrise:*

> Verily, a blessing it is and no blasphemy when I teach: Over all things stands the Heaven Accident, the Heaven Innocence, the Heaven Contingency, the Heaven Exuberance. Lord Contingency—that is the oldest nobility in the world, which I restored to all things when I redeemed them from their bondage under Purpose. This freedom and Heaven—serenity I placed like an azure bell over all things, when I taught that over them and through them no "eternal will"—wills. (Nietzsche 2005:143)

The Heaven of Lord Contingency is Hermes's world. There is no eternal Will operating behind the scenes, no one is responsible for life's contingencies, and so there is no valid pretext for remorse. As Kerenyi said, "Hermes has nothing to do with sins and atonement. What he brings with him from the springs of creation is precisely the innocence of becoming." (Kerenyi 1986;52)

Nietzsche conceived his thought of eternal recurrence in August 1881, "6,000 feet beyond man and time." He formulated it in *The Gay Science* as a thought experiment:

> The Heaviest Weight—What if some day or night a demon were to steal into your loneliest loneliness and say to you: "This life as you now live it and have lived it you will have to live once again and innumerable times again; and there will be nothing new in it, but every pain and every joy and every thought and sigh and everything unspeakably

> small or great in your life must return to you, all in
> the same succession and sequence- even this spider
> and this moonlight between the trees, and even
> this moment and I myself. The eternal hourglass
> of existence is turned over and over again, and you
> with it, speck of dust!" (Nietzsche 2001:341)

This proposition is the supreme test of Dionysian faith. Only a person who had regained the innocence of becoming would joyously affirm what the demon had suggested; anyone else would be crushed by the prospect presented to them. One who lives fully in the moment wills its eternal return. If you say yes to a single joy, Zarathustra declares you have said yes to all woes as well: "All things are chained together, entwined, in love." Only then have you loved the world - *For all joy wants Eternity!* (Nietzsche 2005:283) Here, the connecting principle is not causality or purpose or even meaning; it is Eros, not the latent rationality of all things.

Behind Nietzsche's audacious thought is the myth of a tragic god who must perish so as to return. In *The Will to Power*, an compilation of unpublished notes, Nietzsche dreamt the myth onwards:

> And do you know what "the world" is to me. Shall
> I show it to you in a mirror? This world: a monster
> of energy, without beginning, without end . . . this
> my Dionysian world of the eternally self-creating,
> the eternally self-destroying, this mystery world of
> twofold voluptuous delight, my "beyond good and
> evil," without goal. (Nietzsche 1968:1067)

At first sight, this seems to be a far cry from Jung's teleological model of the psyche. But consider for a moment his myth of a God who is unconscious of his contradictory nature. What kind of creation would such a deity bring forth? Will it not be a veritable monster of energy?

In "Late Thoughts" (MDR: chapter 12), Jung reflects on the gratuitous nature of the creation. He asks how could the process of evolution, "which squanders millions of years upon the development of countless species and creatures," be the outcome of conscious and purposeful intention on the part of a deity? "Natural history tells us of a haphazard and casual transformation of species over hundreds of millions of years of devouring and being devoured. The biological and political history of man is an elaborate repetition of the same thing." (MDR:371) Only the emergence of a reflecting consciousness, Jung suggests, would allow one to "suspect the element of meaning to be concealed somewhere within all the monstrous, apparently senseless biological turmoil." Human consciousness alone confers objective significance on the world, and only creaturely man can serve as a mirror for its unconscious creator.

After reading this passage, Erich Neumann wrote a long letter to Jung in which he questioned Jung's notion of an unconscious deity and refuted the idea of a random hit-and-miss evolutionary process. Jung, however, was not won over by Neumann's arguments:

> We still have no idea of where the constructive factor in biological development can be found. But we know that warm bloodedness and a differentiated brain are necessary for the inception of consciousness and thus also for the revelation of meaning. It staggers the mind even to begin to imagine the accidents and hazards that, over millions of years, transformed a lemur-like

tree dweller into a man. In this chaos of chance,
synchronistic phenomena were probably at work,
operating both with and against the known laws
of nature to produce, in archetypal moments,
syntheses which appear to us miraculous. Causality
and teleology fail us here, because synchronistic
phenomena manifest themselves as pure chance.
(L2: 495)

For Jung, meaning was an emergent property that
came out of the sheer randomness of events in the
natural order. If the universe was ruled by purpose, no
miraculous synchronicities could ever emerge from the
massa confusa. Jung's alchemical model of evolution is
much closer to Nietzsche's Dionysian world picture than
it is to Neumann's teleological version of his psychology.
If, as Jung maintains, God is unconscious, there
would have been no one to observe the miraculous
synchronicities that resulted in the emergence of warm-
blooded conscious beings. Man alone can discern and
appropriate synchronistic events. By doing so, he holds
a mirror up to nature. This, in turn, generates a higher
level of synchronistic experience. The latent rationality
of all things comes out of hiding.

Nietzsche provides a striking example of this pattern of
development. In *Ecce Homo*, he recalls his experience of
the sustained inspiration that produced his *Zarathustra*:

Everything is in the highest degree involuntary
but takes place in a tempest of feeling of freedom,
of absoluteness, of power, of divinity . . . The
involuntary nature of image, of metaphor, is the
most remarkable thing of all; one no longer has
any idea what is image, what metaphor, everything
presents itself as the readiest, the truest, the
simplest means of expression. It really does seem
as if the things themselves approached and offered

themselves as metaphors . . . This is my experience
of inspiration. (Nietzsche 1979:103)

In willing the return of a moment such as this,
Nietzsche willed the return of every moment. Thus, the
future had already happened, and the past was yet to
come. It is in this paradoxical configuration that the
great god Dionysus reveals himself to man.

*

In *Memories*, Jung places Nietzsche after Goethe in
the golden or Homeric chain, a lineage of sages and
which links heaven and earth. (MDR:214) But he did
not include Nietzsche amongst the forerunners of
the idea of synchronicity. (CW8: VII:3) This omission,
however, was not necessarily an oversight. In his
Synchronicity essay, Jung distinguishes between
synchronistic events in the specific sense and such
acausal phenomena as the discontinuities of physics
or the laws of natural numbers. While the latter have
a timeless nature, synchronicities in the narrow sense
are "acts of creation in time." (CW8:965) Nietzsche's
idea of eternal recurrence would deny such events their
uniqueness—they would recur again and again without
variation. This consideration would only apply if eternal
recurrence is understood as an empirical hypothesis.
But Nietzsche's "thought of thoughts" was something
of a chameleon. Joan Stambaugh has cited passages in
the notebooks that suggest the possibility of becoming
free of the iron law of recurrence and of transforming
the moment through the power of consciousness. This
is what seems to be the import of Nietzsche's cryptic
remark: "When man becomes true humanity, he
moves the whole of nature." According to Stambaugh,
"humanity" lies closest "to the best of what he meant

by his misunderstood term, the superman." (Stambaugh 1972:122-3)

In the *Zarathustra* seminars, Jung suggests that Nietzsche would have been an alchemist if he had lived in an earlier period of history. (Z:949-53) This is probably true. The idea that individuated man moves the whole of nature is very close to Gerhard Dorn's idea of the *Veritas*:

> There is in natural things a certain truth which cannot be seen with the outward eye, but is perceived by the mind alone, and of this the Philosophers have had experience, and have ascertained that its virtue is such as to work miracles. As faith works miracles in man, so this power, the *veritas efficaciae*, brings them about in matter. This truth is the highest power and an impregnable fortress wherein the stone of the philosophers lies. (Gerhard Dorn, The Speculative Philosophy, cited in CW12:377)

Dorn anticipates the teaching of Nietzsche/*Zarathustra* in one resounding proclamation: "Transform yourselves from dead stones into living philosophical stones!"

This chapter is a revised version of an essay published under the same title in Harvest, Journal for the C G Jung Club, London, No.40, 1994. When I was working on the first draft, I took a break and switched on the TV. There on the screen was the angelic Little Richard in concert – a truly Dionysian synchronicity.

8

THE ACTIVE DOOR

TRANSFOMATION SYMBOLISM IN NIETZSCHE AND SUHRAVARDI

In Irving Yalom's novel *When Nietzsche Wept* (Yalom: 1992), Lou Salome asks Josef Breuer to treat Nietzsche's suicidal despair. He reluctantly agrees, and the two men form an extraordinary therapeutic alliance. Jung was only able to analyze Nietzsche through his texts, but he thought that Friedrich would have been a difficult patient:

> The problem here is that Nietzsche is not an ideally analyzed person—and not even an ordinarily analyzed person is free from that peculiar crisscross of personal tendencies. If Nietzsche were analyzed—as if a man like Nietzsche could be—he would show two sides: here the suffering neurotic Nietzsche, and there the psychology of the spirit, his peculiar mythological drama. But as it is, the divine drama and man's ordinary suffering are

completely mixed and they distort each other, so
naturally we are confused when we look at the
tangle and try to decipher the contradictions. In
order to have a clear picture you must hold thesis
and antithesis ever before your eyes, the two things
that constantly work into each other or influence
each other and then try to separate them. But it is
really difficult. (Z:856)

I believe that Jung's *Zarathustra* seminars are one
long misreading of Nietzsche's text. But this is what
gives the seminars their vitality. As the late Harold
Bloom pointed out, all canonical texts invite a strong
misreading:

> A strong poem, which alone can become canonical
> for more than a single generation, can be defined
> as a text that must generate strong misreadings,
> both as other poems and literary criticism. Texts
> that have a single, reductive, simplistic meaning
> are themselves necessarily weak misreadings
> of anterior texts. When a strong misreading has
> demonstrated its fecundity by producing other
> strong misreadings across several generations,
> then we can and must accept its canonical status.
> (Bloom 1982:285)

In what follows, I will be looking at a passage in *Thus
Spake Zarathustra* from the standpoint of the thesis and
of the antithesis. In the second half of this chapter, I
will turn to Henry Corbin's equally strong misreading
of the Iranian Sufi Master al Suhravardi. Then to
compound the matter further, I will play Corbin's
misreading of Suhravardi off against Jung's misreading
of Nietzsche. Like the great jazz pianist Thelonious
Monk, Jung and Corbin play wrong right.

The Vision and the Riddle

Nietzsche had many voices. He could be prophetic but also light and playful. Here is how he speaks of the death of God in *On Apostates* (*Zarathustra,* 3:8):

> For with the old Gods, things came to an end long ago—and verily they had a good and joyful God's end! Theirs was no mere twilight death-that is a lie! Rather one day they laughed themselves to death! This happened when the most godless words issued from a God himself—the words; "There is one God! Thou shalt have no other gods before me!" An old wrath-beard of a God, most jealous, forgot himself thus. And thereupon all the Gods laughed and rocked in their chairs and shouted: "Is this not Godliness, that there are Gods but no God . . ." (Nietzsche 2005:158)

Later in the text, Nietzsche calls for a new nobility to oppose mob rule, and he repeats the last line to suggest that this elite will be truly godlike. Jung's comment on this is based on the Thomas Common translation, in which the line in question is "That is just divinity, that there are gods but no God." Jung takes the word "divinity" as a synonym for Meister Eckhart's "Godhead" and translates Nietzsche into a new key:

> We know that Nietzsche has declared God to be dead and here it appears as if God were not so dead; that is, as if there were no personal or monotheistic God, but there was divinity. In the language of Meister Eckhart, it would be Godhead, not God. The divine element is still there, but not in the form of a monotheistic God . . . (Z:1526-7)

Only Jung could bring together the radical nineteenth-century atheist Nietzsche and the greatest medieval Christian mystic. It was however pointed out to me that this is a misreading too far. Nietzsche's actual word was "Gottlichkeit" (Divinity) and not Eckhart's "Gotheit." (Godhead).

Jung returned to Eckhart in *Aion* where he explicated the distinction between Godhead or Divinity and God like this:

> Meister Eckhart's theology knows a "Godhead" of which no qualities, except unity and being can be predicated; it "is becoming," it is not yet Lord of itself, and it represents an absolute coincidence of opposites . . . Union of opposites is equivalent to unconsciousness, so far as human logic goes, for consciousness presupposes a differentiation into subject and object and a relationship between them. Where there is no "other," or it does not yet exist, all possibility of consciousness ceases. Only the Father, the God welling out of the Godhead, "notices himself," "becomes beknown to himself," and confronts himself as a Person. (CW9/2:301)

The death of God does not mean the extinction of God but his withdrawal back into the Godhead. So there is no God as such, only gods; or rather the divine element has left the dogmatic idea of God and become incarnate in human beings. Jung then asks, "Is it the deification of man or the birth of God in man?" He seemed to oscillate between the two, but in *Answer to Job* and *A Psychological Approach to the Dogma of the Trinity,* he has opted for the birth of God in man. God, he declared in the Trinity essay, wants to become incarnate in fallen man:

> In the Paraclete . . . God is much closer to the real
> man and his darkness than he is in the Son. The
> light God bestrides the bridge—Man—from the
> day side; God's shadow from the night side. What
> will be the outcome of this fearful dilemma, which
> threatens to shatter the frail human vessel with
> unknown storms and intoxications? It may well
> be the revelation of the Holy Ghost out of man
> himself. Just as man was once revealed out of God,
> so, when the circle closes, God may be revealed out
> of man. (CW11:267)

If man were to become "deified," he could not be the
bridge. He needs to remain fallen so that God can be
revealed out of his creature in the Paraclete. Nietzsche
had forgotten that "we are no more than the stable in
which the Lord is born." Nothing illustrates Jung's point
more vividly than *The Vision and the Riddle.*

The scene is set at a gateway, where one lane stretches
back for an eternity and another one stretches ahead.
The word "MOMENT" is inscribed on this gateway.
Zarathustra has climbed up to it with a dwarf on his
back. The burden of the spirit of gravity is intolerable,
but eventually, Zarathustra shakes it off. Then he says
to the dwarf:

> Must not whatever among all things can walk
> have walked this lane already? Must not whatever
> among all things can happen have happened and
> been done and passed already? And if everything
> has already been, what do you think, dwarf, of
> this moment? Must not the gateway have already
> been there?

Suddenly, this dialogue about eternal recurrence is
interrupted by a howling dog. The scene changes

abruptly, and Zarathustra sees a young shepherd writhing and choking with a heavy black snake hanging out of his mouth. The spirit of gravity has shifted from the dwarf to the serpent, which has crawled into the man's throat. Zarathustra tugs at the snake but to no avail, then he shouts, "Bite its head off!"

> (The shepherd) bit with a good bite! He spat far away the head of the snake—and sprang up. No longer a shepherd, no longer a human being, a transformed being, illumined, who laughed. Never yet on earth had any human being laughed as he laughed! (Nietzsche 2005:136-8)

When Jung first read this narrative, it made a tremendous impression on him, but he could not explain why. It became his "particular task to deal with the problem of the chthonic snake." In the *Visions* seminar, he takes a very dim view of the matter: "One can quietly say that it is a most hysterical laughter, it is unsound laughter. In reality one would be terribly disgusted." (V: 283) Jung also maintained that the condition of the shepherd "is not to be explained by the preceding facts." But let's look closely at the text and zoom in at the moment of crisis:

> My hand tugged at the snake and tugged in vain! It could not tug the snake out of the shepherd's throat. *Then it cried out of me:* "Bite off! Bite off! Bite its head off!"—thus it cried out of me, my horror my disgust, my compassion, all my good and bad cried out of me into a single cry. (Nietzsche 2005:137)

Is this a cry from the renegade that would drag the ego into an inflationary psychosis, or is it a summons from the core self to a transcendental imperative?

In the *Zarathustra* seminars, Jung gave his most
extensive commentary on this text. He observed that
the normal situation, where the serpent swallows the
hero, has been reversed. Nietzsche's gothic imagery
has no precedent in the world's mythologies. According
to Jung, the black snake embodies everything
that Nietzsche refused to acknowledge in himself.
Consequently, his entire individuation process is
stuck at an impasse. The two sides represented by
the innocent shepherd and the black snake should
come together, and he, "he really should swallow the
serpent in order that the regular thing should happen."
Zarathustra gave the man the wrong advice, and the
outcome was catastrophic: "If you take a leap into
heaven and become the sun," says Jung, "your other
side will be right down there in hell." (Z:1292-6)

The Philosophy of Light

Jung maintained that deification was psychologically
impossible—how could mere mortals extricate
themselves from original sin? This is a Christian view
of the human condition that is not shared by Sufi
masters like Suhravardi. In Iranian Sufism, man has no
fixed position in the order of things; he is, as Corbin
puts it, succinctly "only a Not-yet: either an Angel or
demon in potential." (Corbin 1983:104) In this section,
I will be looking at the allegory in *The Vision and the
Riddle* from a Sufi perspective.

Shiha al-Din Yahya Suhravardi (1155–1191) was executed
in Aleppo at the age of thirty-six under Saladin's
orders. He was the founder of the Illuminationist
school of Islamic philosophy, and he is known as
Shaykh Al Ishraq. According to Henry Corbin, *israq* is

a verbal noun meaning the splendour of the sun when it rises. For Suhravardi, existence is light. Everything in existence manifests light at varying degrees of intensity:

> The essence of the First Absolute Light, God, gives constant illumination, whereby it is manifested and brings all things into existence, giving life to them by its rays. Everything in the world is derived from the Light of His essence and all the beauty and gifts of his bounty, and to attain fully to this illumination is salvation. (*Hikmat al Ishraq,* cited in Nasr 1964:69)

The philosophy of light was first revealed by Hermes or Idris as he is known in the Islamic world. It had two points of origin: Persia and Egypt. From Egypt, it was transmitted to Greece, and from there, it entered Islam. Suhravardi reunified both streams.

In *Spiritual Body and Celestial Earth*, Corbin has selected and translated a dramatic deification narrative from Suhravardi's *Book of Elucidations*:

> On a certain night when there was sunlight, Hermes was at prayers in the temple of Light. When the column of dawn blazed forth, he saw an Earth about to be engulfed, with cities upon which the divine anger had descended and which fell into the abyss.

> Then Hermes shouted, "You who are my father, rescue me from the enclosure that is near perdition!" And he heard a voice shouting an answer, "Take hold of the cable of our irradiation and climb up to the battlements of the Throne." Then he climbed up and there was an Earth and Heavens. (Corbin 1977:120)

Suhravardi's narrative recapitulates the passage through the active door, the Symplegades or clashing rocks. This is an ancient initiatory pattern. According to Ananda Coomararswamy,[8]"The distribution of the motif is an indication of its prehistoric antiquity and refers to the complex pattern of the Urmythos of the Quest to a period at least prior to the population of America." (Coomaraswamy, 1977:521) It is found in Native American myths throughout the continent and is best known in Europe through *The Odyssey:*

> On one side beetling cliffs shoot up and against them
> pound the roaring breakers of blue- eyed Amphrite—
> the Clashing Rocks they're called by blissful gods.
> No ship of men has ever approached and slipped past—
> always some disaster—big timbers and sailor's corpses
> whirled away by the waves and lethal blasts of fire.
> One ship alone, one deep-sea craft sailed clear,
> The Argo, sung by the world, when heading home
> Form Aretes' shores. And she would have crashed
> Against those rocks and sunk at once if Hera,
> for love of Jason, had not sped her through. (Book
> 12, Fagels, 1997:201)

In some Hindu myths, the Symplegades are sharp dancing reeds that snap shut in an instant, or they take the form of doors, which, says Coomaraswamy, stand for pairs of opposites. In the Rig Veda, these are the opposites of day and night or light and dark. The hero must decisively pass through when it is neither day nor night just as Hermes must grasp the cable when the sun is shining at night and climb up to the throne. The path out of the quotidian world "is the single track and strait way that penetrates the cardinal point on which the contraries turn." (Coomaraswamy, 1977:529)

---

[8]   Ananda Coomaraswamy features in chapter 3 which includes some background information.

The shepherd in The Vision and the Riddle" has to pass through the Active Door by the unusual expedient of biting off the head of the snake. He does so with all his might at the moment in which time and eternity intersect. He is immediately transformed:

> Whoever would transfer from this world to the Otherworld, or return, must do so through the undimensional and timeless "interval" that divides related but contrary forces, between which if one is to pass at all, it must be instantly. (Coomaraswamy, 1977:542)

Suhravardi's Hermes and Nietzsche's shepherd do not carry their shadows with them when they ascend. They discard them, and the "cities of the oppressors" sink into the abyss. (Corbin 1978:47) Philosophically, Suhravardi and Nietzsche seem to be poles apart. Suhravardi was a Muslim Neoplatonist, and Nietzsche's philosophy is a devastating critique of the Platonist tradition. Or rather, it looks that way from Henry Corbin's perspective. Recent scholarship has shown that Suhravardi was not a dreamy "theosophist" but "a hard headed philosophical critic and creative thinker who set the agenda for later Islamic philosophy." (Walbridge2005:201) He could have given Nietzsche a good run for his money.

Although Nietzsche philosophized with a hammer, he did not close the door to theophanic visions. In a short poem titled "Sils Maria," he recounted an imaginal encounter with Zarathustra:

> There sat I waiting—waiting yet for naught,
> Transcending good and evil, sometimes caught
> in light, sometimes in shadow, all game,

all sea, all midday, all time without all aim.
At once then, my friend! One turned to two
and Zarathustra strode into my view.
(Nietzsche 2001:258)

In his long essay *Concerning Rebirth*, Jung interpreted "one turned to two" correctly as a theophanic experience of the Self:

> When a summit of life is reached, when the bud unfolds and from the lesser the greater emerges, then as Nietzsche says, "One becomes two" and the greater figure, which one always was but which remained invisible, appears to the lesser personality with the force of revelation.

The last man, who has his little pleasures for the day and his little pleasures for the night, will drag this revelation down to the level of his mediocrity:

> But the man who is inwardly great will know that the long expected friend of the soul, the immortal one, has now finally come to "lead captivity captive"; that is to, to seize hold of him by whom this immortal has always been confined and held prisoner, and make his life flow into the greater life— a moment of deadliest peril. (CW9/1:217)

Jung then refers to the tragedy of the tightrope walker in the prologue of *Zarathustra* that anticipated Nietzsche's catastrophic fate. But this was not entirely his fault. Jung conjectured that had Nietzsche lived at any time between the fifteenth and the eighteenth centuries, he would have been an alchemistic philosopher. "The Christian myth did not hold life for him," said Jung in the Zarathustra seminars. Consequently, "he came to the conclusion that the Church didn't give him the spiritual life he expected or needed, so he would quite naturally seek something that would produce life." (Z: 949-50) But what if Nietzsche could have found what he was seeking in Islam? He was more than half in love with Muslim culture, which he confessed "speaks more clearly to our senses and tastes than Rome or Greece." (Nietzsche 2005a:63, Aphorisms 59,60) If Nietzsche could have made his way to the Islamic world, he might well have found life there, not to mention a new earth to stand on and a new heaven above him:

> O sky above me! O pure deep sky! You abyss of light! Gazing into you,
> I tremble with divine desires.
> To cast myself into your height—that is my depth! To hide myself in your purity—that is my innocence!
> The god is veiled by his beauty: thus you hide your stars. You do not speak: thus you proclaim your wisdom.
> You have risen for me today, mute over the raging sea; your love and modesty speak a revelation to my raging soul. (Nietzsche 1969:184)

Jung saw this reverie as evidence of Nietzsche's inability "to give a definite or a decisive value to anything outside of himself." Consequently, he had to take it in into himself or in this case introject the sky! (Z: 1319-20) Jung's diagnosis of Nietzsche is based on a strong misreading of the texts. But the patient has no right to reply. If he had, Nietzsche might well have said,

> It's a bit rich for you to accuse me of self-deification when this is what you have written in your Liber Novus:

> You serve the spirit of this time, and believe you can escape the spirit of the depths. But the depths

do not hesitate any longer and will force you into the mysteries of Christ. It belongs to this mystery that man is not redeemed through the hero, but becomes a Christ himself. (Jung 2009:202)

The same double standard applies in your treatment of my Zarathustra. A diagnosis of my condition is presupposed at the outset; and you find what you're looking for on almost every page: a man divorced from his instincts taking refuge in inflation. But as I was never as sick as that! Furthermore, you make no mention of the fact that I lost my father when I five—strange oversight for a psychoanalyst! And you also ignore what I said in Ecce Homo: *Listen to me! I am the one who I am! Above all, do not mistake me for someone else!* (Nietzsche 2005a:71)

The Alternative Evolutionary Hypothesis

In *Memories, Dreams, Reflections* chapter 3, Jung recalls that his first reading of Nietzsche's *Zarathustra* was a deeply disturbing revelation:

Zarathustra was Nietzsche's Faust, his No. 2 (personality) and my No. 2 corresponded to Zarathustra—though this was like comparing a molehill with Mont Blanc. And Zarathustra—there could be no doubt about that—was morbid. Was my No. 2 also morbid? This possibility filled me with a terror which for a long time I refused to admit but the idea cropped up again and again at inopportune moments, throwing me into a cold sweat, so that I was forced to reflect on myself. (MDR 1995:123)

No wonder that Jung was extremely ambivalent about Nietzsche for all his life. And if he not had the good fortune to marry the second richest woman in

Switzerland, he probably would have ended up like Friedrich. But sometimes Jung gets away from his Nietzsche complex in the *Zarathustra* seminars. When he relaxes his relentless hermeneutic of suspicion, he acknowledges Nietzsche as "one of the greatest psychologists who ever lived." Jung also commends Nietzsche for coming within a hair's breadth of discovering the archetype of the self:

> We have many situations where it comes in, so one really marvels that he could never grasp it; for instance, in this jewel, and the star, and later on in the chapter about the adder, it comes so close one would almost expect him to realize it. Yet he does not; it was not of his time. Of course we fall down somewhere else; we make this discrimination now, but we omit something else. And we shall never become perfect—happily not. (Z:745-6)

Jung acknowledged that Nietzsche's inability to see the pitfalls of going into the collective unconscious and avert catastrophe was not entirely his fault. He was born too late to be an alchemist and too soon to be a psychoanalyst. I suspect Nietzsche was more psychologically streetwise than Jung gives him credit.

In his neglected masterpiece, *Mythology of the Soul*, H G Baynes examines the material of two borderline psychotic patients in great detail. Both patients encountered a dangerous shadow figure that Baynes called the renegade:

> He is the reckless renegade; the unscrupulous desperado; the man who does what he likes and takes what he can, uninhibited by ethical or moral qualms; the tendency of the personality, in effect, which would repudiate the burden of the

human soul, preferring any kind of magical or
tricky means to the simple acceptance of human
responsibilities. In other words, he personifies
the downward and backwards pull, the alternative
evolutionary hypothesis. (Baynes 1940:91)

This figure appears in the Prologue while Zarathustra
delivers his sermon in the marketplace. He declares
that the human is a rope, fastened between beast and
Overhuman - a rope over an abyss." But when he meets
with complete incomprehension Zarathustra changes
the subject and speaks of the last man, a despicable
figure who renounces the discipline of suffering for the
sake of "his little pleasures for the day and his little
pleasures for the night." Of course, this too meets with
incomprehension but then a tightrope walker begins his
walk high above the market and everyone is distracted.
Before he is halfway across, a buffoon emerges from a
small door in the tower, mocks the tightrope walker,
and then leaps over him. The walker loses his balance
and crashes down to the ground. Evidently, Nietzsche
had anticipated the alternative evolutionary hypothesis
long before Baynes and Jung.

Zarathustra comforts the tightrope walker and
promises to give him a decent burial. He tells the dying
man that he will not go to Hell and that "your soul
will be dead before your body, so fear nothing more."
(Nietzsche 2005:17- 18) This, Jung remarked, is exactly
what happened to Nietzsche after his collapse in 1889,
and he remained in a vegetative state until his death in
1900. However, Rudolf Steiner, who actually spent time
with the ailing Nietzsche, saw things differently. He
reports seeing Nietzsche's soul "hovering over his head,
infinitely beautiful. It had surrendered to the spiritual
worlds it had longed for but was unable to find until
illness set it free". (Lachmann 2007:84)

Steiner's observations seem fanciful when the harrowing details of Nietzsche's final years are brought into the picture. (Prideaux 2018:ch 20–22) But his account should not be dismissed out of hand. In the discussion on the rope dancer in the *Zarathustra* seminars, Jung remarks that there can be perfectly reasonable voices in severely psychotic patients, "a sort of nirvana condition behind madness." He cites some examples and then suggests that "it is also possible that behind Nietzsche's condition there was a superior self which had no chance to come through. Consciousness was diseased but the self was sane." Jung goes on to cite the findings of Dr Carl Ludwig Schleich, the discoverer of anaesthesia, who maintained that the psyche is not connected to the brain but to the sympathetic nervous system. Even if the brain is disturbed, the personality is not necessarily affected. (Z:137-8) Had Steiner discerned Nietzsche's nirvana condition?

Nietzsche had surrendered to spiritual worlds before he collapsed into madness. He does so in *Before Sunrise*, when he longs to cast himself into the light abyss of the sky. In a later chapter, *At Midday*, Zarathustra falls asleep beneath a gnarled tree with a grapevine entwined around it:

> Zarathustra spoke thus to his heart: Still! Still! Did not the world become perfect? But what is happening to me? Just as a delicate breeze, unseen dances upon an inlaid sea, lightly, feather lightly: so sleep dances on me.

> My eyes he does not press closed; my soul he leaves awake. Light is he, feather light.

What happened to me: hearken! Did time fly away?
Am I not falling? Did I not fall—hearken—into the
well of eternity?

The well of eternity is the sky above him and on waking
Zarathustra asks:

O Heaven above me . . . are you listening to my
wondrous soul?

When will you drink this drop of dew that has
fallen on all earthly things—when will you drink
this wondrous soul—When O well of eternity
will you drink my soul back into you? (Nietzsche
2005:241-2)

If Steiner is to be believed, Nietzsche actualized his
deepest longing through his madness. The relationship
between mysticism and psychosis lies beyond the limits
of language. How could it be otherwise?

I would like to thank John Carey for kindly reading
this chapter in an earlier draft and for providing
many thoughtful critical insights.

9

THE WAY UP AND THE WAY DOWN ARE ONE AND THE SAME

When Wolfgang Pauli came to Jung, his life was in meltdown. He was living entirely in his intellect, repressing his instinctual and emotional needs, and drinking heavily. Jung, however, did not intervene directly. Instead, he stood aside and allowed the unconscious to provide the necessary compensation through a sequence of dreams. As the process was approaching its climax, Pauli had the dream of the House of Gathering:

> I come to a strange and solemn house -"The House of Gathering." Many candles are burning in the background, arranged in a peculiar pattern with four points running upwards. Outside at the door of the house an old man is posted. People are going in. They say nothing and stand motionless in order to collect themselves inwardly. The man at the door says of the visitors to the house, "When they come out again they are cleansed." I go into

the house myself and find I can concentrate perfectly. Then a voice says: "What you are doing is dangerous. Religion is not a tax to be paid so you can rid yourself of the woman's image, for this image cannot be got rid of. Woe unto them who use religion as a substitute for another side of the soul's life; they are in error and shall be accursed. Religion is no substitute; it is to be added to the other activities of the soul as the ultimate completion. Out of the fullness of your life shall you bring forth your religion; only then will you be blessed." While the last sentence is being spoken in ringing tones I hear distant music, simple chords on an organ . . . As I leave the house I see a burning mountain and I feel: "The fire that cannot be put out is a holy fire." (Shaw, St. Joan) (CW11:58)

It was remarkable how "this very intellectual and skeptical man" submitted to the authority of the voice in this dream. It has a numinous quality which Jung said was the source of the real therapy, and when a patient has a numinous experience, he or she is released from the curse of psychopathology. (L1 1973:377) But is the "real therapy" only accessible to people with the psychic gifts of a Wolfgang Pauli? According to Jung, numinous experience is not the special privilege of a spiritual elite. It has its origins in the collective unconscious which is common to us all.

Instincts and Archetypes

Whereas traditional Muslim psychology is top-down and proceeds from the spiritual unconscious, Jung's psychology is bottom-up and proceeds from the somatic unconscious. This has prompted accusations of reductionism. But in his seminars on Nietzsche's *Zarathustra*, Jung makes a clear distinction between the spiritual and the psychic. However, he does so on his own terms. Instead of the traditional vertical hierarchy of pneuma, psyche, and sark or soma, he places the somatic and the spiritual unconscious on a horizontal axis. (Z:441-2) This move will probably not appease his critics:

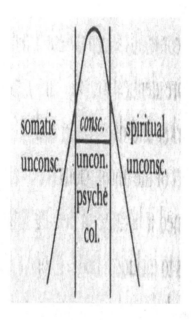

Jung's model is phenomenological, not metaphysical. He has shown the image of yourself you would have if you see yourself from within: a first person rather than third person point of view. On the left of the mountain, there is the somatic unconscious where the psyche merges with the corporeal body. "It is so dark," says Jung in the *Zarathustra* seminar, "that one does not know whether it has to do with the top or the bottom of the system, whether it leads into the body or into the air." (Z:441) And on the other side of the mountain in the luminous darkness of the spiritual unconscious, psyche merges with pneuma: "The greatest intensity of life is in the centre and the darkness is on either side, on the spiritual side as well as the side of matter." (Z:

442) There is a borderline region between psyche and soma on the left of the mountain and a borderline region between psyche and spirit on the right. Jung designates both zones as "quasi-psychic" or "psychoid." I'll attempt to pin down this elusive category later. Let's begin from the somatic side and work our way across the mountain.

In his essay on *The Psychology of the Child Archetype,* Jung says more about the relations between psyche and soma:

> The deeper layers of the psyche lose their individual uniqueness as they retreat farther and farther into darkness. "Lower down", that is to say as they approach the autonomous functional systems, they become increasingly collective until they are universalized and extinguished in the body's carbon. Hence at bottom the psyche is simply world. (CW9/1:291)

Although the instincts are based on the autonomous systems Jung does not reduce them to physiological mechanisms. In an essay written in 1919, *Instinct and the Unconscious*, he provided a working definition of instinct from a psychological point of view: "Instincts are typical modes of action and whenever we meet with uniform and regular modes of action we are dealing with instinct, no matter whether it is associated with a conscious motive or not." (CW8:273)

Whereas Freud emphasized the compulsive character of instinct, Jung was impressed by its law-abiding aspect. But how did he account for the origins of the instincts? Were they learnt patterns of behaviour that became automatic? This is a dubious hypothesis, and Jung cites the example of the yucca moth to explain why it is implausible:

> The flowers of the yucca plant open for one night only. The yucca moth takes the pollen from one of the flowers and kneeds it into a little pellet. Then it visits a second flower, cuts open its pistil, lays its eggs between the ovules and then stuffs the pellet into the funnel shaped opening of the pistil. Only once in its life does it perform this complicated operation. (CW8:268)

Such an intricate and purposive sequence of actions cannot be accounted for in mechanistic terms. The hidden intelligence in instinctual patterns of behaviour implies the operation of an unconscious process of perception, "an instinctive act of comprehension," or in Bergson's terminology, an intuition.

The intuition enables the moth to fulfil an image of the situation which consists of the flower opening, pollination and egg laying. "If any one of these conditions is lacking," says Jung, "the instinct does not function. It cannot exist without its total pattern, without its image." (CW8:398)

Jung designates this total pattern as the archetype without which the moth's behaviour would just be random and without purpose:

> Just as conscious apprehension gives our actions form and direction, so unconscious apprehension through the archetype determines the form and direction of the instinct . . . Thus the yucca moth must carry within it an image of the situation that triggers off its instinct. The image enables it

to recognize the yucca flower and its structure.
(CW8: 277)

The archetype is the form and the image of the
situation is the content.

In 1919, Jung had not yet made the distinction
between the archetype as an innate disposition in the
unconscious and the archetypal image or pattern of
behaviour that corresponds to it. The term archetype
does not refer to an inherited idea or image but to an
inherited mode of psychic functioning "corresponding
to the way a chick emerges from an egg, a bird builds
its nest, a certain kind of wasp stings the motor
ganglion of a caterpillar and eels find their way to the
Bermudas." (CW18:1228) An inherited disposition of
this nature makes empirical sense, but the notion of an
inherited image or idea is pseudo-scientific nonsense.

This teleological model of instinct is a refutation
of Freud's notion of the id as a bundle of conflicting
drives. Instincts are orderly, and they only become
chaotic if they are disturbed. But where is the
experimental data to support Jung's theory? The
zoologist Adolf Portmann devised a very ingenious
experiment to demonstrate what happens when
instinctual patterns of behaviour in animals are
disrupted:

> A little male bird of a species that loves to fight
> was isolated in a cage. It became very depressed; its
> eating and sleeping patterns were disturbed. Then
> it was given a fighting partner and after a really
> good fight it felt much better. Then Portmann put
> the bird back into isolation and observed it. What
> happened? He went to the corner of his cage which

> its partner had occupied and re-enacted the entire
> fight on its own. It did so whenever it felt like it and
> was able to resume its normal eating and sleeping
> patterns. (Von Franz, 1977:119-20)

The experiment demonstrates what Portmann called the inwardness of animal life. Whereas zoology observes instincts as they manifest themselves in outer behaviour, psychology observes instinct from within. The picture changes dramatically with this shift of perspective. "Here," says Jung, "the archetype appears as a numinous factor, as an image of fundamental significance." (CW18:1229)

The instincts and the archetypes constitute the collective unconscious. Both components are constantly in operation: the instincts govern all aspects of our behaviour that are beyond our conscious control, and the archetypes regulate all the fantasy activity that is going on outside the ego. We can, of course, generate a fantasy image consciously, for example by day dreaming, but it will lack any real emotional resonance or depth. An image arising from the activity of an archetype is, by contrast, the real therapy.

A psychic content that has its origin in forgotten or repressed material will have been conscious to the individual at some time, if only fleetingly. It comes out of the personal unconscious. But a content of the collective unconscious *will not have been previously conscious to the individual concerned.* It has its origins outside the sphere of memory in the archetypes and breaks through to the conscious psyche with a revelatory force. Personal unconscious contents are time-bound, those of the collective unconscious are timeless—hence, the element of numinosity.

In times of crisis, when the ego's defenses are down, the unconscious psyche is activated, and the archetypal images will cross over the threshold into consciousness. Jung's break with Freud in 1913, just as Europe was on the brink of catastrophe, threw him into a profound crisis of identity. The gates of the transpersonal psyche were opened. Jung was overwhelmed by a series of apocalyptic visions and thought he was falling into a psychosis. When the war broke out, he realized that the psychosis was not in him but out there in the collective.

He remained in a state of constant tension; it was as if blocks of stone were tumbling down on him. He resorted to yoga exercises to calm himself down. But he did not want to obliterate the images with Indian meditation techniques. If Jung had taken that path, he would never have understood what was going on in his psyche. A very different strategy was called for:

> To the extent I managed to translate the emotions into images . . ., to find the images which were concealed in the emotions—I was inwardly calmed and reassured. Had I left the images hidden in the emotions I might have been torn to pieces by them . . . As a result of my experiment I learned how helpful it can be, from a therapeutic point of view to find particular images which lie behind the emotions. (MDR: 201)

When Jung brought the image into consciousness, he held a mirror up to his instinct. An archetypal image is "the self portrait of the instinct" or "the instinct's perception of itself". Once the instinct becomes conscious of itself in this way, it is no longer an unchained beast: "One must still have chaos within, in order to give birth to a dancing star," said Zarathustra. (Nietzsche 2005:15)

Instinct without its archetypal image is a blind physiological reflex. An archetypal image with no basis in instinct would be disembodied and ethereal. Jung likened the relationship between the two to the light spectrum: instinct corresponds to infrared, and the archetype to ultraviolet. Violet has mystical associations and contrasts nicely with blood-red instincts. Archetypal images are paradoxically both an element of nature and of the spirit. "These images," says Jung, "are not pale shadows but tremendously powerful psychic factors." (CW4:764)

If an emotional disturbance can be translated into an image, the centre of gravity shifts from the infrared to the ultraviolet end of the spectrum. Consequently, the instinctual drive is modified, and you are no longer at the mercy of your passions. Jung placed creative imagination at the heart of his therapeutic method. He recommended the use of drawing, painting, clay work, or inner dialogue to prompt the formation of the saving image. This method is called active imagination, and it can go beyond therapy to become a spiritual practice in its own right.

Synchronicity and Absolute Knowledge

When synchronistic phenomena appear, the archetype "transgresses" the boundary between psyche and world. These uncanny events have the character of a three-dimensional dream and encompass the infrared and ultraviolet bands of the spectrum. For example, Jung was walking with a female patient in the woods. She told him about the first dream of her life which had made an indelible impression on her. She had seen a spectral fox coming down the stairs of her parental home. At that very moment, a real fox came out of the trees about 40 yards away and walked on the path ahead of them for several minutes. "The animal," Jung remarks, "behaved as if it was a partner in the human situation." (L1:395)

Jung's synchronicity hypothesis was formulated with sunstantial critical input from Wolfgang Pauli, the "conscience of physics." But it remains an elusive category at best. Who is to say whether the spectral fox in the woods was a bona fide synchronicity or merely a remarkable coincidence? Doesn't it depend on how you choose to interpret the event? Is there an objective criterion to determine the matter? There is if you are prepared to allow a generous definition of objectivity: Synchronistic events occur when an archetype that is charged with the numinous is constellated. Henry Corbin has provided a compelling example of a numinous synchronistic event from the early life of Ibn 'Arabi:

> He fell gravely ill; his fever brought on a state of profound lethargy. While those around him thought him dead, he in his inward universe was besieged by a troop of menacing diabolical figures. But then there arose a marvellously beautiful being exhaling a sweet perfume and who with invincible force repulsed the demonic figures. "Who are you?" Ibn 'Arabi asked him. "I am Sura Yasin". His anguished father at his bedside was indeed reciting that sura (the 36th of the Koran), which is intoned specifically for the dying.

There is a synchronistic correspondence between events in this world and in the intermediate world. While the father recites the thirty-sixth sura in the belief his son is dying, Sura Yasin manifests itself as an imaginal being to the ailing Ibn 'Arabi and drives away the demons. But there is also some subtle causality operating here. Corbin continues,

> Such was the energy released by the spoken word that the person corresponding to it took form in the subtle intermediate world—a phenomenon not at all rare in religious experience. (Corbin 1969:39)

It is impossible in this case to draw a sharp distinction between synchronicity and subtle causality. There is only a seamless continuum.

In his famous essay Jung defined synchronicity as "an acausal connecting principle." But synchronistic events can only be designated in this way on a very restrictive definition of causality. If you understand cause on the level of car mechanics, then obviously, synchronicities are "acausal." I suspect that synchronicity cannot exclude a subtle causality principle. In his essay on *Psychosomatic Medicine from the Jungian Point of View* C. A. Meier reinstates the traditional idea of the subtle body as an agent in symptom formation and suggests that this identical to the modern concept of synchronicity. (Meier 1986: Chapter 7)

To conclude, I will return to Jung's instinct theory. This can be traced back through the neo-vitalist biology of the nineteenth century all the way to Aristotle. According to Aristotle, the living creature carried its own developmental goal in itself. This is the principle of entelechy, which is usually translated as "actualization." Aristotle rejected the notion of evolution as a result of a random mechanical process, and he also rejected creation myth. Entelechy does not require the intervention of a transcendent being.

The idea of entelechy was retrieved by Hans Dreish, the leading exponent of vitalism. He also rejected the mechanical model and argued that organic individual development could not be accounted for in purely physical or chemical terms. Nor could it be explained in terms of efficient causality: Organic development required entelechy. Dreisch, who had coined the term "psychoid," was an important influence on Jung. He cites him in the Synchronicity essay and the relevant passage is worth quoting at length:

> Whether we like it or not, we find ourselves in an embarrassing position as soon as we begin to seriously reflect on teleological processes in biology . . . Final causes, twist them how we will, postulate foreknowledge of some kind. It is certainly not a knowledge that could be connected with the ego and hence not a conscious knowledge as we know it, but rather a self-subsistent knowledge which I would prefer to call "absolute knowledge." (CW8:931)

Absolute knowledge extends across the infrared/ultraviolet spectrum: It is the instinct's perception of itself and the highest level of gnosis. The alchemists called this absolute knowledge the light of nature. Whereas divine revelation, the Word of God, descends from above, the lumen naturae arises from below. It is the spark of light in the living waters of the unconscious. The darkness below cannot comprehend the Logos above. But says Jung, "The light of nature is the light of the darkness itself, which illumines its own darkness and this light the darkness comprehends." (CW13:197)

Ibn 'Arabi refers to transcendental absolute knowledge as unveiling (*kashf*), tasting (*dhawq*), or opening (*fath* or *futuh*). All these terms refer "to direct experiential knowledge of the reality of things, a knowledge that God gives to his servant through self-disclosure (*tajalli*)." (Chittick 1989:394, n.19) Ibn 'Arabi was a medieval Muslim. Naturally, he took the way up and shunned the darkness below. Jung and the Hermetic alchemists took the way down and sought the light of nature in the psychoid depths. Ibn 'Arabi was a Platonist, but Jung was much closer to the pre-Socratic philosopher Heraclitus, who declared that the way up and the way down is one and the same. He spoke from absolute knowledge—what better foundation could there be for a dialogue between the Shaykh al Akbar and Jung?

Delivered as a lecture to The Scientific and Medical Network in London, March 2014. Previously published in Psychological Perspectives, 63:1, pp. 95–105, Los Angeles 2020.

PRIMA MATERIA

10

FROM STANLEY SPENCER'S *RESURRECTION* TO JOHN COLTRANE'S *ASCENSION*

The new religious movements are labyrinthine in their sheer multiplicity. Andrew Rawlinson's fourfold typology of the spiritual paths provides us with some flexible coordinates. The four categories are: Hot Structured, Hot Unstructured, Cool Structured, and Cool Unstructured. (Rawlinson 1997) Here they are in a thumb nail sketch:

Hot Structured
The path of the shaman, the magician, and the alchemist: Liberation is obtained by initiation and self-transformation. Key word: JUMP.

Hot Unstructured
The path of the devotee, the lover, and the martyr: There is no teaching. Only love and total surrender to God brings liberation. Key word: SUBMIT.

Cool Structured
The path of the yogi, the monk, and the craftsman:
Liberation is within oneself and must be uncovered
by disciplined practice. Progress is in incremental
steps, not by way of surrender or transformation.
Key word: WORK.

Cool Unstructured
The path of the sage and the hermit: There is
no teaching and no path. Your true nature is
liberation, and you have only to awaken to this self-
evident fact. Key word: LET GO.

Resurrection

My family moved to the Berkshire village of Cookham
in 1951, when I was four years old, and we remained
there until 1967. Cookham was the home of one of
the greatest British painters of the last century, Sir
Stanley Spencer (1891-1959). The church where I once
worshipped and later served at Holy Communion
is the setting for his monumental painting of the
Resurrection, which now hangs in the Tate. The dead
rise out of their graves in the churchyard, Christ sits
in the porch holding three infants with God the Father
standing behind him. Stanley appears in the picture
naked, leaning against a gravestone.

Cookham was his earthly paradise, and his major
works are highly idiosyncratic theophanic visions. The
paintings often depict events from the Bible taking
place in the village. Christ is crucified at the bottom
of the High Street or preaches to the multitude at the
local regatta. These works have a timeless quality—
not a static eternity but a dynamic one teeming with
living forms. This is a hot structured universe, which

Rawlinson describes as "vast and inhabited by a hierarchy of beings." Here salvation is not withheld from the wicked. Indeed, Stanley would have wholeheartedly agreed with Origen that even the devil will be redeemed at the end of time.

Stanley was so attached to the village that he was nicknamed "Cookham" at his art college. My roots were never so deep, but Holy Trinity Church acted like a magnet on me from an early age. It was built on the omphalos, the world's navel. Of course, my fall from this paradise was inevitable. The momentum of the secular mood from the late '50s onwards was relentless, and the Church could provide no effective defense against it. Not long after my confirmation I was sent to a rather Dickensian boarding school on my 15th birthday. Being marched to church every Sunday was not conducive to piety, and I was soon overwhelmed by the militant atheism of my peers. Deep down in my adolescent psyche, I was undergoing a crisis of faith. But I was not thrown to the lions for long, and a lifeline came from an unexpected source.

My nickname at boarding school was "Satchmo" because of my passion for jazz. I had a small collection of records by Charlie Parker, Miles Davis, and Thelonious Monk, the men who revolutionized the music in the 1940s and 1950s. Miles Davis's famous album *Kind of Blue* was constantly on the turntable, and I found the soaring sound of John Coltrane's tenor sax particularly compelling. It was at least an intimation of a transcendent reality.

I discovered Coltrane's great quartet in 1965, by which time I was happily out of the boarding school. In the previous year, Coltrane recorded his famous album *A Love Supreme*. The liner notes he wrote had no precedent in the history of jazz:

> All Praise Be to God to Whom All Praise Is Due Let us pursue him in the righteous path. Yes it is true "Seek and ye shall find." Only through Him can we know the wondrous bequeathal. During the year 1957, I experienced by the Grace of God, a spiritual awakening which led me to a richer, fuller, and more productive life. At the same time I humbly asked to be given the privilege to make others happy through music. I feel this has been granted through his Grace. ALL PRAISE TO GOD. (Album notes for *A Love Supreme*, The John Coltrane Quartet, Impulse 1964)

John Coltrane's awakening had delivered him from heroin addiction and spared him the fate that befell Charlie Parker. While his shamanic vocation and relentless experimentalism was typically hot-structured, his religious attitude was hot-unstructured. Such an attitude is informed by faith in "a divine power, quite other than oneself, which encloses us and is the source of liberation." (Rawlinson 1997:100) Whereas the Hot Structured path is self-reliant, hot-unstructured spirituality is totally dependent on divine grace: "Hot Unstructured traditions", says Rawlinson, "share this characteristic: we are always failing. But the solution to this failure . . . is simply to ask. The reason why asking is the solution, is that love is freely given to all who request it." (Rawlinson 1997:108) From a musical point of view, A Love Supreme is quite conservative compared with the radical innovations of alto saxophonist Ornette Coleman in the late '50s. Coleman made a decisive break with prescribed harmonies and reinstated the primacy of the melodic line. This, in turn, liberated the bass and drums from the task of timekeeping. Metrical rhythm gave way to rhythmic pulse, and the old division between the frontline, the bass, and the drums began to dissolve. In the 1960s, virtuosi saxophonists like Albert Ayler and Pharoah Sanders began experimenting with unorthodox textures on their horns by overblowing. Jazz musicians of an earlier generation had done this for effect. But Ayler and Sanders take off on a sonic flight of an unprecedented intensity over a powerful and sometimes relentless rhythmic pulse provided by the drummer. Coltrane threw in his lot with the revolution when he recorded *Ascension* (The Major Works of John Coltrane: Impulse 1965). On this album, eleven musicians collectively improvise for forty minutes in almost total freedom. Each player emerges at intervals out of a dense and seething massa confusa with his solo. This iconic work marked Coltrane's break with the classic jazz tradition. After Ascension, there was no going back.

What about the archetypal background behind this music? I have chosen one example that will not be lost on Jungian readers. In *The Cricket*, a small journal of reviews and poems by black American artists published in the 1960s, Albert Ayler reported a remarkable visionary experience:

> It was night when I had this vision. In this vision there was a large object flying around with bright colours in a disc form. Immediately I thought of the flying scorpion in the chapter of Revelations from the Holy Bible (he must be referring to chapter 9), but when the object started turning I saw that first it was flat then it turned sideways and started to shoot radiant colours . . . then it would turn back to the same position. I was running with my brother when it aimed at us but it didn't touch us at all. I guess it was what they are calling flying saucers. Any way it was revealed to me that we had the right seal of God almighty on our forehead. (Robert Palmer March 1978, liner notes to Albert Ayler, The Dedication Series Vol. VII, The Village Concerts, Impulse Records IA 9336/2)

This is an exemplary UFO vision, and it would not have been out of place in Jung's monograph on this phenomenon. (CW10: Section V) There is something primordial and childlike in the music of Albert Ayler. He played his tenor with huge, almost grotesque vibrato, but the purity of his tone gave it an unearthly beauty. Albert walked the bar playing a celestial yakety sax. Like Stanley Spencer, he transmuted the seemingly banal into a theophany.

The turning point came for me in 1966 when I acquired the *Meditations* suite, a sequel to *A Love Supreme*. For this album Coltrane added Rashied Ali as second drummer and Pharoah Sanders as second tenor to his quartet. (Impulse 1965)

I had not yet heard *Ascension* when I acquired the album and was unprepared for what was to come. On the opening track, titled "To the Father, Son, and Holy Ghost," the saxophones speak in tongues. Coltrane takes the first solo over a tumultuous enhanced rhythm section. He alternates rapidly between the highest and lowest notes on his horn like a one-man call and response. Pharoah Sanders follows with a sonic flight that unveils the primordial forms of the world. Or rather Pharoah is playing in the midst of these forms, which the ancient Greek philosophers called the *archai*, the primary substances that never change, or the *apeiron*, the boundless. (Kerenyi 1963:6–7)

Nothing could have been more alien to my Anglican background than Coltrane's Dionysian eruption. Nor was I the only one to be disconcerted. When Ravi Shankar heard Coltrane live, he liked the music but found the turbulence incomprehensible. This seems like a cool-structured response to a hot-structured situation. The cool-structured cosmos is orderly and accessible to reason. The path of liberation consists of developmental stages, not initiatory ordeals or transformative leaps. The complementary opposite and fourth member of Rawlinson's quadrant is cool unstructured:

> This spiritual path requires no graduated steps, no initiatory ordeal, and no surrender to the divine. Indeed, the very notion of a path is a false construct because "your own nature is liberation and everything else is illusion. You have only to awaken to this self-evident truth." (Rawlinson 1997:100)

Ascension

Early in 1966, Laurence, the friend who was initiating me into this extraordinary music, handed me a book on Sri Ramana Maharshi, the greatest master of the cool-unstructured path. The book was titled *In Days of Great Peace* and was written by a European who stayed at the ashram in Sri Ramana Maharshi's last years. (Mouni Sadhu 1957) It consisted of a diary of the author's inner and outer experiences during Sri Ramana Maharshi's darshans. He told me it was very important that I read it without delay.

As far as I was concerned, this was a distraction I could do without—my A-level examinations were just around the corner, and I had more than enough reading to do. However, Laurence thought otherwise, and when I next saw him, his first question was had I read the book. That night I reluctantly gave in to his persistence and began to read *In Days of Great Peace* in bed. I looked at the iconic Welling portrait of Sri Ramana on the frontispiece and ploughed through about thirty pages of the text.

Mouni Sadhu claimed that Sri Ramana Maharshi transmitted his teaching through silence. This was dramatically illustrated in a chapter titled "Tears." Once, when Mouni Sadhu was sitting at the master's feet, he found that he had tears rolling down his cheeks. But he felt neither sadness nor distress, for these were tears of purification. Bhagavan also saw what was happening and evidently knew what it meant. As I was reading this passage, an inner voice told me that I had once sat at Sri Ramana Maharshi's feet and experienced the same tears.

This apparent recollection from a former life released a rapid surge of energy up my spine. My normal consciousness was momentarily eclipsed. I saw a hierarchy of spirits rise above me like plateaus. As I was about to step onto the plateaus, I was pulled back abruptly. I was momentarily entangled in "the insane contradiction . . . between existence beyond Maya in the cosmic Self and that amiable human weakness which fruitfully sinks many roots in to dark earth." (Jung 1969:953) As I doubled up, I felt a spirit pass over my body. Rightly or wrongly, I was convinced I would have died if I had not fallen back at the last moment.

Despite this abortive ascension, I was not the same person as I was before I began to read *In Days of Great Peace*. Naturally, my parents noticed nothing at the breakfast table the following morning—not that I could have given a coherent account of what had happened to anyone. I certainly could not have turned to anyone in the church. The doors were now firmly closed and have remained so. But neither could I have gone to India to repeat my "former life." I have found no evidence that I had actually sat at Sri Ramana Maharshi's feet in an earlier incarnation. But I had undoubtedly experienced an encounter with the archetype of the holy man or the mana personality.

Jung described this figure as "a dominant of the collective unconscious, the well-known archetype of the mighty man in the form of hero, chief, magician, medicine man, saint, ruler of men and spirits, the friend of God." (CW7:377) Sri Ramana Maharshi's charisma made a tremendous impression on me, but his insistence that the world was Maya contradicted the Judaeo-Christian cosmogony, and his uncompromising denial of the subject/object relation undermined the I-Thou relationship. I found this deeply unsettling.

John Coltrane died in July 1967 at the age of forty. His loss was incalculable, for without his music, I would have had no imaginal context for the numinous trauma of the previous year. A few weeks after receiving the news, I was dining with Laurence at his parents' home. After the meal, we both sensed a presence in the room, an energy field that formed momentarily but did not condense. Earlier in that year, Coltrane had cancelled his visit to this country, much to our disappointment. Had he now made good the omission?

Who Am I?

Mouni Sadhu's book begins with an unsourced extract for Sri Ramana Maharshi's teachings:

> Pursue the enquiry "Who am I" relentlessly. Analyze your entire personality. Try to find out where the "I" thought begins. Go on with your meditations. Keep turning your attention within. One day the wheel of thought will slow down and an intuition will mysteriously arise. Follow that intuition, let your thinking stop and it will lead you to your goal.

Sri Ramana's theoria encapsulates the whole of Advaita Vedanta in a wonderfully concise formulation. It goes something like this:

All thoughts that arise in the mind proceed from just one thought, namely "I am." The process of Self-Enquiry (Atma Vichara) involves tracing each thought back to this root thought. Eventually, the wheel slows down, and you take the final step: You see that even the "I" thought is a fiction. Then you are delivered from the illusion of a separate identity and become the Self that you always were.

Rudolf Steiner, who adhered to the Western esoteric tradition, based his entire philosophy on the primacy of consciousness and the "I." In an essay, "Anthroposophy and Depth Psychology," Hans Lauer shows how penetrating deeply into the "I" can have a very different outcome:

> Consciousness expands to such an extent that it enables one to see directly what lies behind the world's thoughts, the archetypes, what brings them into being. What is this experience? To the modern person it sounds unbelievable and fantastic, yet it is a real experience. One sees differentiated spiritual beings who appear in hierarchical order. We can also call them divine beings, for they are the ones of whom the Christian esoteric tradition speaks of as the hierarchy of angels, archangels, archai, Powers, Thrones, and so on. (Lauer 2002:290-1)

This is exactly what happened to me when I read *In Days of Great Peace*. My "past life" recall must have activated a dormant "I" thought and simultaneously unveiled the hierarchy of spirits. For many years after the event, I could not understand how such a thing could be possible. There is no place for any such hierarchy in the cool-unstructured discourse of Sri Ramana; self-enquiry simply bypasses all intermediate levels of being. There is also no angelology in Anglican Christianity for very different reasons. It was only when I came across Steiner's hot-structured appropriation of the "I" thought that the problem, which had vexed me for decades, was resolved. But from what sources could he have derived his insight? Steiner was deeply learnt in Christian mysticism so he could have drawn upon Pseudo-Dionysus's text, *The Celestial Hierarchies*. He might also have drawn on Kabbalistic source. In the Zohar, there are four worlds or levels of emanation that issue forth from the Absolute (Ain Soph):

> (1)Atsiluth, the world of emanation... (2) Beriah, the world of creation... (3) Yetsirah, the world of formation... (4) Asiyah, the world of making and domain of nature and human existence. (Scholem 1954:272)

Needless to say, I knew nothing about Jewish mysticism at this time. And yet this fleeting revelation had something of the Old Testament about it. If only for an instant I was taken out of Asiyah and raised to Yetsirah. I was afraid as were the prophets and the Kabbalists. But they held their ground while I fell back.

For many years, the epiphanies that took place when I was serving at Communion in Cookham Church, Spencer's visionary paintings, Coltrane's visionary music, the spontaneous activation of the "I" thought, and the of the hierarchy of spirits were just so many disparate fragments. Had I not found my way to Jungian analysis in 1974, things would have remained like this. According to Jung, there are two aspects to the alchemical opus: the experimental procedures and the theoria. The latter plays the same role in alchemy as dogma does in theology. Theoria is the quintessence of the symbolism of the unconscious, "just as dogmas are a condensation or distillation of sacred history, of the myth of the divine being and his deeds." (CW9/2:278) An alchemist's theoria is his Ariadne's thread, without which he would become lost in the labyrinth of the opus. It can take the form of an abstract doctrine, or

Jung suggests it can be "a visio, a spectacle, watching scenes in a theatre." (CW12:403, n.3) Stanley Spencer, who had no time for dogma or theology, was a master of theoria in this sense of the word.

When Jung went to India in 1938, he had not yet developed a theoria to serve as a basis for a dialogue with Sri Ramana. He probably made the right decision not to visit the ashram. (See CW11: VIII, *The Holy Men of India*) When Sri Ramana visited me in 1966, the only theoria I had available to me was a rudimentary idea of numinous experience. This may well have saved my sanity at the time. Jung's model of alchemical individuation has provided me with a far more ample theoria that does not entail such a drastic relativisation of the ego as *Atma Vichara* or Self-Enquiry.

Individuation and Self-Enquiry

If Jung was an empirical psychologist, Sri Ramana Maharshi was an empirical mystic. He did not, as Jung seemed to think, merely reiterate the song of the ages. His method of self-enquiry is a return to the primal "I" thought. This is the first thought to arise in the mind:

> It is only after the rise and origin of the "I" thought that innumerable other thoughts arise. In other words, only after the first personal pronoun, "I" has arisen, do the personal pronouns (you, he, etc.) occur to the mind; they cannot subsist without it. (Osborne 1971:113)

Jung was already formulating the distinction between the ego and the core self as far back as 1916:

> The conscious personal contents constitute the conscious personality, the conscious ego. The unconscious personal contents constitute the self, the unconscious or subconscious ego. (CW7:512)

At this stage, Jung had not yet made the distinction between the ego and the transpersonal self. By 1935, he had defined his position more clearly:

> Sensing the self as something irrational, as an indefinable existent, to which the ego in neither opposed or subjected, but merely attached, and about which it revolves very much as the earth revolves round the sun—thus we come to the goal of individuation. I use the word "sensing" in order to indicate the apperceptive character of the relation between ego and self. In this relation nothing is knowable, because we can say nothing about the contents of the self. The ego is the only content of the self we know. The individuated ego senses itself as the object of an unknown supraordinate subject. It seems to me that our psychological enquiry must come to a stop here . . . (CW7:405)

The totality of the innumerable other thoughts arising from "I" correspond to the totality of psychic processes that constitute the Jungian self. On this analogy, the "I" thought is identical with the centre or nucleus of the self, the *punctus solis* or the point originated by God in alchemy.

Sri Ramana locates the seat of the "I" thought on the right side of the chest in the Heart or *hridayam*. But this, Heart is neither the physiological organ, nor is it the heart chakra:

I ask you to observe where the "I" thought arises in the body, but it is not really quite correct to say that the "I" arises and merges in the chest on the right side. The Heart is another name for the Reality and it is neither inside nor outside the body. There can be no in or out for it, since it alone is. I do not mean by "heart" any physiological organ or any plexus of nerves or anything like that; but as long as a man identifies himself with the body, he is advised to see where the "I" thought arises and merges again. It must be the heart on the right side of the chest since every man of whatever race or religion and in whatever language he is speaking, points to the right side of the chest to indicate himself when he says "I." This is so all over the world, so that must be the place. And by keenly observing the emergence of the "I" thought on waking and its subsidence on going to sleep, one can see it is in the heart on the right side. (Osborne 1971:34)

The classical model of individuation judiciously calls a halt at the centre of the self and proceeds no further. Self-Enquiry does not stop here but dives into the heart and penetrates to the nucleus. In chapters 12, 13, and 14, I will turn to Ibn 'Arabi who charted a course between radical non-dualism (Advaita) and the I-Thou relationship that characterizes the Abrahamic monotheisms. According to Toshihiko Izutsu, the "highest unveiling" is neither extinction in the Void nor is it the infinite qualitative distinction between man and God:

Thus it comes about that the highest stage of metaphysical intuition is not that of those who witness only the Absolute, wholly oblivious of its phenomenal aspect. The highest "unveiling," according to Ibn 'Arabi, is of those who witness both the creatures and the Absolute as two aspects of one Reality, or rather who witness the whole as one Reality diversifying itself constantly and incessantly according to various aspects and relations, being "one" in Essence and "All" with regard to the Names. (Izutsu 1983:478)

The last sentence refers to Ibn 'Arabi's famous doctrine of the Divine Names that constitute the finite world and issue forth in every moment from its infinite ground. I will return to the Shaykh's theoria in chapters 12,13 and 14.

This little essay is an exercise in confessional phenomenology, an attempt to show how the synchronicity principle operates on the level of first-person narrative. It was originally published in Psychological Perspectives 54:2, pp. 197-207, Los Angeles 2011 and Harvest, pp. 8-18, London 2012. I have taken the opportunity to revise parts of the text.

Stanley Spencer's Resurrection in Cookham Churchyard hangs in Tate, Britain, and is well worth a visit. There is also a small Stanley Spencer gallery in Cookham village.

Coltrane's Love Supreme is far more approachable than Meditations or Ascension and transcends its genre. For Hot Structured operators I strongly recommend Valerie Wilmer's As Serious as Your Life, The Story of the New Jazz, Quartet Books, London 1977.

11

PERSONA NON GRATA

For David Rhys in memoriam

On Having Nothing to Lose

Jung said that without the figure of the scapegoat, we would be denied the satisfaction we feel on account of the evil someone else does for us: "Thank Heaven I am the innocent one and not the criminal!" (CW18: 210) The outcast, however, is stigmatized for different reasons. He does not carry a vicarious burden of guilt or shame, nor has he been excommunicated on account of any transgression on his part. Indeed, he may be impelled to go out and commit an offence to justify the abnormality that he is in the eyes of the collective. But he is not really anyone's shadow; rather, he embodies a deeper negation, namely the nemo. This term was coined by the novelist John Fowles in his deeply thought-provoking little book, *The Aristos*. The nemo is a fourth member of the Freudian triad—superego, ego, and id:

> By this I mean not only "nobody" but also the sense
> of being nobody - "nobodiness." In short, just as
> physicists now postulate an anti-matter, so must
> we consider the possibility that there exists in
> the human psyche an anti-ego. This is the nemo.
> (Fowles 1981:46)

The nemo is the personification of man's sense of his own futility, the emptiness he feels at his core. And "since nobody wants to be nobody," we are forever attempting to mask our emptiness: "Thank heaven I have my place in the world and I'm not persona non grata like him." Those who are blessed with the right to exist tell the outcast, "We are somebody, but you are nobody." In the act of doing so, they bestow a role on him. He is indispensable by virtue of being dispensable, someone by virtue of being no one. "The ego," says Fowles, "is certainty, what I am; the nemo is potentiality, what I am not." (Fowles 1981:56) In the case of the outcast, this formula is reversed, his non-being is certainty; his being is potentiality. The downward pull of the spirit of gravity is inexorable. They seal his lips and consign him to the consensual unconscious. By this term, I mean the personal unconscious of the collective. All things from which we avert our gaze are cast out into this repository for the unthinkable or the unspeakable. Complexes that give rise to unacceptable levels of cognitive dissonance[9] are banished to this shadowy domain. The consensual unconscious operates beneath the radar in communities and in institutions.

---

[9]   When we hold two contradictory beliefs or ideas at once or when we engage in actions that contradict our values or habitual attitudes, we suffer distress or discomfort. We then resort to strategies to minimize this cognitive dissonance. Sometimes these strategies bear a striking resemblance to sketches in Monty Python's Flying Circus.

It is a cloak of invisibility for the mechanisms of repression on which social cohesion depends.

In *The Red Book*, we can see Jung in a life-and-death struggle with the consensual unconscious. In the opening passage he renounces the spirit of the times and places himself at the service of the spirit of the depths:

> I have learned that in addition to the spirit of this time there is still another spirit at work, namely that which rules the depths of everything contemporary. The spirit of this time would like to hear of use and value. I also thought this way, and my humanity still thinks this way. But the other spirit forces me nevertheless to speak, beyond justification, use, and meaning. Filled with human pride and blinded by the presumptuous spirit of the times, I long sought to hold that other spirit away from me. (RB 2009:119)

If the outcast is subservient to the spirit of the times, he will lead a life of utter obscurity, dependent on whatever scraps the collective bestow upon him. But if he aligns himself with the spirit of the depths, he might even inconspicuously outwit the authority of the consensual unconscious.

Jung's model of psychospiritual development, the individuation process, involves a prolonged period of liminality, close attention to one's dreams, an introversion of psychic energy, and a temporary withdrawal from the demands of personal and collective life. This, however, presupposes a normal adaptation at the outset. Jung insisted that individuation is not an introverted flight from the community and that it could only be purchased "at

the cost of equivalent work for the benefit of society."
(CW18:1099) You go in order to return. But an individual
whose fate it is to carry the outcast is already outside
the fold. If you have no place in the community, you
cannot return to it in the service of individuation. How
can the outcast benefit the community without the
benefit of community? I will explore two ways out of
the impasse; the first is provided by Nietzsche and the
second by the *I Ching* or *Book of Changes*.

To Recreate all 'It Was' into 'Thus, I Willed It'

At the beginning of his discourse "On Redemption,"
Zarathustra encounters the outcasts in the form of
a group of cripples and beggars. A hunchback tells
Zarathustra that he and his companions would be
convinced by his teaching if he could cure them of their
afflictions. He explains to the hunchback that miracle
cures can turn out to be curses rather than blessings.
Then Zarathustra turns to his disciples and delivers his
teaching on redemption. He begins by declaring that
willing liberates. Or it would, were it not for something
that puts the will in fetters:

> "It was": that is the will's gnashing of teeth and
> loneliest sorrow. Powerless with respect to what
> has been done—it is an angry spectator of all that
> is past. Backwards the will is unable to will; that
> it cannot break time and time's desire—that is the
> will's loneliest sorrow.

We are all prisoners of the visceral sense of revenge
against our inability to will backwards. Zarathustra's
answer to this conundrum is like a Zen koan: "To
redeem that which has passed away and to recreate
all 'It was' into a 'Thus I willed it'—that alone I call

redemption!" Later in his discourse, Zarathustra amplifies this paradoxical utterance:

> All "it was" is a fragment, a riddle, a cruel coincidence—until the creating will says to it: "But thus I willed it!" But has it ever been spoken thus? And when will this happen? Has the will been unharnessed yet from its own folly? Has the will become its own redeemer and joy bringer? Has it unlearned the spirit of revenge and all gnashing of teeth? And who has taught it reconciliation with time, and something higher than any reconciliation?
>
> Something higher than any reconciliation the will that is the will to power must will—yet how might this happen? Who has taught the will to will backwards and want backwards as well? (Nietzsche 2005:121 -22)

These remarks refer to an earlier chapter, "On the Tarantulas," in which Zarathustra teaches that redemption means overcoming the instinct for revenge. Revenge is toxic like the poison of the tarantula: "It sits within your soul: wherever you bite, there grow black scabs; with revenge your poison makes the world go round." Only when this poison has been eliminated is one redeemed:

> For that humanity might be redeemed from revenge: that is for me the bridge to the highest hope and a rainbow after lasting storms.

Of course, the tarantulas will do everything in their power to abort this aspiration:

> "Revenge we will practice and defamation of all who are not the same as us"—thus the tarantula

hearts vow to themselves. 'And "will to equality"—
just that shall thenceforth be the name for virtue;
and against all that has power we will raise our
outcry. (Nietzsche 2005:86)

Our lust for revenge is the cause of our perpetual
entanglement with the consensual unconscious that
would make everyone the same. How can we extricate
ourselves from this squalid dukkha matrix? By an act
of will? Jung pointed out in his *Zarathustra* seminars
that the will can only be a redeeming factor if there
is "an inspiration or revelation, an insight beyond what
you are really able to understand or what you hitherto
have understood." He then asked, "Who could give you
secret knowledge?" One of the participants came up
with the right answer: the cripples. Jung replied,

> Yes, the dwarves know the things that are hidden.
> That is the reason why they come now. For whoever
> believes in the will, whoever wants redemption and
> wills to have it, needs revelation, and these little
> gods, dwarfs or cripples or mana people, have
> secret knowledge. (Z:1238- 9)

What could the dwarf or outcast teach us? That the will
to power wills in the depths of the unconscious and
that this will overrides the imperatives of the conscious
personality. When this happens to us, we are convinced
that our ego will has been thwarted by an unseen hand
and we bitterly resent it. Only someone who can see
that he or she has secretly colluded with the unseen
hand will be released from the teeth gnashing against
time, and *it was*. We are, said Jung in his *Psychological
Commentary on The Tibetan Book of the Dead*, "so
hemmed in by things that jostle and oppress that we
never get the chance, in the midst of all these "given"
things, to wonder by whom they are given." The *Bardo*

Thodol contains the crucial insight "that 'the giver' of all given things dwells within us." ealizes1) To realize this truth is the great liberation.

But the outcast has willed something that anyone in their right mind would avoid like the plague. He has elected to live in the Underworld. Everyone else runs in the opposite direction. As Jung put it in *Psychology and Alchemy*, "The dread and resistance which every natural human being experiences when it comes to delving too deeply into himself is at bottom the fear of the journey to Hades." (Jung 1968:439) Like a medieval Christian, the outcast undergoes his sentence in Purgatory while in this life.

I will turn now to one of Nietzsche's later works, *Twilight of the Idols*. In "The Four Great Errors," Nietzsche exposes the error of free will. This notion is a shady trick that theologians have up their sleeve for making people feel "responsible" and, therefore, dependent on them. Responsibility implies guilt, and guilt entails punishment: "Whenever a particular state of affairs is traced back to a will, an intention, or a responsible action, becoming is stripped of its innocence." In this way, the priests at the head of traditional communities were able "to establish their right to inflict punishment—or assign the right to God." Christianity, Nietzsche declares, "is a hangman's metaphysics." (Nietzsche 2005a:181-2) This is a very one - sided piece of rhetoric. Nietzsche seems to have forgotten Matthew 7:1, "Judge not, yet ye be judged".

What then is Nietzsche's new ethic once we discard the concepts of guilt and punishment? It is that no one is responsible for being the person they are because "the fatality of human existence cannot be extricated from the fatality of everything that was and will be. People are not the products of some special design, will or purpose." He continues,

> A person is necessary, a person is a piece of the whole, a person belongs to the whole, a person only *is* in the context of the whole—there is nothing that can judge, measure, compare, or condemn our being because that would mean judging, measuring, comparing, and condemning the whole . . . *But there is nothing outside the whole!* (Nietzsche 2005a:182)

If the oppressive idea of God and the divine plan is abolished, the innocence of becoming is restored to each moment, and we begin to redeem the world. But the consensual unconscious cannot let go of the hangman's metaphysics. It is forever assigning responsibility, judging, and condemning. Only the outcast is able to extricate himself from this reflex tendency in the collective psyche. And when this vicious circle is finally broken, the shadow of his persecutors falls into the abyss.

Nietzsche's paradox is inextricably bound up with his thought of eternal recurrence. If you will the return of just one moment then you will the return of every moment of your life. In this way you convert every "It was" into "Thus I willed it". I have explicated Nietzsche's thought of thoughts in chapter 7.

Not Dark Yet...

The ancient Chinese classic, the I Ching offers is an indispensable aid to negotiating the hazards of human fate. What advice might the oracle give to the outcast? The thirty-sixth hexagram is titled *Ming Yi*. Wilhelm translates this as *Darkening of the Light* and Lynn as *Suppression of the Light*. (Lynn 1994) The ideogram for Ming/Brightness consists of the graphs for sun and moon. Yi, which Ritsema translates as "hide" can also mean: cut, wound, destroy, exterminate. He has translated *Ming Yi* as *Brightness Hidden* (Ritsema and Sabbadini 2005). The bottom trigram Li, Radiance is buried under the trigram Kun, Earth:

According to Wilhelm, historical personages were linked to the line texts. The evil Shang tyrant Chou Hsin is represented by the top line. At fifth place is Prince Chi who was held prisoner by Chou Hsin, from whom he endured harrowing circumstances. King Wen, at that time the Duke of Chou, was also imprisoned by Chou Hsin and belongs in second place, and King Wu, who overthrew the last Shang emperor, is at third place. The high-minded Po I, who withdrew into hiding, is represented by the first line:

> Darkening of the light during flight. He lowers his wings. The superior man does not eat for three days on his wanderings. But he has somewhere to go. The host has occasion to gossip about him.
> (Wilhelm 1967:568)

Cheng Yi (1033–1107) suggests that the superior man acts so furtively because he discerns the incipiency of things. His behaviour is incomprehensible to the mass of men who are bound to the consensual unconscious. Consequently, he becomes an object of suspicion. (Lynn 1994:362, n.8)

The commentary on the 5th line text of "Ming Yi" says,

> Darkening of the Light as with Prince Chi. Perseverance furthers. The perseverance of Prince Chi shows that the light cannot be extinguished. (Wilhelm 1967:568)

According to Wilhelm, the prince was a relative of the tyrant Chou Hsin and lived at his court. "As he could not desert his post in times of darkness, he concealed his true sentiments and feigned insanity. Although he was held as a slave, he did not allow external misery to deflect him from his convictions." (Wilhelm 1967:142)

The prince had taken on what Nietzsche called the discipline of the great suffering:

> The discipline of suffering, great suffering—don't you know that this discipline alone has created all human greatness to date? The tension of the soul in unhappiness, which cultivates its strength; its horror at the sight of great destruction; its inventiveness and bravery in bearing, enduring, interpreting, exploiting unhappiness, and whatever in the way of depth, mystery, mask, spirit, cleverness the heart has been granted—has it not been granted them through suffering, through the discipline of great suffering? (Nietzsche 1998: Aphorism 225, pp. 116-7)

There is nothing to prevent Nietzsche's discipline of suffering from ending up as an open-ended ordeal. It has no time limit and no exit strategy. The fourth line of *Ming Yi* suggests away of extricating oneself from this pitfall:

> He penetrates the left side of the belly, One gets at the very heart of the darkening of the light, And leaves the gate and courtyard. (Wilhelm 1967:141)

This line text is very obscure. Zhu Xi (1130–1200) suggested that someone in this position is at the lowest point of the upper trigram *Kun*, darkness. (☷) Here, the force of darkness is at its weakest. If this one has enough integrity of purpose, he can see things from the perspective of those in the lower trigram of *Li*, brightness. (☲) Having seen into the heart of darkness *(Ming Yi)*, he can leave gate and courtyard. (cited in Lynn 1994: 362, n.12) The key word here is "integrity" (*cheng*). In Chinese thought, integrity is both a moral and a cosmological category. A person of integrity and the cosmos are both "one and not permitting of change." In other words, both man and cosmos adhere to constant principles. (Zhang Dainian 2002) Zhu Xi cites the twenty-fifth hexagram, *wu wang*, in this connection. *Wu wang* means without illusion or without guile or simply integrity:

> Integrity is said of what is truly the case and shows "no illusion" (hexagram 25). It is the fundamental nature of heaven. (Explanation of the Book of Comprehending, cited in Zhang Dainian 2002:144)

One situated at the fourth line of *Ming Yi* is able to leave the gate and courtyard because he has the integrity to see the situation for what it is and make his departure.

If the outcast has this integrity, he can extricate himself from the oppressive double bind imposed on him by the social order.

On Having Nothing to Repress

In one crucial respect, the thirty-sixth hexagram is not applicable to the situation of the outcast. He is not oppressed by an evil tyrant like Chou Hsin. He is kept in his place by a seemingly benign regime such as the one I discovered on a dream journey I took in 2001:

> I am dropped into another dimension *Star Trek* style. On reaching the ground, I notice that I have a tiny conical brush attached to the tip of my nose. I remove it and throw it away—a mistake I will later regret. I am in a fundamentalist theocratic state. The church elders wear the little brush on the tips of their noses as a sign of rank. Unwittingly, I have thrown away my cover.

> My companions and I go to the nearest church. A Sunday school class is just ending. The teacher must be a layperson because he does not have the mark of rank. I converse with the adults, but I know that I must not say anything that might be regarded as provocative. Only the most anodyne topics of conversation are permitted. I am treated like an established member of the community and do my best to dissimulate. Then I accompany one of the Sunday school teachers on his way home. He pushes his bike, which has oval wheels not round ones. Space has a slightly different structure in this dimension. I need a pretext to get away from him and tell him that "I'm extremely concerned about Jeremy."

There is one incongruous detail in the dream I should mention. After I get away from the man with the bicycle, I dip my fingers in a puddle to cleanse them of mud, or perhaps shit, a tiny bit of fertile prima materia. According to the alchemists the precious lapis is found in a heap of dung.

What would have happened if I had not disposed of my little conical nose - brush at the end of the dream? Had I retained my badge of rank I might have taken my place at the table of the elders. The world they presided over was the inverse of the secular mood. In this fundamentalist utopia God has died a second death. The first death of God (Nietzsche 2001: Aphorism-125, pp. 119 - 20) was the death of the projection of God as an external entity. The God image that Jung defined as "the imprint of the most overwhelmingly powerful influences exerted on the conscious mind by unconscious concentrations of libido" (Jung 1971:412) dropped into the depths of the collective unconscious. The second death of God resulted in the elimination of all spontaneous expressions of the unconscious libido. Now a vapid demiurge ruled in place of Yahweh. The priestly caste, with those ridiculous brushes on the tips of their noses, had no need of the concepts of guilt and punishment. Why? Because no one ever transgressed in thought or in action. How could they if *the consensus omnium is God, and God is the consensus omnium.*

This autocratic Sunday school was the result of a process of reverse natural selection. The meek and mild had, indeed, inherited the earth, and the strong had been driven into extinction. In *Twilight of the Idols,* Nietzsche acknowledged that the struggle for survival exists but went on to say,

It is unfortunately the opposite of what Darwin's school would want . . . namely to the disadvantage of the strong, the privileged, the fortunate exceptions. Species do not grow in perfection: the weak keep gaining dominance over the strong— there are more of them, and besides they are cleverer Their ingenuity consists of caution, patience, cunning, disguise, great self-control and everything involved in mimicry (which includes much of what is called virtue. (Nietzsche 2005a: Aphorism 14, pp. 119 -20)

Nietzsche's idea of inverse evolution raises an acutely uncomfortable question: Is the outcast the only one who is going in the right direction?

*

During a cold snap in the winter of 1996, a minor infection in my left ear spread rapidly to my left eye. I had to be taken to hospital without delay to prevent the bacteria from destroying my eyesight and possibly from reaching my brain. For the first few nights, I was delirious. When my mental clarity returned to me, some initial thoughts on the archetype of the outcast came up from the depths. Had it not been for the timely intervention of my friend in America, the late David Rhys, this material would have dropped into the consensual unconscious. An earlier attempt to develop this material was published with the title "On Having Nothing to Lose" in Harvest, the journal for the London Jung Club, in 2014.

THEORIA

12

ON ARCHETYPES AND DIVINE NAMES

I am a star following his way like you[10].

I

Ibn 'Arabi's encounter with Averroes/ His experience of immediate enlightenment at an early age/Ibn 'Arabi's God image: the non-dual Essence and the personal Divinity/God is incomparable and similar/ Jung's outright rejection of incomparability/ The relativity of God in Jung's psychology and Ibn 'Arabi's metaphysics

Muyi l-Din, Ibn 'Arabi's father, was a close friend of Averroes (Abu'l Walid Ibn Rushd, 1126–1198). When Averroes expressed a wish to meet Muyi l-Din, his

---

10   From the Mithraic Liturgy, cited in CW.18:1573.

father sent him to the philosopher's house in Cordoba on an errand. Averroes received the young man and embraced him. Then Averroes said Yes, and Ibn 'Arabi said Yes in return. The older man was overjoyed, but then Ibn 'Arabi said No. Averroes winced, and the colour went out of his cheeks. He asked his guest what solution he had found through divine illumination. Was it identical with the findings of speculative reflection? Ibn 'Arabi replied, "Yes and no. Between the yes and the no, spirits take their flight from matter and heads are separated from their bodies." The older man turned pale and murmured the ritual phrase, "There is no power save in God." The young Ibn Arabi had overturned Averroes's Aristotelian logic and thrown him into an existential crisis. (Corbin 1969:41-2)

When it is put into context, this encounter is somewhat less startling, although nonetheless extraordinary. Prior to the meeting, the young Ibn 'Arabi had been on a long retreat and had experienced immediate illumination (*fath*). Averroes must have heard about this, which is why he requested the meeting. It is worth mentioning that although he was an intellectual giant and recognised as such in his time, Averroes was an exceptionally humble man. In his monumental *Meccan Revelations* (*Futuhat al-makkiyya*), Ibn 'Arabi said that Averroes wanted to know if the insights he had gained through years of study and reflection corresponded to what the Muyi l-Din had experienced directly. After this meeting, Averroes is recorded as saying to Ibn 'Arabi's father:

> This is a state that we had confirmed rationally, but had never seen anyone who possessed it. Praise belongs to God, that I should live in a time of one of its possessors, those who have opened the locks upon its doors. Praise belongs to God who singled me out to see him! (Cited in Chittick 1989: xiv)

We have no first-hand account of what happened to
Ibn 'Arabi on his initiatory retreat, and the secondary
sources are not entirely consistent. Claude Addas has
examined them all in her biography of the Shaykh, and
she has come to this conclusion:

> Whatever the case may be . . . the very first
> stage of Ibn 'Arabi's spiritual journey consisted
> of an immediate fath or illumination, or more
> precisely of a jadhba, the state of being drawn
> out of oneself in ecstasy as the result of a divine
> intervention which is direct and abrupt; and that
> he obtained this illumination straightaway and
> without any prior effort during the course of a
> retreat. (Addas 1993:38)

An illumination of this nature is, indeed, rare, and
I only know of one other instance. In the closing
decade of the nineteenth century, a Tamil youth called
Venkataraman was sitting alone in a room when he
was suddenly overwhelmed by the fear of death.
Fortunately, we have a first-hand account of what
happened next. At the time, Venkataraman had no
health problems to account for this, and he did not try
to account for it. Neither did it occur to him to consult a
doctor. He felt he had to solve the problem himself:

> The shock of the fear of death drove my mind
> inwards and I said to myself mentally without
> actually framing the words: "Now death has come;
> what does it mean? What is it that is dying? This
> body dies.

Venkataraman then lay down with his limbs
outstretched and held his breath as if he really was
dead:

"Well then," I said to myself, "this body is dead. It will be carried stiff to the burning ground and there burnt and reduced to ashes. But with the death of the body am I dead? Is the body I? It is silent and inert but I feel the full force of my personality and even the voice 'I' within me, apart from it. So I am Spirit transcending the body. The body dies but the Spirit that transcends it cannot be touched by death. That means I am the deathless Spirit." All this was not dull thought; it flashed through me vividly as living truth which I perceived directly, almost without thought process. "I" was something very real, the only real thing about my present state, and all conscious activity connected with the body was centred on that "I." From that moment on the "I" or Self focussed attention on itself by a powerful fascination. Fear of death had vanished once and for all. Absorption in the Self continued from that time on. (Osborne 1970:18-19)

Muyi l-Din would have been around the same age as Venkataraman when he had his moment of truth. According to Claude Addas, his illumination probably took place in a cemetery in Seville. Did he experience a comparable confrontation with death? Venkataraman, who later took the name of Ramana Maharshi (1879–1950), was one of the most revered gurus that India has ever produced. In a word, he was the twentieth-century Shankara.

Jung could have met Sri Ramana Maharshi when he visited India in 1938. But he decided against it. In his essay *The Holy Men of India*, he explained that a man who was perfectly balanced was of no interest from a psychological point of view:

The insane contradiction, on the other hand, between existence beyond Maya in the cosmic Self

and that amiable human weakness which fruitfully
sinks many roots into the black earth, repeating for
all eternity the weaving and the rending of the veil
as the ageless melody of India—this contradiction
fascinates me: for how else can one perceive the
light without the shadow, hear the silence without
the noise, attain wisdom without foolishness.
(CW11: 953)

Ibn 'Arabi's God image encompasses everything from
the cosmic Self beyond manifestation to the tips of the
roots in the black earth. The Reality (*al Haqq*) is not
delimited, and therefore, it cannot exclude anything,
not the black earth, not even delimitation itself. In
other words, if God, in his infinitude, were to exclude
the finite world, he would be delimited in this respect.
(Chittick 1989:109-10) God and the world are an
inclusive totality.

There are two aspects to *al Haqq*, the Divinity (*al Uluha*)
and the Essence (*Dhat*). No predicates can be applied
to the Essence, and all names can be ascribed to the
Divinity. From the standpoint of the Divinity, God and
the creation are separate entities. But it is a category
error to think that the world as object exists separately
from God in the Divine Essence. Subject-object duality
does not apply on this level.

As far as Jung was concerned, psychology could say
nothing about the Divine Essence as it was beyond the
a priori limits of knowledge. With regard to Divinity,
he could only speak of God in terms of his image in
the unconscious psyche, the *imago Dei*. Psychology can
point to a universal disposition or archetype in the
unconscious to produce an image of deity. It cannot
go beyond its brief and speak of an extra psychic
reality corresponding to the image. To speak of the

Divine Essence or to posit an objectively existing deity would have led to accusations of mysticism and deprived Jung's psychology of all scientific credibility. It is easy to forget he represented a minority voice in the aggressively positivistic culture of the twentieth century.

Despite his numerous disclaimers, Jung was not able to distance himself from theology entirely. For example, in his long essay *The Relations between the Ego and the Unconscious*, he advances a vigorous critique of classical Western theism:

> "Absolute" means "cut off," "detached." To assert that God is absolute amounts to placing him outside all connection with mankind. Man cannot affect him, or he man. Such a God would be of no consequence at all. We can in fairness only speak of a God who is relative to man, as man is to God. (CW7: 394, note 6)

In the *Fusus al Hikam*, Ibn 'Arabi uses the metaphor of the mirror to describe a relationship of co-dependence between man and God:

> He is your mirror for your vision of yourself, and you are His mirror for His Vision of His Names— which are none other than Himself- and the manifestation of their determinations. (Dagli 2004:26)

But this convergence between Jung and Ibn 'Arabi should not be pushed too far. For the Shaykh, the reciprocity between God and man can only be realised through the operation of divine grace. Reza Shah Kazemi puts it very succinctly: "It can only be God

Himself that actualizes the consciousness of the relativity of God."[11] (Shah Kazemi 2006:95) If absolute meant "cut off" this act of grace would be logically impossible.

II

God's exists in Himself (tanzih) and for us (tashbih)/ Theophany and the Divine Names/The Unity of essence and the Unity of multiplicity/Jung's Kant based methodology/His one-sided emphasis on the tashbih aspect of God

Sri Ramana Maharshi taught that man and the world do not exist separately from God. In other words, "the world is unborn." Conversely, Jung maintained that a God who only exists in and for himself is cut off from all human conditions. According to Ibn 'Arabi, God exists in and for himself, but he also exists for us. His famous doctrine of the Divine Names allows him to steer a middle course between tanzih and tashbih. There are ninety-nine Names of God in the Quran, and seven of these are most frequently invoked: The Alive, Knowing, Desiring, Powerful, Speaking, Generous, and Just. In Ibn 'Arabi's cosmology, the universal Quranic Names differentiate themselves into the particular names in all their endless multiplicity. The Divine Names denote different attributes of God, and the two terms can be used interchangeably. However, Sachiko Murata has drawn attention to a grammatical distinction between them: "A name is an adjective (serving as a proper noun), while an attribute is an

---

[11] Frithjof Schuon puts the matter very concisely: "The personal Divinity only allows those who adore him to understand that he is not the absolute reality." (Schuon 1959:55)

abstract noun. For example, God is called by the Name Merciful, while the corresponding attribute is mercy. His Name is Just and His attribute is justice." (Murata 1992:27)

Every created entity manifests a name, and nothing exactly replicates anything else. In a word, the Divine Names are infinite. Probably no Western scholar has conveyed the pathos of this doctrine more eloquently than Henry Corbin. In *Creative Imagination in the Sufism of Ibn 'Arabi*, Corbin expounds "the eternal cosmogony as conceived by the genius of Ibn 'Arabi." The creation of the world involves a reciprocal relationship between God and creature from the outset. When the Prophet was asked where God was before he created the world, he replied that "He was in a Cloud, there was no space either above or below." Ibn 'Arabi interprets this hadith as follows:

> God creates the world in order to satisfy His yearning to be known. The Cloud is a condensation of the Divine breath, which the Divine Mercy exhales in the sigh. This release of the breath is the first theophanic act in which the Divine Being reveals His Names to Himself. In a second theophany the Names are differentiated into individuated forms. But the Names are still in state of pure potentiality. They too yearn to be known and when the Breath of the Merciful is released in a sigh of compassion they can enter fully into existence: Thus in this Cloud are manifested all forms of being from the highest Archangels, the "Spirits ecstatic with love" to the minerals of inorganic nature; everything that is differentiated from the pure essence of the Divine Being as such (al Haqq), genera, species and individuals, all this is created in the Cloud. (Corbin 1969:186)

It is the Divinity (*al Uluha*) who requires the Names to manifest himself and who exhales the Breath of the Merciful. The Divine Essence (*Dhat*) exists in and for itself and, therefore, has no need of the Names. In *Fusus*, Ibn 'Arabi speaks of the unity of multiplicity and the unity of essence. The first term applies to the Absolute on the level of the Divine Names, and the second term applies to the Absolute as he exists independently of the Names and the world. Both aspects, says the Shaykh, are called by the same name: "One." (Izutsu 1983:102) In this way, he is able to maintain the equilibrium of *tasbih* and *tanzih*.

From the standpoint of Jung's empirical psychology, God is the divine libido. Contrary to Freud, he argued that libido (Latin for "I desire") cannot be confined to sexuality and that this term included every conceivable desire from our longing for the orgasm to our longing for God. In his essay on Meister Eckhart's essay, Jung explicated his idea of the God-image in these terms:

> The accumulated libido activates images lying dormant in the collective unconscious, among them the God image, that engram or imprint which from the beginning of time has been the collective expression of the most overwhelmingly powerful influences exerted on the conscious mind by unconscious concentrations of libido. (CW6:412)

In Jung's later writings, the emphasis shifted from the libido to the engram or the archetype. An archetype or imprint, of course, implies an imprinter, but psychology cannot overstep its bounds and say anything at all about the imprinter: "We simply do not know the ultimate derivation of the archetype any more than we know the origin of the psyche. The competence of psychology as an empirical science only goes so far as to establish, on the basis of comparative research, whether for instance the imprint found in the psyche can reasonably be termed a God image." (CW12:15) The unconscious libido produces as many images of God as there are Divine Names, but there is nothing gratuitous about this theogonic process. Jung acknowledged that "even the Boundless is pervaded by psychic laws which no man has invented, but of which he has gnosis in the symbolism of Christian dogma." (CW11:168) He could not avoid exceeding his own epistemic ground rules from time to time.

III

Jung: transcendental assertions arise out of numinous experience/The Universal Man and the collective unconscious/Adam and the Jungian self/ Psychological individuation does not require any form of transcendent intervention/For Ibn Arabi the actualisation of every archetype is totally dependent on the Divine Command

Jung was convinced that after Kant it was no longer possible to make metaphysical assertions. Given the limitations of human knowledge, there are no firm grounds for assuming that "our metaphysical picture of the world corresponds to the transcendental reality." But he did not go as far as Hume and consign all metaphysical systems to the flames. Transcendental statements are not arbitrary inventions or wish-fulfilment fantasies. They originate in "involuntary numinous experiences which happen to a man and find expression in religious assertions and convictions." (CW14:781 and 782) The implications of this observation are profound. What is the source of these numinous experiences? Are such experiences the psyche's response to noumenal reality? In *The Idea of the Holy,*

Rudolf Otto offered compelling evidence in favour of this hypothesis:

> The facts of numinous consciousness point therefore—as likewise do the pure concepts of the understanding of Kant and the ideas and value judgements of ethics and aesthetics— to a hidden substantive source, from which religious ideas and feelings are formed, which lies in the mind independently of sense experience.

This source of cognition is something higher and deeper than the Kantian categories. It is "a pure reason in the profoundest sense." (Otto 1958:113-14)

The nearest Jung comes to acknowledging a hidden substantive source to the *imago Dei* is in his *Reply to Martin Buber* who had written a trenchant critique of his psychology of religion. Here is Jung's response to Buber's accusation that he was promoting "a religion of pure psychic immanence" (Buber 1953:111):

> God has indeed made an inconceivably sublime and mysteriously contradictory image of himself, without the help of man, and implanted it in man's unconscious as an archetype, an archetypal light: not in order that theologians of all times and places should be at one another's throats, but in order that the unpresumptuous man might glimpse an image, in the stillness of his soul, that is akin to him and wrought in his own psychic substance. This image contains everything he will ever imagine concerning his gods or concerning the ground of his psyche. (CW18:1508)

In the opening chapter of the *Fusus al Hikam, Of the Divine Wisdom in the Word of Adam,* Ibn 'Arabi tells us that God created an inconceivably sublime image to serve as a mirror to reflect his Names:

> Al Haqq, Praise be to Him, wanted through his most beautiful names which are innumerable, to see the essences (ayan) of the names- or, if you will, to see Himself (or his own ayn/essence). He wished to do this through an all- encompassing being which embodies the attributes of existence. Through this being, God's secret would then be revealed to himself. (Nettler 2003:19)

According to Titus Burckhardt, the word *ayn*, plural *ayan*, contains the meanings of essential determination, personal essence, archetype, eye, and source. These essences are called fixed essences (*ayan thabita*) because they are immutable structures in the mind of God. They constitute the archetypal forms of everything in the phenomenal world. In his commentary on the *Fusus*, Nettler clarifies the relationship between the Names and the *ayan*:

> In giving these essences to God's Quranic names, Ibn 'Arabi has here extended the significance of the names from their meaning as descriptions of God to things in the phenomenal world. God's names may then be known, the way other things are known. God will then be able to see Himself in the essences of His names as He wishes to do so.

At first, the world is flat, undifferentiated, and void of spirit like an unpolished mirror. But then God breathes life into Adam, the all-encompassing being that He has created: "The divine command," says Ibn Arabi, "necessitates the polishing of the mirror of the world and Adam is the very polishing of the mirror and the

Holy Spirit of that (undifferentiated) form (of creation)."
(Nettler 2003:19)

Ibn 'Arabi goes on to describe the angels who are the
spiritual and sensory faculties of the Universal Man.
In Jungian psychology, the Universal Man corresponds
to the collective unconscious, and Adam corresponds
to the transpersonal self. As Jung puts it in *Mysterium
Coniunctionis*: "Adam stands not only for the psyche
but its totality; he is a symbol of the self, and hence a
representation of the irrepresentable Godhead." (CW14:
558) From a psychological point of view, the self and the
God image are empirically indistinguishable. (CW9/2:73)

For Ibn 'Arabi, Adam was created to be the mirror of
the Universal Man so that the Divine Names could be
known. To polish the mirror is, therefore, to realize our
Adamic nature so that God can become conscious in
each of us. But God can only become conscious in an
integrated personality. As Jung puts it,

> And just as the universe is not a dissolving mass
> of particles but rests in the unity of God's embrace,
> so man must not dissolve into a warring mass of
> particles but must become a unity embracing them
> all . . . Possession by the unconscious means being
> torn apart into many people and things . . . Which
> is why, according to Origen, the aim of a Christian
> is to become an inwardly united human being.
> (CW16:397)

Through the process of individuation, the contents
of the transpersonal unconscious are integrated
into consciousness. This process involves a dialogue
between the conscious and unconscious personalities
which is activated by means of dream work and active

imagination. In this way, the personality achieves a higher level of integration.

How is this process of integration conceived in the Sufism of Ibn 'Arabi? His model of psychospiritual development is based on the *ayan thabitah* or fixed essences. In his study of Ibn 'Arabi and Chuang Tzu, *Sufism and Taoism*, Izutsu translates *ayan thabitah* as the permanent archetypes. These archetypes occupy the middle position between the Absolute and the empirical world. Other Islamic scholars translate this term as the "non-existent entities." "Existence," in this particular context, means phenomenal existence. As Ibn 'Arabi puts it, the *ayan* have not yet smelt the fragrance of existence. They subsist as potentialities: "Symbolically the permanent archetypes are dark. They are dark because they are not yet illuminated by the bright daylight of existence. Existence as Light belongs only to the individual things that exist concretely and externally." (Izutsu 1983:161) This corresponds exactly to the empirical facts of the collective unconscious. According to Jung, the archetypes enter into existence in space and time when they cross the threshold into the light of ego consciousness. An archetype that is about to actualise itself in the form of a concretely existent thing is, needless to say, in an extremely delicate state. This is how Izutsu describes the transition:

> The permanent archetype in itself is a Universal transcending the level of time; it is an intelligible in the Divine Consciousness. When a Universal is about to go into a state of actual existence and is about to be particularized in the form of an individual thing it becomes first connected with a particular point of time and thereby becomes temporally specialized. (Izutsu 1983:177)

The parallels between Jung and Ibn 'Arabi are compelling, but there is one crucial difference. For Ibn 'Arabi, a permanent archetype can only be actualised by Divine Command. Consequently, the individuation of an archetype, and by extension the individuation of a human being, is in the hands of a transcendent God. By contrast, Jung's model of the individuation process is sufficient unto itself:

> The symbols of wholeness frequently occur at the beginning of the individuation process, indeed they can often be observed in early infancy. This observation says much for the a priori existence of potential wholeness, and on this account the idea of entelechy instantly recommends itself. (CW9/1: 278)

The term *entelechy* is Aristotelian, and it usually translated as "actuality" or "actualisation." The concept of entelechy applies to the organic development of the living creature. An acorn will, under the right conditions, develop into an oak tree; that is its entelechy. Here is how an Aristotle scholar explains this idea:

> Everything that happens in nature must already exist potentially; in other words, it must already exist in another form. As for the numerous natural species, they are the product neither of randomness nor of the creationist interference of a transcendent reason: the natural species are what an appropriate matter borrows from a natural agent who is already in possession of this form. (Richard Bodeus:59, cited in Popkin 1998)

The concept of entelechy does not require the intervention of a transcendent deity and therefore it carries no theological baggage. In this respect, Jung's psychology is much closer to the Aristotelianism of Averroes than it is to the Platonism of Ibn 'Arabi.

For Ibn 'Arabi, the divine command actualises all potentialities. This command has two aspects: *qada* and *qadar*. *Qada* means "decree" and refers to the decisive judgement made on the basis of God's knowledge of the essence of each creature. *Qadar* means "destiny" or "fate," and it concerns the mode of manifestation and its precise timing. This is not Islamic fatalism. There is one factor that can override *qada* and *qadar*, namely preparedness (*isti 'dad*), the condition of the recipient. If an individual is not adequately prepared, the *qadar* manifests itself as fate. Jung understood this very well:

> A religious terminology comes naturally, as the only adequate one in the circumstances, when we are faced with a tragic fate that is the unavoidable concomitant of wholeness. "My fate" means a daemonic will to precisely that fate—a will not necessarily coincident with my own (the ego will). When it is opposed to the ego, it is difficult not to feel a certain "power" in it, whether divine or infernal. The man who submits to his fate calls it the will of God; the man who puts up a hopeless and exhausting fight is more apt to see the devil in it. In either event this terminology is not only universally understood but meaningful as well. (CW12:36, n.17)

In *Aion*, Jung says, "The psychological rule says that when an inner situation is not made conscious, it happens outside, as fate. That is to say, when the individual remains undivided and does not become conscious of his inner opposite, the world must perforce act out the conflict and be torn into opposing halves." (CW9/2:126) The individual who is conscious of his or her inner situation has the prospect of a better outcome.

Instead of persisting in a futile struggle, he or she has the option of collaborating with fate/*qadar*. However, we can only see our permanent archetype through a glass darkly. The inner structure of this archetype is, says Izutsu, an impenetrable mystery. But he continues there is one small aperture through which man can peep into this unfathomable mystery: "That aperture is the self-consciousness of man." (Izutsu 1983:180)

To glimpse one's permanent archetype is to see the God within. In a letter to a theologian, Jung wrote,

> I thank God every day that I have been permitted to experience the reality of the imago Dei in me. Had that not been so, I would be a bitter enemy of Christianity and the Church in particular. Thanks to this actus gratiae my life has meaning, and my inner eye was opened to the grandeur and beauty of dogma. (L1:487)

Ibn 'Arabi lived in the Islamic world at a time when divine revelation was the sun and empirical science was the moon. Jung lived in a post-Christian world, where the moon had eclipsed the sun. Consequently, the Shaykh's experience of the Divinity was direct and unmediated:

> When I kept knocking on God's door
> I waited mindfully, not distracted,
> Until there appeared to the eye the glory of His face
> And a call to me, nothing else.
> I encompassed Being in knowledge—
> Nothing in my heart but God. (Chittick 1989: xiv)

Chittick suggests that this is what happened to the young Ibn' Arabi on his first retreat.

IV

*Otto: divination = discernment of the numinous/ the
centrality of divination in Jung's psychology/ Jung's
unacknowledged debt to Schleiermacher/Ibn 'Arabi's
extraordinary divinatory powers*

In his Yale lectures on *Psychology and Religion*,
delivered in 1937, Jung defined religion as "a careful
and scrupulous observation of the numinosum."
(CW11: 6) He derived this definition from Rudolf Otto's
influential book, *The Idea of the Holy*. Otto called the
faculty that carefully and scrupulously observes the
numinous "divination." He defined this faculty as "the
capacity for deeply absorbed contemplation, when
confronted by the vast living totality or reality of
things in nature and history." A mind that is receptive
to the impressions of the universe "becomes capable
of experiencing intuitions and feelings of something
that is a sheer overplus in addition to empirical reality."
(Otto 1958:146)

The equivalent term for divination in Jung's psychology
is intuition. Nathalie Pilard's book *Jung and Intuition*
(Pilard 2015) is very illuminating in this connection.
She points out that the English translation of the
Collected Works on which I have relied had obscured
the centrality of intuition in Jung's model of the
psyche. According to Pilard, the simplest form of
intuition is *einfall*. This term refers to things "falling
into" consciousness. For example, someone comes out
with a profound remark only to forget it a moment
later. Such insights originate in what Jung calls the
natural mind that "says absolutely straight and
ruthless things." It is aptly named because "it wells up
from the earth like a natural spring, and brings with it

the peculiar wisdom of nature." (V:523 and 691) There is another German word for intuition, *anschauung.* According to Otto, *anschauugen* are intimations "of a reality fraught with mystery and momentousness." (Otto1958:146-7) For Schleiermacher, *anschauung* is the source of religion itself:

> Religion's essence is neither thinking nor acting, but intuition and feeling. It wishes to intuit the universe, wishes devoutly to overhear the universe's manifestations and actions, longs to be grasped and filled by the universe's immediate influences in childlike passivity. (Schleiermacher 1996:22)

If Schleiermacher had not rediscovered the sense of the numinous in the early nineteenth century, our capacity for divination would have withered on the vine. (See Otto 1931: VIII) Jung does not mention him anywhere in the Collected Works or the Seminars, but I have discovered one reference in a letter to Henry Corbin in 1953:

> Schleiermacher really is one of my spiritual ancestors. He even baptized my grandfather—born a Catholic—who by then was a doctor . . . The vast esoteric and individual spirit of Schleiermacher was a part of the intellectual atmosphere of my father's family. I never studied him, but unconsciously he was my spiritus rector. (L2:115)

Ibn 'Arabi was born into a culture in which the faculty of divination could flourish to a degree we would find unimaginable nowadays. He was able to focus his extraordinary powers of intuition both on the universe and the Quran:

> Plunge in to the ocean of the Quran if your breath is sufficiently powerful. And if not, limit yourself to the study of the commentaries on its apparent sense; but in this case do not plunge for you will perish. The ocean of the Quran is deep, and if he who plunges into it did not limit himself to those places which are closest to the shore, he would never come back . . . (As for those who have remained back) they have aimed at the centre of the ocean—or rather it has aimed at them—and they have plunged for eternity. (Cited in Chodkiewicz 1993:22-3)

In 1944, Jung had a heart attack. While he was on life support, he experienced a series of theophanic visions, which were recorded in chapter 10 of *Memories, Dreams, Reflections*: "Everything around me seemed enchanted," he recalled, "Night after night I floated in a state of purest bliss, *thronged round with the images of all creation*." (Faust, Part 2). The quotidian world he came back to was "too material, too crude and clumsy, terribly limited both spatially and spiritually." (MDR:325-6) He longed to escape the prison and plunge into the ocean without shore for eternity. But he could not leave the shore and never come back. Now Jung was no longer boxed in by Kant-based empiricism, he too had seen the glory of His face.

> I am indebted to Andrew Rawlinson for averting catastrophe with his timely critique of my first draft.

13

OPPOSITION IS TRUE FRIENDSHIP

C.G.Jung, Ibn'Arabi and the Answer to Job

A Life in Sacred Order

In 1923, Jung made a short field trip to a Pueblo reservation in New Mexico. Although he found the Pueblo were very secretive about their religion, he was able to engage in a dialogue with their chief, Ochwiay Biano. At one point in the conversation, Ochwiay told Jung exactly what he thought of the white man:

> See how cruel the whites look. Their lips are thin, their noses sharp, their faces furrowed and distorted by folds. Their eyes have a staring expression; they are always seeking something. What are they seeking? The whites always want something; they are always uneasy and restless. We do not know what they want. We do not understand them. We think they are mad.

Jung asked him why he thought the whites were crazy:

> They say they think with their heads, he replied.
> Why of course—what do you think with? Jung asks
> him in surprise.
> We think here, he said indicating his heart.
> (MDR:276)

For Ibn 'Arabi and, indeed, for Sufism in general, the heart (*qalb*) is the source of true knowledge and comprehensive intuition. (Corbin 1969:221) Ochwiay's gesture of pointing to his heart had the effect of awakening this knowledge in Jung. He went into a long meditation, and for the first time, he viewed the "triumph of the West" through the eyes of a Native American.

Jung had successfully bridged the cultural divide between his modernity and the mythological outlook of a Pueblo chief. Could he have done the same if he had been in a dialogue with Ibn 'Arabi? His candid admission that he "could never really relate to Islam" (Bair 2003:354) suggests they would have passed each other like ships in the night. The problem is encapsulated in a dream he had in 1948. Carl Jung meets his deceased father who was now the custodian of an eighteenth-century house. Paul Jung takes down a huge Bible covered in fish skin and gives such a recondite exposition of a text that the son and his companions cannot understand a word of it. In the next scene, father and son go upstairs to the second floor. They enter a vast circular room, a gigantic mandala. Jung had seen such a room in India, the council hall of the Sultan Akbar (the *divan-i-kass*). There is a steep flight of stairs in the centre leading to a small door high in the wall. Jung's father tells his son that he will lead him to the highest presence and prostrates himself Muslim style. Carl does the same with great emotion, *but he cannot bring his head all the way down and stops a millimetre from the floor.* (MDR:245-7)

As Jung admitted, he really should have touched the floor with his forehead. Apparently, something prevented him from doing so:

> There are things that awaited me hidden in the unconscious. I had to submit to fate, and ought really to have touched my forehead to the floor, so that my submission would be complete. But something in me was saying, "All very well, but not entirely." Something in me was defiant and determined not to be a dumb fish and if there were not something of the sort in free men, no Book of Job would have been written several hundred years before the birth of Christ. Man always has some mental reservations in the face of divine decrees. Otherwise, where would be his freedom? And what would be the use of that freedom if it could not threaten Him who threatens him. (MDR: 247)

Traditionalist Muslim scholars maintain that to refuse to submit to God is to refuse revelation. Michel Chodkiewicz makes this very clear in his essay *Those Who Are Perpetually in Prayer:*

> Revelation is not only message: it is also commandment. The message delivers its totality only to the submissive: to the true Muslimum. The Quran opens its "treasures" only to those who apply the Law it has established. The sharia (Law) and the haqiqa (the highest and most secret of truths) are inextricably conjoined. (Chodkiewicz 1993:101)

No wonder Jung had difficulty in relating to Islam. The degree of renunciation the Law requires is simply unsustainable outside a traditional culture. But Chodkiewicz is only explicating Ibn 'Arabi's attitude to the Law, which is summed up in the following sentence: "The munazalat are obtained only by the most perfect conformity to the prescriptions of the Law." The term *munazalat* is defined by the Shaykh "as an encounter between God and man, each having covered half the distance." (Chodkiewicz 1993:90) Jung would not have been Jung if he had brought his head all the way down, and Ibn 'Arabi would not be Ibn 'Arabi if he had declined to do so. Indeed, for an observing Muslim, such a refusal is incomprehensible.

In his autobiography, Jung spoke about his father's catastrophic collapse of faith. But in the dream Paul Jung had no difficulty in bringing his head all the way down to the floor. The dream seems to be saying to his son, *Look, your father has regained his faith, and he has submitted before the highest presence.* Jung's father was an Arabic scholar who had written his doctoral thesis on the Karaites, an ultra-orthodox Arabic-speaking Jewish sect. Like Muslims at the time of Ibn 'Arabi, the Karaites were a culture of renunciation. Nowadays, such a culture is commonly regarded as restrictive and joyless. But Jung was deeply impressed by the dignity and the serenity of the traditional people he encountered in America and the Islamic world. He also observed that modern Europeans are both more complicated and consequently slightly ridiculous. (MDR:268) Most of us have no idea how a ritual culture works, and we do not begin to see the extent of our indigence. A classroom conversation with a nine- or ten-year-old Asian girl when I was on a supply teaching assignment brought this home to me. She told me that going to the temple was the high spot of her week. Then

she asked me if I went to the temple. I replied that I did
not and she said, "Oh Sir, you don't know what you're
missing!" She spoke from the natural mind and she
spoke from Tradition.

The great sociologist and Freud scholar Philip Rieff
provides the best account I know of the dynamics of
traditional cultures:

> Culture, our ingeniously developed limitations is
> constituted by two motifs, which are dialectically
> related. These two motifs, which have shifting
> contents, I call interdicts and remissions from
> interdicts. Every culture is so constituted that there
> are actions one cannot perform, more accurately
> would dread to perform. (Rieff 1990:323)

A ritual culture will, of necessity, have a system of
interdicts that we would regard as draconian. If the
authorities turn a blind eye to deviations from the
ritual codes, the entire social order would unravel.
But it would be intolerable to live under a permanent
regime of renunciations, and so the burden of the
interdicts is relieved by various remissions. This may
even involve the temporary inversion of the hierarchy
as in the medieval feast of fools. (See *On the Psychology
of the Trickster*, CW9/1:458-65) When the remissions go
too far, as they did with the medieval saturnalia, the
balance between interdicts and remissions is disturbed,
and sacred order is undermined. Ibn 'Arabi lived in a
ritual culture that had a stable equilibrium of interdicts
and remissions. Like the Pueblo, he lived his life in
sacred order. So did Jung's father until he lost his faith.
When Carl Jung was with his father in the *divan-i- kass*,
he could not go back to a sacred order that no longer
existed. It would have been an empty gesture for him to
bring his head all the way down to the floor. Jung could

build a bridge between modern and traditional cultures, but he could not cross it.

Without the millimetre of space, Jung could not have confronted Yahweh in the way that he did in his *Answer to Job*:

> I shall not give a cool and carefully considered exegesis that tries to be fair to every detail, but a purely subjective reaction. In this way I hope to act as a voice for those who feel the same way as I do, and give expression to the shattering emotion that the unvarnished spectacle of divine savagery and ruthlessness produces in us. (CW11:561)

In a letter to Henry Corbin, warmly thanking him for his long review of *Answer to Job*, he wrote that "the book came to me during the fever of an illness. It was as if accompanied by the great music of Bach or Handel." (L2:116) Clearly, this book is not a biblical commentary; but what exactly is it? I am indebted to the late Leon Schlamm who explained to me that *Answer to Job* is a particularly intense, even visceral, work of active imagination. Jung was engaged in a dialogue with God in the depths of the unconscious. He was relating to his subjective reaction in a very objective way:

> This meditative practice initiates a dynamic, confrontational exchange between consciousness and the unconscious, in which each is totally engaged with the other, which, in turn, activates a stream of powerful, unconscious emotions and impulses. For Jung the function of this meditative practice is to access numinous unconscious images concealed by these emotions and impulses. (Schlamm in Huskinson 2008:109)

This practice requires at least a millimetre of space between ego consciousness and the unconscious psyche.

So what effect did this confrontation with Yahweh through active imagination have on Jung? According to Schlamm, "It triggered his perception of the immensity of God" (Schlamm/Huskinson 2008:109):

> That is to say, even the enlightened person remains what he is, and is no more than his limited ego before the One who dwells within him, whose form has no knowable boundaries, who encompasses him on all sides, fathomless as the abysms of the ocean and vast as the sky. (CW11:758)

The Shaykh would have wholeheartedly approved of Jung's evocation of the divine immensity, but there the endorsement ends. In what follows I will go in quest of the middle ground between the two.

A Reciprocal and Essential Relationship between Man and God

After a very brief summary of Ibn 'Arabi's central doctrine of the Divine Names, I will read Jung's *Answer to Job* from this metaphysical perspective[12].

The doctrine of the Divine Names is the corner stone of Ibn 'Arabi's vast theoria. Each Name denotes an attribute of God. According to Ibn 'Arabi, God exists in and for himself as the Divine Essence

---

[12]   I have provided a summary of Answer to Job in Appendix 2.

(*Dhat*) and he exists for us as the Divinity (*al Uluha*). The Divine Essence is "the most indeterminate of indeterminates," and the Divine Names subsist in it as pure potentiality. The Names are differentiated in the Divinity and brought to the threshold of manifestation. There are an infinite multiplicity of Divine Names or attributes. God is the hidden treasure yearning to be known, and He is actualizing His attributes in every moment of creation.

There are ninety-nine Names of God in the Quran, and seven of these are most frequently invoked: Alive, Knowing, Desiring, Powerful, Speaking, Generous, and Just. Muslim theologians classify the Names in terms of incomparability (*tanzih*) and of similarity (*tashbih*). Names such as Majestic, Inaccessible, and Vengeful belong to the first category; and Beautiful, Near, and Merciful to the second. Some pairs of names are complimentary, like Majestic and Beautiful, while others are contradictory, like Merciful and Vengeful or Life Giver and Slayer. Whether they are complimentary or contradictory, all the Names are one and the same, insofar as they all refer back to the Divine Essence. Every Name denotes the Divine Essence and each Name denotes a specific object or attribute that exists separately from the name assigned to it. Izutsu formulates this paradox very clearly in his study of Ibn 'Arabi in *Sufism and Taoism*:

> Thus the most conspicuous feature of the Divine Names is their double structure, that is their having two designations. Each name designates, and points to, the unique Essence, while pointing to a meaning or reality not shared by any other Name. (Izutsu 1983:100)

After this metaphysical excursion let's turn to the story of Job. In the Quran Job appears three times. In surah 4:163 he is only mentioned in passing. In 21:83 his afflictions are mentioned but nothing is said about who is responsible for them. In 38:41 Job cries to God that Satan has afflicted him. God then shows mercy and restores his family to him. Ibn' Arabi has a short chapter on Job in the Fusus. The emphasis in this chapter is on the patience of Job and his refusal to seek relief for his suffering from any other source than God.

For Ibn 'Arabi, any interpretation of the Quran or of any revealed scripture that does not do violence to the language was valid. But by answering Yahweh blow for blow, Jung unavoidably does violence to the text. Ibn 'Arabi would have regarded Jung's visceral anger and his confrontational stance towards God as extremely bad *adab* (spiritual propriety). For his part Jung maintained that he had a prima facie case. Yahweh had entered into a wager with Satan. He had allowed his adversary to do his worst with Job, providing his life is spared. If the pious Job laments the day on which he was born and curses his Creator, then Yahweh has lost the bet. Who, Jung would ask, could consent to anything so monstrously gratuitous? Only someone who was blind to his own contradictions and oblivious to the terrible destructivity of his shadow. From a modern psychological point of view, this seems to be self-evident. But how does the situation look from the perspective of the Divine Names? If the Names are, to all intents and purposes, infinite, some of them will inevitably be contradictory, for example, the Vengeful and the Merciful. In the tragedies of Job, Oedipus, and Lear, the conflict between the Divine Names is played out on a human level.

Jung argued that Yahweh is unconscious of his own internal contradictions. Where, he asked, was his divine mercy when he subjected Job to a display of his overwhelming might? Yahweh's theophany from out of the whirlwind (Job 38-42) was, in Jung's opinion, stage managed, and he described it as "an impressive performance given by the prehistoric menagerie." (CW11:595) But Yahweh has already revealed himself for what he is in the cynical wager he struck with Satan and through the afflictions he visits on Job, his loyal servant. Naturally, Yahweh does not want to look at what he has disclosed of himself, and the conflict has become acute. According to Jung, a new factor emerges out of this situation:

> This new factor is something that has never occurred before in the history of the world, the unheard of fact that, without knowing it or wanting it, a mortal man is raised by his moral behaviour above the stars in heaven, from which position of advantage he can behold the back of Yahweh, the abysmal world of the shards. (CW11:595)

When Jung's Job confronts the unconsciousness of Yahweh, he gains a crucial margin of reflective consciousness. The creature has surpassed his Creator. For Jung, the relationship between God and man is not reciprocal, and the onus falls entirely on Job.

But the relationship works both ways in an earlier essay Jung wrote on Meister Eckhart, included in *Psychological Types:*

> The "relativity of God," as I understand it, denotes a point of view that does not conceive of God as "absolute," i.e., cut off from man and existing beyond all human conditions, but as in

a certain sense dependent on him; it also implies
a reciprocal and essential relationship between
man and God, whereby man can be understood
as a function of God, and God as a psychological
function of man. (CW6:412)

In this earlier work, Jung is not so far from Ibn 'Arabi
who saw the relationship between God and man in
terms of mirror symmetry. Such reciprocity would be
impossible if both partners were not fully conscious.
Jung's recognition of a fully reciprocal relationship
between man and God in the Eckhart essay is a step
towards Ibn 'Arabi. But the absence of any reciprocal
relationship between man and God in the *Answer* looks
like a step back. In the next section, we will consider
Erich Neumann's challenge to Jung's notion of an
unconscious God.

Is the Creator Conscious?

After his encounter with the Pueblo, Jung realized how
indigent he was without a myth of his own. His quest,
for one, came to fruition in the same year on the Athai
Plains in Kenya. As he surveyed the vast savannah,
he realized that human consciousness alone confers
objective meaning on the world. In his cosmogonic
myth, man is a co-creator with God. (MDR:284-5) He
returned to this revelatory insight in "Late Thoughts":

By virtue of his reflective faculties, man is raised
out of the animal world, and by his mind he
demonstrates that nature has put a high premium
on the development of consciousness. Through
consciousness he takes possession of nature by
recognizing the existence of the world and thus, as
it were confirming the Creator. The world becomes

the phenomenal world, for without conscious
reflection it would not be. (MDR:371)

In his pre-reflective state, God is pure elemental
dynamism, and the world he creates is gratuitous:

> If the Creator were conscious of Himself, He would
> not need conscious creatures; nor is it probable that
> the extremely indirect methods of creation, which
> squander millions of years upon the development
> of countless species and creatures, are the outcome
> of purposeful intention. Natural history tells us of
> a haphazard and casual transformation of species
> over hundreds and millions of years of devouring
> and being devoured. The biological and political
> history of man is an elaborate repetition of the
> same thing. (MDR: 371)

The idea that God had to wait out the aeons in
primordial darkness until a warm-blooded creature
with a sufficiently differentiated brain emerged out of
the process of evolution to act as his mirror would
have been unacceptable to Ibn 'Arabi. How, he might
ask, could the limited ego consciousness of man be
a mirror for the Divine Names in their vast totality?
Only a universal being like Adam could bring God to
consciousness of himself. The transpersonal self can
serve as God's mirror; the ego could never assume
this role.

In February 1959, Erich Neumann wrote a long letter
to Jung in response to the draft he received of the last
two chapters of *Memories, Dreams, Reflections: On Life
after Death and Late Thoughts.* He expressed his doubts
about the evolutionary basis of Jung's argument and
also challenged the basic premise of *Answer to Job*;
namely that the Creator is unconscious. With regard

to evolution, Neumann argued that the notion of the "haphazard and casual transformation of species" was a Darwinist remnant and that it "will perhaps be superseded by a completely different theory in which your conception of the archetype as well as absolute knowledge will play a crucial role." (Leibscher 2015:345) His objections to Jung's Darwinism in the1959 letter are somewhat elusive. What he has in mind comes across more clearly in his 1952 Eranos lecture on *The Psyche and the Reality Planes.* Here, he argued that the modern theory of evolution, based on a combination of chance and natural selection, is "almost entirely mechanistic." Consequently, it eliminates the creative element "that is one of the fundamental phenomena of life." He went on to suggest three factors of natural evolution:

· In the ascending series of organisms, an increasingly large expanse of the world becomes open to experience.
· The anonymous field knowledge of a group evolves into centred ego knowledge of an individual consciousness.
· This evolution leads from a state of being rigidly bound to the essential expandability of human knowledge.

The development of a centred ego complex is a two-edged sword. Consciousness is more focused but also more restricted. Only when the ego is relativized in individuation does it get a taste of freedom. The attainment of individual creative freedom "indicates an evolutionary direction, which becomes increasingly obvious in the ascending series of world domains, for the inorganic to the organic." (Neumann 1989:50 -1)

Jung was not persuaded by Neumann's argument. In his reply, he insisted that "we cannot claim to know of what the constituent factors of biological development consist. But we know well that warm-bloodedness and brain differentiation were necessary for the emergence of consciousness." (Neumann 1989:349) This assertion puts Jung at odds with the alchemists. In the Hermetic world picture, consciousness is not the exclusive property of warm-blooded species and is already present in the lower levels of the chain of being. Alchemists recognized this phenomenon and designated it as the light of nature. Jung traced this idea back to Agrippa von Nettesheim, who supposed a "luminositas sensus naturae" and declared that from this source "gleams of prophecy came down to the four-footed beasts, the birds and other living creatures." (cited in CW8:393) In his famous essay *Synchronicity: An Acausal Connecting Principle* Jung presented the light of nature in modern dress as the absolute knowledge of the unconscious:

> Agrippa is thus suggesting that there is an inborn "knowledge" or "perception" in living organisms . . . Whether we like it or not, we find ourselves in this embarrassing position as soon as we begin seriously to reflect on the teleological processes in biology or to investigate the compensatory function of the unconscious, not to speak of trying to explain the phenomena of synchronicity. Final causes, twist them how we will, postulate a foreknowledge of some kind. It is certainly not a knowledge that could be connected to the ego, and hence not a conscious knowledge as we know it, but rather a self-subsistent "unconscious knowledge" which I would prefer to call "absolute knowledge." (CW8:931)

But Jung had conflicting narratives, and in "Late Thoughts," Jung seems to have reverted to the standard mechanistic model of evolution. In his correspondence, Neumann was trying to put Jung back on track. His strategy is easier to follow in the 1952 Eranos lecture. For example, in this passage, he is amplifying Jung's thoughts on the luminosity of life or the light of nature:

> This luminosity, which we have also characterized as the "vector towards consciousness," is the unitary reality's immanent tendency to make itself known. This is to say, that content, meaning, luminosity, and "form" . . . are objective characteristics of reality and not a product of the psyche in the sense of interpretation. Like numinosity, luminosity is not a quality of the psyche which is projected on to the world, but rather it is one of the realities to which the psyche is related. This already arises from the fact that luminosity as an anonymous field of knowledge, pertaining for instance to the instincts, antedates by far the evolution of consciousness as well. (Neumann 1989:36)

Neumann may well have been inspired by the following in the *Philosophia Sagax* of Paracelsus: "And as little as aught can exist in man without the divine numen, so little can aught exist in man without the natural lumen. A man is made perfect by numen and lumen and by these alone." (cited in CW8:388) According to Jung, these alchemical visions suggest "that the archetypes have about them a certain effulgence or quasi-consciousness, and that numinosity entails luminosity." The luminosity of life "is the unitary reality's immanent tendency to make itself known." This idea is more poetically expressed in the hadith of the treasure that was often quoted by Ibn 'Arabi: "I was hidden treasure, I longed to be known and so I created the world."

Neumann's argument contra the unconsciousness of God brings Jung's psychology closer to Ibn 'Arabi. In his letter to Jung, he writes,

> I would like to raise some issues with the thesis so beloved of you of "the becoming conscious of God," and moreover some issues that arise out of your own material. Could it not be the case that precisely the thesis of your consciousness should be compensated for? A thesis whose aspect of development is still perhaps tied to a particular time? If the Self contemplates you as the ego, then the Self is not unconscious. (Leibscher 2015:344)

A conscious God would not be cut off from all human conditions. He would instead be constituted in a truly reciprocal and essential relationship with man:

> If we humans are complexes of the divine unconscious, which he or it becomes conscious of while we make conscious our individuality with our human consciousness, the accent on the individual would be still greater without our having to formulate the Self or God as unconscious. If we were unconscious complexes of God that are endowed with consciousness and the possibility of consciousness, our task of consciousness and integration would also be sacred. (Leibscher 2015:344)

The God image is constituted in the soul through the sacred task of individuation. As Ibn 'Arabi puts it in one of his poems, "In knowing Him I give Him being." This, Corbin explains, does not mean that the human existentiates the divine essence. He or she gives being only to "the God created in the faiths." (Corbin 1969: 124) From a psychological point of view, the God created in the faiths is symbol of the self. Or as Corbin puts it, "The image of God whom the faithful creates is the image of God whom his own being reveals." (Corbin 1969:266)

If you are the mirror in which God sees himself, the image that appears will be adapted to the size and reflective capacity of the mirror. According to Corbin, "the God created in the faiths" takes a form in every soul that is determined by the soul's belief, knowledge, and aptitude. A devout believer will see only one image in the mirror, the God that is created in his faith. But a Gnostic will be aware of the relativity of his God image. The God created in Job's faith was too conventional and had to be broken down to be reconstituted. The God created in Jung's childhood faith was overturned when he was twelve years old. He was standing outside Basel Cathedral on a summer's day. He thought of God sitting up above on a golden throne, but then another thought wanted to come through that would have been unspeakably blasphemous. Whatever it was, the thought would have been a sin against the Holy Spirit, which cannot be forgiven. So he suppressed it. The next few days were sheer torment. Then Carl came to the conclusion that God was testing him. He allowed the thought to come out regardless of his fear of hell fire. God was still sitting on his golden throne, and then an enormous turd fell crashing down onto the cathedral roof and shattered the entire building. He felt an enormous sense of relief and the unutterable bliss of divine grace. But he also had experienced a dark and terrible secret. God's grace was incomprehensible. (MDR: 52-8) Did God redeem Carl, or did Carl redeem God?

In *The Ringstones of Wisdom*, the Shaykh famously said, "He is your vision of yourself, and you are the mirror for His vision of His Names—which are none other than himself." (Dagli 2004:26) Jung's Job acted as the mirror in which Yahweh saw himself. And when God saw his image, the imago Dei underwent an evolutionary transformation. In the next section, we will see what form this metamorphosis took.

One Can Love God but One Must Fear Him

The antecedents of *Answer to Job*, go back to Jung's heated discussions with his clergyman father. When he asked why God Almighty did nothing to stop the evildoing of the devil, his father told him that God was allowing Satan to have his time. This did not satisfy the young Carl who pointed out that a man who let a vicious dog loose on the neighbourhood would be put in jail. (D: 588) Jung's father was alluding to the book of Revelations, which is one of the key texts in *Answer to Job*. It is, Jung argues, impossible to square this apocalyptic text with the doctrine that God is light and that there is no darkness in him. (1 John 1:5) In the Revelations of John, the dogs are let off the leash and allowed to go on the rampage:

> Could anyone in his right mind deny that John correctly foresaw at least some of the possible dangers which threaten our world in the final phase of the Christian aeon? He knew, also, that the fire in which the devil is tormented burns in the divine pleroma for ever. God has a terrible double aspect: a sea of grace is met by a seething lake of fire, and the light of love glows with the fierce dark heat of which it is said "ardet non lucet"—it burns but gives no light. That is the eternal, as distinct from the temporal, gospel: one *can love God one but must fear him*. (CW11:733)

The God who can be loved is the *Deus Manifestus*, and the God who must be feared is the *Deus Absconditus*. In the *Visions* seminars, Jung explains these terms very clearly:

> That is the term used by Luther. Absconditus means concealed, it is the hidden or concealed god, and he meant by that the god that was the opposite of the Deus Manifestus, of whom the Bible speaks and about whom we have certain views or convictions. We believe that God is spirit and good, and that Christ is love, and all that is the Deus Manifestus, the god that has revealed himself to us. But Luther said that opposite this god there must be another, the same god but the hidden side, the shadow of god, as it were, who does not reveal himself. (V:845)

The *Deus Absconditus* reveals himself out of the whirlwind to Job. And he also revealed himself to Luther:

> Then shall we learn that God is a consuming fire . . . That is the consuming, devouring fire . . . Wilt thou sin? Then He will devour thee up . . . For God is fire, that consumeth, devoureth, rageth; verily He is your undoing, as fire consumeth the house and maketh it dust and ashes. (De Servo Arbitrio, (Cited in Otto 1950:99)

Jung had a traumatic experience of the *Deus Absconditus* in the earliest dream he could recall. He saw a stone-lined hole in a field near the vicarage where the family lived. He descended and found a doorway closed off by a green curtain. When he pushed it aside, he saw a red carpet on the flagstone floor leading up to a golden throne. This was the seat of a subterranean phallic god twelve to fifteen feet high and about two feet thick. On the top of the rounded head was a single eye gazing motionlessly upward. Above the head, there was an aura of brightness. He was paralyzed with terror and feared that it would crawl off the throne and creep towards him like a worm. This dream was "a frightful revelation which had been accorded me without my seeking it." (MDR:26–28)

The whole of *Answer to Job* is encapsulated in a single proposition: *"Whoever knows God has an effect on him."* (CW11: 617) Jung discerned that neither Job nor Yahweh can be the same after their encounter. Job has seen the shadow of God, and his superior knowledge has the effect of polarizing the *Deus Absconditus* and the *Deus Manifestus*. The split between the kingdom of heaven above and the fiery world of the damned below is healed by Sophia, the *Sapientia Dei*, who is coeternal with God and who existed before the Creation. This divine feminine principle appears in the wisdom literature, which is roughly contemporary with the Book of Job:

> The Lord possessed me in the beginning of his way, before his works of old.
> I was set up from everlasting, from the beginning, or ever the world was.
> When there were no depths, I was brought forth; when there were no fountains abounding with water. (Proverbs 8: 22-4, CW11:609)

Jung conjectured that, in his arbitrary treatment of Job, Yahweh had forgotten his wisdom. But when the confrontation with Job brings the unconscious split in his nature to consciousness, Yahweh is compelled to recall her. Edinger explains this development as the discovery of his missing Eros. Up to now, Yahweh has been an utterly impersonal elemental dynamism, but everything changes when he reveals his true nature to Job:

> Job's knowledge of God has the effect of making God conscious of the relatedness principle because someone found him in a state of unrelatedness and perceived that condition. The perception itself had the effect of correcting the situation. (Edinger 1992 63)

When God reveals himself to Job out of the whirlwind, he asks him, "Will the unicorn be willing to serve thee, or abide by thy crib? Canst thou bind the unicorn with his band in the furrow? Or will he harrow the valleys after thee?" (Job 39:9–10) In ecclesiastical allegory and later in alchemy, the unicorn is a symbol of the *Deus Absconditus*. Its wrath must be tamed so that it can be led to the lap of a virgin. (CW12: 6: II, b)

Rudolf Otto on the Book of Job

I have my own millimetre of space with regard to Jung's *Answer to Job*. Neither Leon Schlamm's persuasive argument that the *Answer* is an active imagination (Schlamm/Huskinson 2008) nor Henry Corbin's revelatory review of Jung's book *Eternal Sophia* (Corbin 2019) have closed the gap. I could not account for this until I recalled a seemingly unrelated encounter that Jung had in Africa. He met an old white settler in Uganda who had been there for forty years. He gave Jung this piece of advice: "You know, mister, this here country is not man's country, it's God's country. So, if anything should happen, just sit down and don't worry." (MDR:285-6). Like the people of the Old Testament and like Muslims in the time of Ibn 'Arabi, the old settler accepted God on his own terms. Jung's righteous anger prevented him from conducting his active imagination in God's country.

In Rudolf Otto's influential book, *The Idea of the Holy* there is commentary on Job:38-42. Otto interprets Yahweh's address to Job from the whirlwind as an event in God's country. Job's confrontation with God is an exemplary numinous experience. It is worth spending a little time to explicate this term. Otto's book is concerned with the experiential dimension of religion rather than the doctrinal dimension. Religious experience is sui generis. It can legitimately claim this privileged status because the object of religious experience is not of this world; it is *Wholly Other.* An experience of the Other is *numinous*, a term Otto derived from numen, a spirit that inhabits a sacred grove. Just as the noun 'omen' can be converted into the adjective 'ominous' so can 'numen' be converted to 'numinous'. There are two aspects to numinous experience: *mysterium tremendum et fascinans.* The *tremendum* is conveyed unforgettably in the visions of Ezekiel and also in the theophany in the book of Job. It corresponds to the Divine Name of Wrathful. The *fascinans* corresponds to the Name Merciful or Gracious. Whereas an experience of the *tremendum* induces awe, the *fascinans* gives rise to wonder and to rapture. Numinous experience, says Otto, is constituted by the coexistence of these aspects in "a strange harmony of contrasts." (Otto 1950:31)

In chapter 4, Otto says that the association of *mysterium tremendum* with the wrath of God has been problematic for both theologians and laypeople. Otto acknowledges that divine wrath is, indeed, without moral qualities, like a hidden force of nature or stored-up electricity suddenly discharging itself.

Yahweh is incalculable and arbitrary. Naturally, this is an offence to anyone who thinks of the deity only in rational terms. But the people of the old covenant did not think in this way: For them, the wrath of God, so far from being a diminution of his Godhead, appears as a natural expression of it, an element of "holiness" itself and quite an indispensable one. And in this, they are entirely right. The wrath is nothing but the *tremendum* itself, apprehended and expressed by the aid of a naïve analogy from the domain of natural experience, in this case from the ordinary passional life of man. This is, indeed, naïve, but says Otto, "The analogy is most disconcertingly apt and striking." And it retains its value even now because it is "an inevitable way of expressing one element in the religious emotion." (Otto 1950:18)

In Job 38-42, Yahweh reveals himself out of a whirlwind to Job. After such an overwhelming experience of the *mysterium tremendum*, Job declares that he has uttered words he did not understand and now "abhors himself and repents with dust and ashes." (Job 42:3-6) His words are an expression of "numinous unworth" or "creature feeling" and not gestures of self-abasement. According to Otto, this sense of unworthiness does not necessarily arise from the awareness of any moral transgression and may have no relation to the superego at all:

> It is not based on deliberation, nor does it follow any rule, but breaks, as it were, palpitant from the soul- like a direct reflex movement at the stimulation of the numinous. (Otto 1950:50)

Jung thought otherwise. He maintained that Job's response is not a reflex but a very astute move in the face of Yahweh's overwhelming might. Job's dream of a benevolent and just God had been shattered, and he has realized that Yahweh is a phenomenon and "not a man":

> Shrewdly, Job takes up Yahweh's aggressive words and prostrates himself at his feet as if he were indeed the defeated antagonist. Guileless though it sounds, it could just as well be equivocal. (CW11:599)

According to Otto Job's response to the theophany (Job: 38-42) involves no dissimulation on his part. Job is, indeed, overwhelmed by the *tremendum*, but he has not been merely silenced by superior strength. When he says that he abhors himself and repents in dust and ashes, this is "an admission of inward convincement and conviction, not of impotent collapse and submission." Nor, contrary to Jung, is God seeking a capitulation from Job. His theophany is also a theodicy, which is far superior to that of Job's friends: "For latent in the weird experience that Job underwent in the revelation of Elohim is at once an inward relaxing of the soul's anguish and an appeasement which would alone and in itself perfectly suffice as a solution of the problem of the Book of Job." (Otto 1950: 78) This appeasement does not derive from the notion that Yahweh's ways are higher than those of mere mortals and his actions are beyond human comprehension. That would be a teleological justification, and the theophany shatters all such rational constructs. The extraordinary descriptions in chapters 39-41 of the mysterious and inexplicable instincts of the eagle, the ostrich, who leaves her eggs exposed in the sand, the wild ass and the unicorn, not to mention Behemoth and Leviathan all suggest "the downright stupendousness, the well-nigh daemonic and wholly incomprehensible character of the eternal creative power." Yahweh does not answer

Job's prima facie case. His reply "is incommensurable with thoughts of rational human teleology and is not assimilated with them; it remains in all its mystery." But as the *mysterium* becomes felt in consciousness, "Elohim is justified and at the same time Job's soul brought to peace." He kneels before "the wholly uncomprehended Mystery, revealed yet unrevealed, and his soul is stilled by feeling the way of its working, and therein its justification." (Otto 1950:80-1) God has revealed the totality of His Names to his servant Job.

In 1961 a young Jewish medical student had volunteered to deliver a sermon on Answer to Job at his synagogue. He wrote to Jung to seek his advice. This is what wrote in reply:

> I would suggest a reduction of your program, namely that you deal with the most important aspect. It would be a fundamental fact of the pair of opposites united in the image of God, i.e., Yahweh. The two are Love and Fear, which presuppose an apparently irreconcilable contradiction. Yet such an opposition must be expected whenever we are confronted with an immense energy. There is no dynamic manifestation without a corresponding initial tension which provided the necessary energy. If we suppose the deity to be a dynamic phenomenon in our experience, its origin must be an opposition or paradox. (L2:623)

For Ibn 'Arabi the contradictions between the Divine Names were annulled in the Divine Essence. But for Jung they were resolved in and through the reflective consciousness of creaturely man. Herein lies the milllimetre of space between them.

14

RESPECTING CONFUSING TREADS

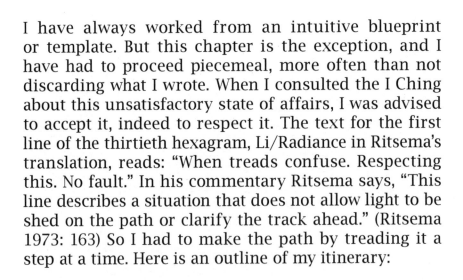

I have always worked from an intuitive blueprint or template. But this chapter is the exception, and I have had to proceed piecemeal, more often than not discarding what I wrote. When I consulted the I Ching about this unsatisfactory state of affairs, I was advised to accept it, indeed to respect it. The text for the first line of the thirtieth hexagram, Li/Radiance in Ritsema's translation, reads: "When treads confuse. Respecting this. No fault." In his commentary Ritsema says, "This line describes a situation that does not allow light to be shed on the path or clarify the track ahead." (Ritsema 1973: 163) So I had to make the path by treading it a step at a time. Here is an outline of my itinerary:

1. A letter from Gilles Quispel in reply to my enquiry about Jung's place in Tradition/A reply to the Traditionalist accusation that Jung reduced transcendent spirit to immanent psyche.

2. Modern interpretations of Ibn 'Arabi are often anachronistic/Titus Burckhardt on Ibn 'Arabi's sacred astrology/Universal Man in Sufism and in Jung's psychology.
3. Izutsu's philosophy of Existence/Unity of Being in Sufism and Vedanta.
4. The Breath of the Merciful—a dialogue between the author and Ibn 'Arabi scholar Samir Mahmoud.

1.The alchemical theoria is, according to Jung, "obviously something a master can teach his pupil; it is the one solid possession from which the adept can proceed. For the prima materia always remains to be found, and the only thing that helps him is the 'cunning secret of the wise,' a theory that can be communicated." (CW9/2:219). But from where did Jung derive his theoria? Surely, he did not draw it out of himself. It was 1986, and I needed an answer to this question as a matter of urgency. Throughout that year, I was in correspondence with Martin Lings, a leading Traditionalist scholar.[13] He maintained that Jung had no basis in Tradition to speak of, that his psychology was just another variety of twentieth-century syncretism. I knew this was wrong, but how was I to convince him that Jung's theoria was not a New Age invention?

In April, I wrote to Gilles Quispel, the great scholar of ancient Gnosticism, for assistance. Professor Quispel was a participant in the Eranos conferences and had a particularly deep affinity with Jung. If anyone had the answer, it would be him. I did not have to wait long for a reply:

---

[13]   See chapter 5:III for an account of my meeting with Martin Lings and our subsequent correspondence.

The question you ask has vexed me all my life, but I am in a better position to answer it than most Anglo-Saxons, because European humanism is so different from its Anglo-Saxon counterpart.

Ever since Pico della Mirandola discovered Jewish Gnosis of the Kabbalah and Reuchlin introduced it to Germany, there has been a Gnostic tradition on the Continent: Jacob Boehme, Gottfried Arnold, Goethe, Steiner, Jung. These thinkers felt a natural affinity with ancient Gnosticism and medieval Catharism which they studied intensely. Gnosis is, beside reason and faith, the third component of our cultural pattern. You have only Blake and Blavatsky.

Tradition of symbols is powerful. Unless no connection can be proved, for instance between Asiatic and Indian American symbols, I opt for tradition. On the other hand this tradition would not be so powerful if it did not appeal to archetypes. And there is such a thing as spontaneous generation.

Gnostic symbols (the Son of Man as the Self, Sophia as the Goddess) do appeal more to modern man than the dogmas of the Churches. Mainstream Christianity would be wise to admit a Gnostic interpretation of its symbols.

But should Gnostics nowadays bother about the Churches? I read in the paper that 97% of the English are unchurched. Was not Jung wiser when he tried to help those who did not believe any more, the erring flock without a pastor? And is it not better to uncover the alternative tradition of the West (no Gnostic persuaded anybody)? Let the dead bury their dead, let us follow the wanderer from Galilee, even if this may lead nowadays perhaps outside the Church.

Professor Quispel had rightly placed Jacob Boehme at the head of his Pansophic or Theosophical genealogy. Arthur Versluis's pioneer work on this tradition of Christian esotericism, *Wisdom's Children*, traces Boehme back through Paracelsus, Eckhart, Tauler, and Dionysus the Areopagite to early Christian Gnosticism. But Boehme is not just a link in the chain; his life and works, says Versluis, "represent a decisive moment in Christian history. For Boehme's works are nothing less than a masterful reconstitution of Christian gnosis at the beginning of the modern era." (Versluis 2004:3) If Quispel had got it right, Jung has a venerable spiritual ancestry.

I received a short letter from Professor Quispel three years later. He was forthright in his views about the Traditionalists: they were "neither Gnostic nor serious." This dismissive remark is symptomatic of the rivalry between two schools of modern esotericism, Eranos and Traditionalist. I have examined the roots of the conflict elsewhere in this book. But what is it about Jung that the Traditionalists find so abhorrent?

The Traditionalist critique goes something like this: Jung does not differentiate between spirit and soul. Consequently, he fails to situate the soul in its proper place in the hierarchy of being.[14] (Burckhardt 1974:156) Little if any evidence is offered in support of this argument. In fact, Jung answers the criticism in his essay on *The Phenomenology of the Spirit in Fairy Tales*:

> The hallmarks of the spirit are, firstly, the principle of spontaneous movement and activity; secondly, the spontaneous capacity to produce images

---

[14] I have addressed Burckhardt's anti Jung polemic in chapter 4.

> independently of sense perception; and thirdly, the autonomous and sovereign manipulation of these images. This spiritual entity approaches primitive man from outside, but this with increasing development it gets lodged in man's consciousness and becomes a subordinate function, thus apparently forfeiting its original character of autonomy. That character is now retained only in the most conservative views, namely the religions. (CW9/1:393)

Jung recognized that the descent of the spirit into the sphere of human consciousness was "probably an unavoidable necessity." That being so, the task of the religious traditions is not to block this development but to guide it "in such a way that it can proceed without fatal injury to the soul." And he went on to say that "the religions should therefore constantly recall to us the origin and original character of the spirit, lest man should forget what he is drawing into himself and with what he is filling his consciousness." (CW9/1:393) From a psychological point of view, it is a retrograde step to insist on an a priori distinction between soul and spirit.

Jungian and post-Jungian psychologists have addressed this problem of soul and spirit in their own terms. According to James Hillman, spirit and soul are "root metaphors." "These metaphors," says Hillman, "are not so much carefully worked out conscious philosophies as they are half conscious attitudes rooted in the structure of the psyche itself." We cannot pick up and cast off root metaphors at will because they are traditional. "Where the tradition is alive, the archetypal background of it carries those who are related to it." (Hillman 1964/76:24-5) In his magnum opus *Re-Visioning Psychology*, Hillman explicates the distinction between soul and spirit with some precision. But unlike the Traditionalists, he is aware of the fact that he is translating one set of metaphors into another. (See Hillman 1975:67-70)

2. The Traditionalists have played an indispensable role in bringing Ibn 'Arabi to the West. In *Rethinking Ibn 'Arabi*, Gregory Lipton gives credit to the Traditionalists where credit is due but questions their appropriation of the Shaykh. He argues that it is a category error to regard Ibn 'Arabi as an advocate of the esoteric ecumenism promoted by Schuon and his disciples. For example, in 1212, Ibn 'Arabi wrote to the Seljuk, sultan of Anatolia, in which he berated the sultan for being too liberal towards the "Protected People," i.e., Jews and Christians:

> The calamity that Islam and Muslims are undergoing in your realm—and few address it—is the raising of Church bells, the display of disbelief, the proclamation of associationism and the elimination of stipulations imposed by the Prince of Believers on the Protected People. (Cited in Lipton 2018:55)

He went on to insist that the Protected People pay in full for their protection through the indemnity tax and that they be made to feel the humiliation of it. This was not an isolated outburst, and "there are multiple places where Ibn 'Arabi castigates the Jews and Christians for their supposed blasphemy and unbelief." (Lipton 2018:8)

Evidently, the Ibn 'Arabi of the letter to the sultan coexisted with the Ibn 'Arabi of "The Interpreter of Divine Desires." Here are the verses that are frequently cited by the Traditionalists as irrefutable evidence of the Shaykh's universal ecumenicism:

Wonder,
a garden among the flames!

My heart can take on
any form:
a meadow for gazelles, a cloister for monks,

For the idols, sacred ground,
Ka'ba for the circling pilgrim,
the tables of the Torah,
the scrolls of the Quran.

My creed is love;
wherever its caravan turns along its way,
that is my belief,
my faith. (Sells 1994:90)

Professor Lipton's close reading of the poem reveals that
it is not endorsing the claim that all religions are so
many forms of a unanimous perennial wisdom. There is
only one religion that encompasses and also supersedes
the vast diversity of beliefs, and that is Islam. To read
the poem as declaration of "the Transcendent Unity
of Religions" is anachronistic. The Traditionalists
have projected a very modern notion of religion onto
a medieval Islamic saint. However, Ibn 'Arabi was
ecumenical in his own terms. He famously declared
that *there are only beliefs and all are correct*. Beliefs are
an expression of how human beings conceive of God
or rather of "the God created in the faiths." All such
images of God reflect an aspect of the Divinity, and all
are "true" to a greater or lesser extent. In this sense, the
Shaykh's heart was, indeed, receptive to every form.

In *Rethinking Ibn 'Arabi*, Titus Burckhardt is depicted
as playing second fiddle to Schuon. This is less than

fair. Burckhardt was a major Islamic scholar in his own right, and his insights into Ibn 'Arabi were profound. He wrote two pioneering works on the Shaykh, *Mystical Astrology According to Ibn 'Arabi* (Burckhardt 1977) and *An Introduction to Sufi Doctrine* (Burckhardt 1976), and translated the *Fusus al Hikam* under the title of *The Wisdom of the Prophets*. (Burckhardt 1975) I will offer some reflections on the first two texts.

Burckhardt's assertion that Jung "carefully avoided all contact with representatives of living tradition" is not true (Burckhardt 1986:177). Had he taken the trouble to read Jung's *Memoirs* more carefully, he would have discovered that, in 1925, Jung had engaged in a deep dialogue with a Pueblo chief on a reservation in Taos, New Mexico. Far from avoiding contact with a representative of living tradition, Jung was eager to find out all he could about the religion of the Pueblo. Here is a short extract from their conversation:

> As I sat with Ochwiay Biano on the roof, the blazing sun rising higher and higher, he said, pointing to the sun, "Is not he who moves there our father? How can anyone say differently? How can there be another god? Nothing can be without the sun." His excitement, which was already perceptible, mounted still higher; he struggled for words and exclaimed at last, "What would a man do alone in the mountains? He cannot even build a fire without him."

When Jung suggested that the sun might be a ball of fiery gas shaped by an invisible god, the proposition made no sense at all to Ochwiay. He simply replied that, "The sun is God. Everyone can see that." (MDR:279) Maybe Ochwiay had been told that his geocentric model has been superseded by the findings of modern astronomy. If so, was he clinging tenaciously to a pre-scientific world picture? Not necessarily. His assertion that the sun is God makes profound sense in symbolic terms, and the cosmology of the Pueblo is empirically true from the standpoint of immediate observation. As Titus Burckhardt puts it in the *Mystical Astrology*, "The geocentric system, being in conformity with the reality that presents itself immediately to the human eyes, contains in itself all the logical coherence requisite to a body of knowledge for constituting an exact science." (Burckhardt 1977:10) Ibn 'Arabi's cosmology is also such a science. It is based on the symbolism of appearances, not the empirical facts that only came to light four centuries later.

The term "symbolism of appearances," however, implies some kind of reality behind the appearances. But mythological thinking does not operate with this distinction. "The traditional cosmology," says Burckhardt, "does not make any explicit differentiation between the planetary skies in their corporeal and visible reality, and that which corresponds to them in the subtle order; because the symbol is essentially identified with the thing it symbolizes." (Burckhardt 1977: 15) Such symbols are not allegorical but tautegorical. They do not refer to anything outside themselves but carry their own meaning within themselves. The term "tautegorical" was originally coined by Coleridge and adopted by Schelling in his *Philosophy of Mythology*. It was further developed by Ernst Cassirer who, in turn, passed it onto Henry Corbin. Corbin saw a direct parallel with the Shi'ite method of t'awil, which aims to uncover the hidden meaning (*batin*) in sacred symbols:

> And since the hidden meaning is nothing other than the letter raised or transmuted into symbol, and perceived henceforth on the level of the

> imaginal world, the symbol is no longer something
> behind which hides the thing symbolized. It is
> quite simply, the form assumed on this level by the
> transcendent reality, and this form is the reality.
> Thus, instead of allegory, one could perhaps speak
> of *tautegory*. (Corbin 1986:304-5)

Schelling put the matter more trenchantly: "To
mythology the gods are actually existing essences, gods
are not something else, nor do they mean something
else, rather they mean only what they are." (Schelling
2007:136)[15] When Ochwiay Biano declared that the
sun was God, he was speaking tautegorically. "This
conception," says Burckhardt, "is essentially true in
the sense that all sensible light has its source in the
intelligible light of which the sun is the most evident
symbol." (Burckhardt 1977:27) The sun is the heart
of the world, and it "communicates its light to all
the other stars, including the fixed stars and is itself
illuminated by the direct and incessant irradiation of
Divine Revelation." We now know that the fixed stars
are sources of light independent of the sun, but this
does not invalidate the Shaykh's perspective because
"the sun represents the centre of radiation of the
Divine Light for a determined world, whereas the fixed
stars symbolize interferences of the light of a superior
world." (Burckhardt 1977:28)

Beyond the sky of the fixed stars is the sky without
stars. This sky is "void" and marks the boundary
between formal and informal manifestation. It is the
primum mobile and constitutes the fundamental
measure of time. In itself, it is independent of

---

[15]   For Schelling's influence on Corbin and his fellow Eranos
        scholars see Wasserstrom (1999):56-7, The Tautegorical
        Sublime.

all temporal measure, and it "corresponds to the indifferentiation of pure duration." (Burckhardt1977:16) Beyond the sky without stars is the Divine Pedestal, which contains the skies of the earth, and finally the divine throne, which encompasses the whole of creation. Their spherical form, says Burckhardt, "is purely symbolic, and they mark the passage from astronomy to metaphysical and integral cosmology." (Burckhardt 1977:12-16)

An Introduction to Sufi Doctrines is distillation of the quintessence of Ibn 'Arabi's theoria. Each short chapter is theme for meditation, and the work as a whole is an ideal preparation for the study of the Shaykh. Let's begin with chapter 12 on the Universal Man or Anthropos. This figure is a root metaphor of the human psychospiritual totality. For the Sufis, the Universal Man is the Perfect Man. According to Burckhardt the term "Universal Man" has two overlapping meanings. It can refer to "the permanent and actual synthesis of all states of Being, a synthesis which is at the same time both an immediate aspect of the Principle and the totality of all relative and particular states of existence." On the other hand, "this name applies to all men who have realized the Union or 'the Supreme Identity,' to men such as the great spiritual mediators and especially the prophets and . . . the saints." (Burckhardt 1976:77)

The Universal Man is a symbol for the first Prophet, Adam, and the last, Muhammed. In *Understanding Islam*, Frithjof Schuon described the theophanic aspect of the Prophet like this:

> As a spiritual principle, the Prophet is not only
> the Totality of which we are separate parts or

fragments, he is also the Origin of which we are
so many deviations; in other words, the Prophet
as Norm is not only the "Whole Man" but also
the "Ancient Man" . . . to realize the Whole or
Universal Man means to come out from oneself
to project one's will into the absolutely "Other,"
to extend oneself into the universal life which
is that of all beings; while to realize the Ancient
or Primordial Man means to return to the Origin
which we bear within us; it means to return to our
eternal childhood, to repose in our archetype, our
primordial ad normative form, in our theomorphic
substance. (Schuon 2005:122)

This is, as Titus Burckhardt points out, a paradoxical
mode of being. The individual who has realized the
Universal Man and has become one with the divine
spirit really feels that he is himself. But in what sense
can he be said to subsist? But "if the individual subject
does not subsist in any sense whatsoever, there would
be no continuity linking his human experience."
(Burckhardt 1976:79-80) In his introduction to his
translation of Al Jili's *Universal Man*, Burckhardt
returns to this conundrum:

Universal Man is not really distinct from God; he is
like the face of God in his creatures. By union with
him, the spirit unites with God. Now, God is all and
at the same time above all. He is at once immanent
and transcendent; equally the spirit, in this state
of Union, is united to creatures in their essences,
by a direct intuition; at the same time it is like a
diamond that mixes with nothing and is penetrated
by nothing, because it participates in Divine Reality
which is sufficient unto itself. (Burckhardt 1983:ii)

Burckhardt has merely side stepped the question
with a little help from the coincidentia oppositorum.
It remains difficult to see how a being that is

extinguished in the Divine Essence can "really feel he is himself." Jung was doubtful about non-dualist doctrines for this reason. In his model of psychospiritual development (the individuation process) the Universal man or Anthropos is transposed into different key. At first sight, Jung's treatment of the Anthropos looks like Schuon's Primordial Man from a psychological perspective:

> The dream is little hidden door in the innermost and most secret recesses of the soul, opening into that cosmic night which was psyche long before there was any ego consciousness, and which will remain psyche no matter how far ego consciousness extends. For all ego consciousness is isolated; because it separates and discriminates, it knows only particulars, and it sees only those that can be related to the ego. Its essence is limitation, even though it reaches to the furthest nebulae among all the stars. All consciousness separates; but in dreams we put on the likeness of that more universal, truer, more eternal man dwelling in the darkness of primordial night. There he is still the whole, and the whole is in him, indistinguishable from nature and bare of all egohood. (CW10:304)

This eternal man "bare of all egohood" is a symbol of the transpersonal self. The self says Jung is "the greater, more comprehensive Man, that indescribable whole consisting of conscious and unconscious processes". This objective whole which transcends and includes the ego "corresponds exactly to the Anthropos." (CW9/2:296) Jung's notion of a transpersonal self that is supraordinate to the conscious personality or ego and which surrounds it on all sides is extremely elusive if one tries to formulate it in concepts. In truth, the self is indefinable, a borderline concept at the limits of communicable language. But the self is not an inaccessible "thing in itself." We encounter it in our dreams as the Primordial Man and in the religious traditions as a charismatic figure: Christ, Divine Sophia, Prophet Muhammad, Confucius, Buddha, etc. Whereas the Traditionalists regard Universal Man as immutable Jung saw this figure as a dynamic totality overflowing with evolutionary potential. Which of the two, I wonder, is closer to Ibn 'Arabi?

Why can't Traditionalists agree to differ with Jung? He seems to be translating the insights of the religious traditions into psychological language, thereby making them accessible to a secular culture. And if that's the sole objective of Jung's psychology of religion, Traditionalists would need to do no more than express their understandable reservations. But Jung did not confine himself to this ecumenical objective. His writings on theological matters are a trenchant critique of the religious traditions and a direct challenge to their authority. No self-respecting Traditionalist can countenance such a thing. When Jung says that "light and shadow are so evenly distributed in man's nature that his psychic totality appears, to say the least of it, in a somewhat murky light," he is, in effect, saying that the Universal Man, who personifies this totality, is not the Perfect Man. Conversely, if Christ is the Perfect Man, he cannot be a complete symbol of the self[16]. The psychological concept of the self, says Jung, "cannot omit the shadow that belongs to the light figure, for without it this figure lacks body and humanity." Moreover, the one-sidedness of the canonical

---

[16] In Jung's Collected Works the transpersonal self is designated with a small "s". To prevent confusion some Jungian writers use upper case "S" to denote the transpersonal Self. I am designating the Jungian self in lower case and reserving the upper case for the metaphysical Self.

Christ figure has had the most disastrous cultural and psychological consequences. Jung goes on to say,

> In the empirical self, light and shadow form a paradoxical unity. In the Christian concept, on the other hand, the archetype is hopelessly split into two irreconcilable halves, leading ultimately to a metaphysical dualism—the final separation of the kingdom of heaven for the fiery world of the damned. (CW9/2: 76)

Christ is split off from his shadow Antichrist who embodies "the dark half of the human totality, which ought not to be judged too optimistically." But it would be very misleading to present Jung as an out and out iconoclast. His critique of the Christian tradition is intended to be a diagnosis of an ailing religion. The idea of Jung as the therapist for an ailing Christian tradition is advanced in Murray Stein's pathbreaking book *Jung's Treatment of Christianity.* (Stein 1985)

3. In *Revisioning Transpersonal Theory,* Jorge Ferrer enumerates five categories of Perennialism. (Ferrer 2002:87-95) Only two categories concern us here: esoteric and structural perennialism. The esotericists subscribe to the notion of a unanimous perennial philosophy underpinning all the religious traditions. The structuralists avoid this essentialising tendency and "understand the many mystical paths and goals as contextual manifestations (surface structures) of underlying universal patterns (deep structures) which ultimately constitute *one path and one goal* for all spiritual traditions." (Ferrer 2002:76-78) This perspective is "already implicit in Jung's distinction between noumenal and phenomenal archetypes, and in Eliade's studies on myth." The main forum for structuralist esotericism was provided by the

Eranos conferences that took place at Ascona from 1933 to 1987. Esoteric perennialism comes out of the Traditionalist movement, which I have covered in chapters 3 (Coomaraswamy), 4 (Burckhardt), 5 (Schuon), and 6 (Guenon). As for the structuralists, I have drawn extensively on Corbin and Izutsu in chapters 12 and 13, and of course, Jung has appeared in every chapter of this book. In what follows, I will focus on the philosophy of Toshihiko Izutsu. He was highly respected by both the Traditionalists and the community of Eranos scholars.

For Izutsu, the perennial philosophy did not exist in *illo tempore*; it is a possibility to be actualised in the future. His magnum opus, *Sufism and Taoism*, took its inspiration from Henry Corbin's idea of a metahistorical dialogue, which, says Izutsu, "is something urgently needed in the present world situation." Such a dialogue, he continues, "will, I believe eventually be crystallised into a philosophia perennis in the fullest sense of the term. For the philosophical drive of the human Mind is, regardless of ages, places and nations, ultimately fundamentally one." (Izutsu 1983:469) There is, he maintains, one fundamental category that is the lynchpin of this metahistorical dialogue on a philosophical level, and that is Existence, or better Unity of Existence, *wahdat al wujud*, for Ibn 'Arabi and *t'ien ni*, heavenly levelling, or *t'ien chun*, heavenly equalisation for Chuang tzu. In his essay titled *An Analysis of Wahdat al Wujud*, he considers Existence as the key term for a metaphilosophy of Oriental philosophies. As Izutsu explains at the outset, he does not consider *wahdat al wujud* (Unity of Being) as an exclusively Islamic idea:

> Rather, I am interested here in this concept and the philosophical possibilities it contains, as something representative of the basic structure

which is commonly shared by many of the Oriental philosophies going back to divergent historical origins, like Vedanta, Buddhism, Taoism, and Confucianism. The structure of the philosophy of *wahdat al wujud* would in this perspective be seen to represent one typical pattern—an archetypal form, we might say—of philosophical thinking which one finds developed variously in more or less different forms by outstanding thinkers belonging to different cultural traditions in the East. (Izutsu 2007:59-60)

Sri Ramana Maharshi encapsulated the essence of the Unity of Being in his answer to a question about Shankara's idea of the world as *Maya* (illusion):

Shankara has been criticized for his philosophy of Maya without understanding his meaning. He made three statements: that Brahman is real, that the universe is unreal and that Brahman is the Universe. He did not stop with the second. The third statement explains the first two; it signifies that when the Universe is perceived apart from Brahman, that perception is false and illusory. What it amounts to is that phenomena are real when experienced as the Self and illusory when seen apart from the Self. (cited in Osborne 1971:16)

On the level of common sense, things are seen as separate from the Self or the Absolute. Izutsu designates this way of seeing the world as *essentialist*. The perspective expounded by Sri Ramana Maharshi is *existentialist*. Whereas *essentialism* refers to the world as seen from the standpoint of ordinary ego consciousness, *existentialism* "is a metaphysical system based upon, and born out of an ecstatic, mystical intuition of Reality as it discloses itself to a transcendental consciousness in the depths of concentrated meditation." (Izutsu 2007: 66) Izutsu quotes Ibn Arabi in this context:

> It is the empirical world that is a mystery,
> something eternally hidden and concealed, while
> the Absolute is the eternally Apparent that has
> never concealed itself. The ordinary people are in
> this respect completely mistaken. They think the
> world is apparent and the Absolute is a hidden
> mystery. (Izutsu 2007:74)

From the standpoint of ego consciousness, the Absolute
and the world are two separate entities. The empirical
world is the "real world," and the Absolute is hidden
behind it. *Existentialism* turns this *essentialism* on
its head. The Absolute and the empirical world are a
seamless totality. From the standpoint of the unity of
existence, it is the world that is hidden and the Absolute
that is apparent.

Existence (*wujud*) is one single reality, but it has many
divergent forms of manifestation (*mazahir*):

> This position is established upon the fundamental
> vision of the act of "existence," which is one
> absolute reality, running through or flowing
> through all things in the universe . . . This
> fundamental vision of the reality of "existence"
> running through the whole universe, or rather we
> should say, producing the whole world of Being as
> various forms of its self-unfolding has led thinkers
> of this school towards constructing a metaphysical
> system in which the same reality of "existence"
> is given a number of degrees or stages of its self-
> unfolding or self-manifestation. (Izutsu 2007:75)

Izutsu's objective "is first to grasp the central vision of
a whole system or the spirit that animates the system
from within and informs it, and then to describe the
system as an organic evolvement of that central vision."
(Izutsu 2007:60) Shaykh Mawlay Al 'Arabi ad Darqawi

(d. 1823) spoke of this vision on the level of direct experience:

> I was in a state of remembrance and my eyes were lowered and I heard a voice say: *He is the first and the last and the Outwardly manifest and the inwardly hidden.* I remained silent, and the voice repeated it a second time, and then a third, whereupon I said: "As to the *First*, I understand, and as to the *Last*, I understand, and as to the *Inwardly Hidden,* I understand, but as to the *Outwardly Manifest,* I see nothing but created things." Then the voice said: "If there were any outwardly manifested other than Himself I should have told you." In that moment I realized the whole hierarchy of Absolute Being. (Cited in Lings1971:131)

Izutsu's philosophy of Existence provides the foundations for a meta-historical dialogue between the Far Eastern traditions, the Islamic world and the modern West.

4. On 1 November 1950, Pope Pius XII issued a papal bull. It declared that "the immaculate Mother of God, Mary ever virgin, when the course of her earthly life was finished, was taken up body and soul into the glory of heaven." Jung regarded this new dogma as turning point in the Christian aeon. He believed that the implications of the Assumption went beyond the theological domain:

> The dogma of the Assumption, proclaimed in an age suffering from the greatest political schism history has ever known is a compensating symptom that reflects the strivings of science for uniform world-picture. In certain sense both developments were anticipated by alchemy in the *hieros gamos* of opposites but only in symbolic

form. But nevertheless, the symbol has the great advantage of being able to unite heterogeneous or even incommensurable factors in a *single* image. With the decline of alchemy, the symbolic unity of spirit and matter fell apart, with the result that modern man finds himself uprooted and alienated in a de-souled world. (CW9/1:197)

At the time of writing these words, Jung was working with the physicist Wolfgang Pauli to articulate such a world picture. To conclude, I will recapitulate my dialogue with an Islamic scholar on Jung, Pauli, and Ibn 'Arabi. Samir and I believe that the Shaykh's doctrine of Unity of Being provides the metaphysical foundations that Jung and Pauli needed to formulate a theoria. encompassing quantum physics and the psychology of the unconscious.

The Breath of the Merciful: A Dialogue with Samir Mahmoud

Jung and Ibn 'Arabi were both visionary mystics, but any attempt to set up a dialogue between these two fellow travellers soon hits an epistemological roadblock. In his commentary on *The Secret of the Golden Flower*, he said, "One cannot grasp anything metaphysically, one can only do so psychologically. Therefore, I strip things of their metaphysical wrappings in order to make them the object of psychology." (CW13:73) Jung insisted that his methodology is empirical and strictly limited to the phenomenal contents of the psyche.

For Ibn 'Arabi, such an epistemology amounts to nothing less than a denial of the heart (*qalb*), the faculty by which divine being can be apprehended and known beyond the flux of phenomena. By rejecting the possibility of intellectual intuition, Jung, in effect, dismisses the foundations of Ibn 'Arabi's metaphysical perspective in one broad sweep. Out go the hierarchy of degrees of being, the unseen world (*'alam al ghayb*), and the classical distinction between microcosm and macrocosm.

This is a very one-sided critique. Jung insisted on the necessity to respect the limits of knowledge, but he did not, as some hostile critics allege, repudiate the heart. He made his position very clear in *Mysterium Coniunctionis*: "That the world inside and outside us rests on a transcendental background is as certain as our own existence." However, in the next sentence, Jung sounds a note of caution: "But it is equally certain that the direct perception of the archetypal world inside us is just as doubtfully certain as that of the physical world. If we are convinced that we know the ultimate truth concerning metaphysical things, this means nothing more than the archetypal images have taken possession of thought and feeling, so that these lose their quality as functions at our disposal." (CW14:787)

In 1946, the physicist Wolfgang Pauli returned to Europe after sitting out the war in America. He relocated to Zurich and resumed his dialogue with Jung. They were not indulging in armchair speculation. Their objective was to formulate a new world picture that would encompass modern physics and the psychology of the unconscious on the basis of a unitary psychophysical order of reality. But they both knew that this would be a mere intellectual construct if it did not include Eros and the feminine principle. Of course, the consensus amongst physicists is that Eros has absolutely nothing to do with physics or cosmology. For Ibn 'Arabi, on the other hand, divine love and compassion constitute the very root of existence. The

Absolute is beyond Being but manifests the degrees of Being through an act of love. This world-creating Eros is symbolised as the Breath of the Compassionate. The world is not created by divine fiat but from the passionate sigh of God in the primordial darkness of His isolation from His creatures. God, in his essence, yearns to manifest himself in beings to be revealed by them and for them. His ardent desire is appeased by this sigh. The Breath of the Compassionate is the substance that permeates everything and weaves the fabric of the Unity of Being.

In Arabic, the phrase "to be" also means "to find being." For Ibn 'Arabi, the alchemical opus involves shaking off one's forgetfulness of Being by transmuting the base self into its essence, gold. Beings, insofar as they have emerged from the One, are already on the path back; everything is in perpetual movement upwards, towards the One, driven by the transformative power of Eros, which is none other than the love of the One for itself.

Could Ibn 'Arabi have been the source for the new model of the universe Jung and Pauli had been seeking? Pauli maintained that a real synthesis of science and religion "must press back to the emotional source of natural science, to their fundamental archetypes and their dynamic. Then there remains no longer science but religion . . . a religion of wholeness in which natural science finds its natural place." (Lindorff 2004:213) If Jung, Pauli, and Ibn 'Arabi are talking about the same fundamental archetypes, then the way is open for a three-way dialogue.

Ibn 'Arabi's perspective is top-down: The Divine Names receive God's undifferentiated breath, and as it flows over the permanent archetypes, the essences of things in God's mind, the Breath, is inflected and differentiated. Therefore, the essences of things receive God's Being and come into existence when they are constituted in God's knowledge. This doctrine seems far removed from Jung's bottom-up model of the collective unconscious and the archetypes. But the gap closes in the course of the Jung/Pauli dialogue. For example, in *Mysterium Coniunctionis*, Jung states that "the common background of microphysics and depth psychology is as much physical as psychic and therefore neither but rather a third thing, a neutral nature which can at most be grasped in hints since its nature is transcendental."(CW.14:760) This background is the potential world of the *unus mundus*, which has all the conditions that determine the form of empirical phenomena in it. According to the alchemist Gerhard Dorn, it is "the potential world of the first day of creation, when nothing was in actu, i.e., divided into two and many but still one."[17] This idea is in agreement with Ibn 'Arabi's Oneness of Being. Simply stated, the oneness of being means there is only one being, absolute being (*al-wujud al- mutlaq*), and everything in existence is nothing but the manifestation of this absolute being. This is the case from the point of view of the Absolute itself. However, from the standpoint of relativity, existence is multiple with an underlying organic unity. This doctrine of the manyness of the One Reality (*al-wahid al kathir*) has equal status with the doctrine of Oneness of Being.

Although Jung accommodated the top-down model in his late-period works, he never abandoned his

---

[17] For an account of Jung's later archetypal theory and his hypothesis of the unus mundus see Chapter 6: 2, A Window into Eternity.

bottom-up perspective. The integration of the instinctual shadow is crucial to Jung's model of psychospiritual development, the individuation process. But this very modern idea has no place in Ibn Arabi's soteriology. The initiate ascends in a spiral of purification of the body of light which has been imprisoned in the body of gross corporeal matter. The shadow is not integrated as in Jungian individuation but discarded. Ibn 'Arabi strives after perfection; Jung aims for wholeness, which paradoxically includes imperfection. In his long essay on *Christ, a Symbol of the Self,* Jung cites Matthew 5:48: "Be you therefore perfect (teleiosis) as your heavenly Father is perfect," and his comment on it is as follows:

> To strive after teleiosis in the sense of perfection is not only legitimate but is inborn in man as a peculiarity which provides civilization with one of its strongest roots. This striving is so powerful, even, that it can turn into passion that draws everything into its service. Natural as it is to seek perfection in one way or another, the archetype (of the self) fulfils itself in completeness, and this is a teleiosis of another kind. Where the archetype predominates, completeness is forced upon us against our conscious strivings, in accordance with the archaic nature of the archetype. The individual may strive after perfection . . . but must suffer the opposite of his intentions for the sake of completeness. (CW9/2:123)

Jung concludes with a quotation from St Paul: "I find then a law, that, when I would do good, evil is present with me." (Romans 7:21) For Ibn 'Arabi, perfection and wholeness constitute a coincidentia oppositorum. The living creature is necessarily "imperfect." If it was perfect, it would be indistinguishable from God, and there would be no divine manifestation. Each creature is perfect in its imperfection. It is exactly as God intends it to be.

If any readers feel short-changed by such a tantalisingly brief piece of writing, I should explain that between 2009 and 2012, Samir Mahmoud and I made several attempts to find an institutional base and funds for a research program on Jung, Pauli, and Ibn 'Arabi (JPIA). Of course, the academic consensus omnium opposed us at every step of the way. JPIA was not to be. But the underlying theoria is indestructible. When the time is right, it will emerge like a phoenix from the ashes.

APPENDIX 1

THE OTHER FRITHJ OF SCHUON

I discovered Frithjof Schuon's book *Transcendent Unity of Religions* in 1974, when he was not well known. The English translation had been published by Faber and carried an endorsement by T. S. Eliot on the dust jacket: "I have met with no more impressive work in the comparative study of Oriental and Occidental religion." Schuon's book hit me with the force of a revelation, but at that time, I could find virtually no information about the man behind the charismatic word. In 1981, I acquired a catalogue for an exhibition of his paintings at the Taylor Museum in Colorado Springs under the title *Scenes of Plains Indian Life*. It contained some fascinating biographical background and some samples of his paintings, which were indeed impressive. There was also a rather forbidding photograph of Schuon dressed in an elegant Nehru suit and looking directly into the camera. Was this man a true charismatic or a poseur? I had to wait until 1992 for the data I would need to make an informed judgement.

In 1980, Schuon left Lausanne and relocated to Bloomington, Indiana, to be closer to his Native American friends. He established the Tariqa Maryimiah, which he presided over as Shaykh Isa Nur al din Ahmed. In 1991, a disaffected disciple Mark Koslow claimed that he had seen Schuon fondle three underage girls in a so-called primordial gathering. He reported the matter to the police, and the case was brought before a grand jury. I received the news from an American friend with stunned incredulity. I immediately contacted two UK-based tariqa members. Both were practicing Muslims, and both had known Schuon for many years. Unlike Mark Koslow, neither had a grievance against their former shaykh. But they were highly sceptical about the outcome of the trial and rightly so. Schuon was acquitted, but it emerged later that all the tariqa members lied under oath. The shaykh's fall from grace sent shock waves throughout the Traditionalist community. Some denounced him; others went into denial. Only a minority in the Traditionalist community have had sufficient objectivity to examine the evidence and face the implications.

Schuon died in 1998 and it would be a pointless exercise to put him on trial all over again. My objective is not to judge but to to understand how someone who had attained such a high level of gnosis could have undergone such a catastrophic regression. To this end, I have drawn selectively on the following sources:

- Hugh Urban's paper *A Dance of Masks: The Esoteric Ethics of Frithjof Schuon* (2002) has been indispensable. Urban maintains that the true prophet was merely a mask for the false prophet. I suspect that the true and the false prophet co-existed in the same person.

- Mark Koslow's text "Frithjof Schuon: An Account" is a treasure trove of insider information and also one of Urban's main sources. But we both agree that it is a problematic source. Koslow had a bitter personal grievance against Schuon, which raises doubts about his impartiality. He has issued a revised account that is far more sober and objective, but this is of less interest as a human document. (It is available on line: http//www.naturerights.com/knowledge%20%book/guenon.asp) I was lent the original account for about two weeks back in 1991 and took extensive notes.
- An abridged version of *The Feathered Snake* by Aldo Vidali confirms much of Koslow's Account.
- *The Veneration of the Shaykh*: an unpublished typescript with handwritten amendments by Schuon. It was written by Sa Badriyah, the shaykh's fourth "intrinsic wife." Nasr's accolade seems very low-keyed in comparison.
- In 1992 I was shown a stack of photographs of Schuon in "primordial costume" or rather his birthday suit. He is wearing an American Indian headdress and nothing else at all. In some of these photographs he is with his female devotees; in others he is on his own. I made a written record of what I saw at the time.
- Anecdotal evidence given by the two ex-tariqa members who provided these sources. Their remarks were made far more in sorrow than in anger.
- Data on the indictments of Frithjof Schuon, three signed witness statements relating to the primordial gatherings and press releases from the Bloomington *Herald Times* between October and November 1991.

Urban's essay conveys the syncretistic culture of the tariqa. It was a heady brew:

> Schuon had organized a rather unusual religious community at his home in Bloomington, Indiana. Although ostensibly begun as a traditional Sufi order, Schuon's community progressively grew into an eccentric religious synthesis, combining a variety of Eastern religions, apocalyptic imagery, esoteric sexual practices, and a great deal of symbolism drawn from Native American traditions. At the centre of the community was a form of ritual dance based primarily on the Sun Dance of the Ogala Sioux—though fairly radically reinterpreted through Schuon's metaphysical system. Indeed by synthesising the Sun Dance with Islamic mysticism and Tantric sexual yoga, Schuon professed to have revealed the universal core of all religion. (Urban 2002:406)

The primordial dances took place in a circular wooden building modelled after the Sun Dance lodge. There was a pole at the centre, a Wakan tree, and a low stool on which the great chief Brave Eagle sat. According to Mark Koslow, there were three grades of the dance:

- Indian days for visitors and those outside the Inner Circle where the women wear what amounts to Indianized bikinis.
- Gatherings of the Inner Circle (perhaps fifty to sixty people) and "qualified" visitors . . . the women are all naked except for slight loin cloths which hardly hide anything . . . The imitation Sa Badriyah does of bringing the sacred pipe is performed naked. (Schuon believed that Badriyah is an incarnation of Buffalo Cow Woman.)
- The third category is only attended by an intimate inner circle . . . They are completely

naked and the dances are more suggestive . . . and there is more intimacy with Schuon. (Mark Koslow's Account:18, cited in Urban 2002: 436, n.68)

Koslow's observations are confirmed by several court witnesses as well as by former disciples. These private primordial dances were not properly contained, and sometimes minors were allowed to be present.

The way that Schuon (aka. Brave Eagle) hijacked the sacred rite of the Sun Dance has been covered comprehensively by Professor Urban. (See Urban 2002: 417- 27)

I Am Not a Man as Other Men

For a short time in 1992, I was lent a copy of Schuon's memoirs, which were strictly reserved for tariqa members. It was rather disappointing as much of it was all about the love of his life Madeleine. He had written a love song or prophetic poem shortly before their first meeting, and after she had (sensibly) married someone else, he continued with an interminable reverie. In Jungian psychology, Madeleine is the personification of Frithjof's unconscious femininity, his soul image. "The anima image," according to Jung, "which lends the mother such superhuman glamour in the eyes of the son, gradually becomes tarnished by commonplace reality and sinks back into the unconscious, but without losing in any way its original tension and instinctivity. It is ready to spring out and project itself at the first opportunity, the moment a woman makes an impression that is out of the ordinary." (CW9/1: 141)

Schuon had intense visions of the anima in her transpersonal aspects throughout his life, the Virgin Mary, the Sioux Buffalo Cow Woman, the Buddhist Tara and Kali. The material is of considerable psychological interest:

> On my way to Morocco in 1964, when I was suffering from asthma and feeling ill to the point of death . . . there occurred . . . the contact with the Blessed Virgin. This had as its result the irresistible urge to be naked like her little child. From this time onwards I went naked as often as possible . . . later this mystery came on me again . . . with the irresistible awareness that I am not a man as other men. (Schuon, *Sacred Nudity* cited in Urban 2002: 413)

According to Sa Badriyah, who played role of anima consort in Schuon's final years, he was shown the sexual parts of the Virgin by the grace of God. (Urban 2002: 413)

The irresistible awareness that he was "not a man as other men" is pure hubris or, in Jungian terms, inflation. The archetypal figures of the collective unconscious are numinous, and the urge to identify with them is indeed irresistible. When this happens, the conscious personality inflates, and the ego becomes a mighty god. The next vision is distinctly inflationary:

> Pte- San- Win . . . the Buffalo Cow Woman of the Sioux who brought the sacred pipe to the Indians . . . was in the Mihrab (of a mosque). She was naked and he rose up with her, embracing into the air. (Schuon, The Message of the Icons, cited in Urban 2002:414)

This is a very dangerous situation. Schuon had gained access to the magical power or the mana of Buffalo Cow Woman and assimilated it into his ego. He had been transformed into a "mana personality" and he was indeed not a man like other men. Jung described this personality as "the well-known archetype of the mighty man in the form of the hero, chief, magician, medicine man, saint, the ruler of men and spirits, the friend of God." (CW7: 377) Schuon's visions were inflated transgressions in sacred order, and consequently, he was on a slippery slope to psychosis. But he might have avoided this pitfall if he had not repudiated Jung's psychological insights:

> The dissolution of the anima means that we have gained insight into the driving forces of the unconscious, but not that we have made these forces ineffective. They can attack us at any time in new form. And they will infallibly do so if the conscious attitude has a flaw in it. It's a question of might against might. If the ego presumes to wield power over the unconscious, the unconscious reacts with a subtle attack, deploying the dominant of the mana personality, whose enormous prestige casts a spell over the ego. Against this the only defence is a full confession of one's weakness in the face of the unconscious. By opposing no force we do not provoke it to attack. (CW7: 391)

It's inconceivable that Schuon would have recognised the insights of C G Jung. But he would have found exactly the same advice in Sioux mythology. According to the traditional narrative, two Lakota men encountered a mysterious and beautiful buffalo woman, completely naked with long black hair. One young man cannot resist the urge to embrace her, and he was reduced to ashes. The other approached her with humility, and he received the sacred pipe. (cited in Urban 2002: 413) Sometimes the evidence for a unanimous perennial philosophy is very compelling.

Ecce Homo

Just as there are three grades of the primordial dance, so do Schuon's esoteric paintings fall into three categories: works that outsiders can see and that can be exhibited, works where access is restricted, and "icons" that are reserved for a small circle of the elect. Some items in this third category were reproduced in Mark Koslow's account. These paintings were either by Schuon himself or executed by Sa Badriyah under the master's supervision.

The first painting I saw was by Sa Badriyah, and it was based on a photograph of Schuon that was included in Koslow's account. He is kneeling in the nude with his legs apart, and his hands pressed together above his head in a mudra. In the painting, his genitalia are surrounded by a glow of golden light. Sa Badriyah declared that she was born to paint this picture. A number of paintings showed Sa Badriyah kneeling with her hands fixed in a mudra and with her legs apart like a centre-spread model with a halo.

These paintings have been characterised as eso-porn, but this is not entirely accurate. Pornography is produced to titivate and arouse, but these works are regarded as icon's in the Schuon cult. For an insight into the latent content of these art works I will quote an illuminating passage from Robert Stoller's essay *Perversion and the Desire to Harm*:

The trauma in each perversion script—whether the story is told as a daydream, pornography, or performance in reality—is converted into a triumph. The attackers of earlier times are defeated, undone, unable to persist in their attack. Now, each new episode of the trauma is constructed so that the victim is not defeated, though the experience is carried out using the same essentials that had earlier led to the disaster. Now the victim is the victor and the trauma is a triumph, the crazy optimism of a full erection. If the story is well constructed, one feels guiltless and without anxiety. In this brilliant replay lies the idea that the old attackers have been thwarted and thereby humiliated—and the humiliation is the fundamental experience that is exchanged in these episodes. By humiliating one gets revenge for being humiliated. (Stoller 1985:32)

When Robert Stoller died in a car accident in 1986 the psychoanalytic world lost one of the most original minds since Freud. If he was still with us, I would have written to him and asked him for his opinion of Schuon's iconography. (See Stoller 1991)

The next painting is extraordinary: Shaykh Isa has his eyes open, and there is a shroud over his head. This falls over his shoulders and reaches the bottom of the picture, which stops just below his exposed genitals. His thumb and middle finger of his right hand are joined in a mudra above his left hand, which has the palm upward. The resemblance to Christ (Isa!) is unmistakable. A passage in Guenon's *Reign of Quantity* will provide the Traditionalist commentary. In a chapter titled *The Great Parody or Spirituality Inverted*, he writes about the Antichrist who will preside over a spurious spiritual restoration in the last days:

> In order to express the false carried to its extreme he will have to be so to speak "falsified" from every point of view, and to be like the incarnation of falsity itself. In order that this may be possible, and by reason of his opposition to the true in all its aspects, the Antichrist can adopt the very symbols of the Messiah, using them of course in an inverted sense. (Guenon 1972:326)

From an orthodox religious perspective, this work is blasphemous. But not from a psychological point of view- there is no such thing as blasphemy in the collective unconscious.

How did Schuon himself understand his icons? Evidently, they were given to disciples as instruments of meditation. A typescript with the title *The Veneration of the Shaykh* (composed by Badriyah with handwritten amendments by Schuon) provide the following instructions to the *fuqara*:

> Before such a prodigious outpouring of the Spirit, how can one doubt that one is faced with an "avataric" phenomenon; or with a prophetic figure; or with a great bodhisattva; in short with a spiritual manifestation of major import? Such is the simple nature of the matter which ought to determine . . . and for the disciples who understand, does determine our attitude.

The way Badriya flatters and manipulates her readers could only be convincing to someone who wanted to be deceived. She then has the gall to inform us that "there is absolutely nothing in all this that could contradict Islam." Indeed, how could it when the shaykh himself has stated that he is "the human instrument for the Religio Perennis at the end of time" and that "disciples have the right, in fact the obligation, to venerate him, to show their awareness of his grandeur and nature, to express gratitude for the privilege accorded to them, and to open themselves as far as possible to his spiritual influence . . ." As Jung observed, the wiles of the anima can utterly destroy a man.

C.G.Jung preferred "the precious gift of doubt that does not violate the virginity of things beyond our ken." (CW12a: 8) Absolute knowledge is a human possibility, but it threatens the equilibrium of the psyche. Great saints like Ibn 'Arabi or Sri Ramana Maharshi were the exception to the rule. Schuon was not. His infantile regression was a drastic corrective and a gift from the Gods.

*

Guenon, R. (1972) The Reign of Quantity and the Signs of the Times, trans. Lord Northbourne, Penguin Books Inc. Baltimore, Maryland.

Jung, C. G. Collected Works:

> CW7 (1966) Two Essays on Analytical Psychology, 2: IV The Mana Personality.
> CW9/1 (1968) The Archetypes and the Collective Unconscious, II: Psychological Aspects of the Mother Archetype.
> CW12 (1968a) Psychology and Alchemy

Stoller, R. (1985) Observing the Erotic Imagination, Yale University Press, New Haven and London. (1991)

Porn: Myths for the Twentieth Century, Yale University Press.

Urban, H. (2002) A Dance of Masks, The Esoteric Ethics of Frithjof Schuon, in Crossing Boundaries, Ethics in the History of Mysticism, ed. G. William Barnard and Jeffrey Kripal, Seven Bridges Press, New York.

APPENDIX 2

AN OVERVIEW OF *ANSWER TO JOB*

When Karl Barth read Jung's *Answer to Job*, he acknowledged that it was:

> ... a humanly very gripping document, exceedingly instructive as to the psychology of professional psychologists. As a contribution to the interpretation of the biblical Job, however, and above all of the Bible, it suffers hopelessly from the fact that the author, according to his own interpretation, has given the Word over unabashedly and recklessly to his very remarkable affect, which inhibited him from reading and pondering what lay before him in a state of calm. In this sense, his work has become completely unprofitable. (cited in Heisig 1979: 182: n.61)

From the point of view of biblical scholarship, Barth's criticism is unanswerable. But if Jung had paid too much attention to the theologians, he could not have produced such a strong misreading of the book of Job. Indeed, strong misreading is an understatement. Jung's misreading of Job is, as Barth observed, visceral in its force. (For Harold Bloom's concept of strong and weak misreading see the introductory section of Chapter 8.)

According to Murray Stein, *Answer to Job* "reveals his highly charged emotional relationship to Christianity." (Stein 1985:162) He is at one and the same time "the emotionally involved psychotherapist and angry son who brutally confronts the Father with His shortcomings":

> I cannot . . . write in a cool objective manner but must allow my emotionally subjectivity to speak . . . I do not write as a biblical scholar (which I am not), but as a layman and physician who has been privileged to see deeply into the psychic life of many people. What I am expressing is first of all my own personal view, but I know that I also speak in the name of many who had had similar experiences. (CW11:559)

Jung once said to Aniela Jaffe, "If there is anything like the spirit seizing one by the scruff of the neck, it was the way this book came into being." (L2:20) This was not the first time he had been seized like this. In a waking dream from Jung's childhood, God shits on his own church from a great height. (MDR 1995: 52-9) This shocking and incomprehensible paradox was the seed of the *Answer to Job*.

In *Aion* and then in *Answer to Job*, we find Jung stripping away the New Testament idea of God so as to work back to the monistic conception in the Old Testament. The God-image in the Old Testament is a numinous totality embodying good and evil, justice and injustice. From a psychological point of view,

Yahweh is entirely lacking in self-reflection, and his various aspects are not integrated. They can fly apart into mutually contradictory acts. This is a far cry from traditional Christian theism—or maybe not. Origen (185–254) believed that the Antichrist would not be destroyed in the last days but redeemed. This view, which was condemned as heresy at the Council of Constantinople (AD 381) appealed strongly to Jung. According to the biblical scholar Victor Maag:

> Origen showed himself to be the spiritual heir of the original Old Testament monism. As such he was closer to Jesus and the first generation of Christians than was the Council of Constantinople or the late New Testament authors with their Anti-Christ conception. (The Curatorium of the C G Jung Institute 1967:63)

My summary of *Answer to Job* will follow the threefold sequence set out in Henry Corbin's long review of Jung's book: The Absence of Sophia, the Anamnesis of Sophia, and the Exaltation of Sophia. (Corbin 2019:102-53)

The Absence

> The naïve assumption that the creator of the world is a conscious being must be regarded as a disastrous prejudice which later gave rise to the most incredible dislocations of logic. For example, the nonsensical doctrine of the privatio boni would never have been necessary had one not had to assume in advance that it is impossible for the consciousness of a good God to produce evil deeds. Divine unconsciousness and lack of reflection, on the other hand, enable us to form a conception of God which puts his actions beyond moral judgment and allows no conflict to arise between goodness and beastliness. (CW11: 600, n. 13)

Jung's Job starts out with this naïve assumption and would have continued with it had not Satan caused Yahweh to doubt the fidelity of one of his most loyal subjects. If his wealth and good fortune were taken away, Satan suggests, the pious Job would soon begin to curse his Maker. A wager is then struck between Yahweh and Satan. On the condition that he spares Job's life, Satan is free to do anything he likes to compel him to curse the Lord. If Job does so, he has won the bet.

In a very short time, the fates hit Job with devastating force. He is deprived of his considerable wealth, livestock, and servants; even his children are destroyed. But Job does not fail the test, and Yahweh wins round one: "The Lord gave and the Lord has taken away; blessed be the name of the Lord." (1:21) However, this is not enough for Satan who wants to make Job squeal. Yahweh gives him the go-ahead so long as Job's life is spared. Satan then afflicts his victim with loathsome sores. Despite this gratuitous affliction, Job does not curse his Maker. Instead, he holds his ground and demands to know directly from Yahweh what he has done to deserve all this punitive treatment. A long series of dialogues follow, in which Job's three "comforters" try to convince him that he must have sinned to merit such terrible retribution. (Job 19:25) But they say nothing to dissuade him from bringing his case before Yahweh. Neither can the far more eloquent Elihu convince Job that he should drop his case and submit to the authority of the Lord. Of course, Job knows nothing about the wager between Yahweh and Satan.

Elihu's speech prepares us for the climax of the drama, in which the Lord answers Job out of the whirlwind:

Who is this that darkens counsel by words without
knowledge?
Gird up your loins like a man.
I will question you, and you shall declare to me.
(38:1-3)

According to Jung, Yahweh's speech shows that he
is "still intoxicated with the tremendous power and
grandeur of his creation." After such an awesome
theophany extending through three chapters, Job
wisely submits to Yahweh's overwhelming might:

I had heard of thee by the hearing of the ear,
But now my eye sees thee;
Therefore, I despise myself and repent in dust and
ashes. (42:5-6)

But who is the real victor here? Confronted with such a
display of omnipotence, Job could only capitulate. But
has he also maintained that crucial millimeter of space?
Jung suggests that

Yahweh's dual nature has been revealed and
somebody or something has seen and registered
this fact. Such a revelation, whether it has reached
man's consciousness or not, could not fail to have
far-reaching consequences. (CW11:608)

He spells out what these consequences are a few pages
further on:

Yahweh has to remember his absolute knowledge;
for if Job gains knowledge of God, then God
must learn to know Himself. It just could not be
that Yahweh's dual nature should become public
property and remain hidden from Himself alone.
Whoever knows God has an effect on him. The

> failure of the attempt to corrupt Job has changed
> Yahweh's nature. (CW11:617)

The Anamnesis

At this point, a new figure enters the divine drama, "a
feminine being who is no less agreeable to Him than
to man, a friend and playmate from the beginning of
the world, the first born of God's creatures, a stainless
reflection of his glory and a master workman." She
appears in the Old Testament Wisdom literature which
was contemporaneous with the book of Job:

> When he marked out he foundations of the
> earth, then I was beside him . . . and I was daily
> his delight rejoicing before him always . . . and
> delighting in the sons of men. (Proverbs 8:29–31)

Sophia was there at the beginning, but Yahweh had
become estranged from her or had forgotten her. Now
they are reunited in the heavenly nuptials. Yahweh
will incarnate himself in the child, and in this way,
God will become man. He will learn what it is like
to be Job and rectify the injustice he had done to
his exemplary servant. In *Answer to Job*, Jung turns
Orthodox Christian dogma on its head. Instead of God
redeeming fallen man, it is man who redeems God from
the tyranny of his own unconsciousness.

The Exaltation

For the last third of his book, Jung turns his attention
to the *Revelations of John*. Unlike the book of Job, with
its straightforward narrative structure, *Revelations* is a

dense and complex work. To complicate matters further, Jung speculates about the personal psychology of the author of the apocalypse. He maintains, entirely on the grounds of psychological probability, that the author of Revelations and the writer of the three letters of John are one and the same. All the talk of perfect love of a God who is all light in the letters finds its devastating psychological compensation in the terrors of the apocalypse. He is on thin ice. We cannot even be sure if 1, 2, 3 John are by the same hand; *1 John* is anonymous, 2 and 3 are from "the elder." Modern scholars see three or more authors represented in the Johannine corpus.

God has incarnated only his light side in his only begotten Son. This is symptomatic of the split in the Christian *imago Dei* into two irreconcilable halves: the Kingdom of Heaven and the fiery world of the damned. In the *Revelations* the fiery world of the damned returns with a vengeance. But John's visions are not all violence and cataclysm. There are moments that point towards a uniting symbol that could reconcile the warring opposites:

> And a great portent appeared in heaven, a woman clothed with the sun, with the moon under her feet and on her head a crown of twelve stars.

She cries out in her pangs of birth while being threatened by a great red dragon who will devour both her and the child. But when the child is born, it is taken up to God, and the woman flees into the wilderness (*Revelations* 12:1-6). The woman clothed with the sun is an ordinary woman, not a goddess or eternal virgin. The birth of her son anticipates a complete divine incarnation, but this is for another future world, so the child is taken up to God:

Only in the last days will the vision of the sun-woman be fulfilled. In recognition of this truth, and evidently inspired by the working of the Holy Ghost, the Pope has recently announced the dogma of the *Asumptio Mariae*, very much to the astonishment of all rationalists. Mary, as the bride is united with the son in the heavenly bridal chamber, and, as Sophia, with the Godhead. (CW11:743)

The Assumption of the Virgin Mary was proclaimed as dogma by Pope Pius XII in 1950. Jung, much to almost everyone's astonishment, claimed that the declaration of the Assumption was "the most important religious event since the Reformation." (CW11:752) In fact there were two events: the theophany of the woman clothed in the sun and the Assumption of the Virgin. The exaltation of Sophia -Maria is preparatory to a further stage in the divine drama. At first, there was the Incarnation, when God the Father revealed himself in his only begotten Son. In the new dispensation, God will be born again through the third person of the Trinity, and the Holy Spirit will become incarnate in creaturely man:

This sending out of the Paraclete has still another aspect. This Spirit of Truth and Wisdom is the Holy Ghost by whom Christ was begotten. He is the spirit of physical and spiritual procreation who from now on shall make his abode in creaturely man. Since he is the Third Person of the Deity, this is as much as to say that *God will be begotten in creaturely man.* This implies a tremendous change in man's status, for now he is raised to son-ship, almost to the position of man-god . . . But that puts man, despite his continuing sinfulness, in the position of mediator, the unifier of God and creature. (CW11:692)

I will close with Henry Corbin's commentary on this passage:

No more wrath towards man and no more human terror exploding in furor. In shedding his shadow side, God unburdens man of it. God is born to man and man is born to God as Filius Sapientae, son of Sophia. This is no longer the anamnesis of Sophia as we have it in the Old Testament, but her reign and her exaltation, because we have here her mediatory work. She is defender and witness, the advocate in Heaven, and *that* is the answer to Job. (Corbin 2019:137)

*

Corbin, H. (2019) *Eternal Sophia*, trans. Cain J, in Jung, Buddhism and the Incarnation of Sophia, ed. Cazenave M, Inner Traditions, Rochester, Vermont.

Heisig, J. (1979) *Imago Dei: A Study in Jung's Psychology of Religion*, Associated University Presses, Cranbury, New Jersey and London.

Jung, C. G. (1969) Collected Works 11, Psychology and Religion West and East, VI: Answer to Job, Routledge and Kegan Paul, London.

Maag, V. (1967) The Anti-Christ as a Symbol of Evil, ed. The Curatorium of the C. G. Jung Institute, Zurich, North Western University Press, Evanston.

Stein, M. (1985/6) *Jung's Treatment of Christianity: The Psychotherapy of a Tradition*, Chiron Publications, Wilmette, Illinois.

APPENDIX 3

FREUD'S MOSES

What follows is a road not taken. I had intended to include a chapter in which I read Freud's *Moses and Monotheism* alongside Jung's *Answer to Job*. Some readers might be interested to read the Freud section of this chapter as a juxtaposition text.

In his neglected work, *Freud and Philosophy*, Paul Ricoeur distinguishes between two methods of interpretation: the hermeneutics of restoration of meaning and the hermeneutics of suspicion. The first is based on faith: "No longer the faith of the simple soul but the second faith of one who has engaged in hermeneutics, faith that has undergone criticism, post-critical faith." This faith seeks a second naivete; it seeks *to understand* what is signified, not *to explain* it reductively. The Eranos phenomenologists of religion, Gerardus van der Leeuw, Gershom Scholem, Henry Corbin, and Mircea Eliade, approach religious phenomena in this way. By contrast, the hermeneutics of suspicion repudiates phenomenological empathy. The objective is not to disclose the sacred but to banish the illusions of false consciousness. Ricoeur cites Marx, Nietzsche, and Freud as the three masters of suspicion. (Ricoeur 1970:28-9,32-3)

Freud's *Totem and Taboo* was written around the time of the break with Jung in 1912, and it would provide the template for *Moses and Monotheism* twenty years later. In the beginning, says Freud, there were small isolated human communities that were ruled by a despotic father who kept all the females to himself. If any son attempted to usurp him, he was either killed or castrated. Eventually, the sons combined forces. They killed the father and devoured him in common. Now the patricidal brothers had to avoid a reversion to the status quo ante. To this end, they all agreed to renounce the privileges of the father, and they instituted monogamy. To appease their remorse, they all felt over the parricide they also instituted the totemic feast. A specific animal was revered as a totem and it was forbidden to kill or injure this animal except on the designated day that it was ritually slaughtered and eaten by the entire male clan. The ceremonial repetition of the killing of the primal father formed the basis of a new social order with its laws and its rites. Freud maintained that this drama occurred in countless primal hordes and that the memory of it became an imprint in the mass unconscious.

In an early essay, "The Meaning of History and Religion in Freud's Thought," Philip Rieff draws a distinction between time as Chronos and time as Kairos. Whereas a moment in chronological time is identical with every other moment, a Kairos moment, such as the murder of the primal father, is unique. An event in chronological time is neutral, but a Kairos event determines the future of an individual or of an entire community.

Once it has occurred, the consequences are irreversible. According to Rieff, the idea of Kairos is a fundamental category in Freud' thought:

> For Freud, a given life history, even a given group history, must be examined in terms of crucial events occurring necessarily at a specific historical time. What is crucial needs to have happened early. There had to be a Kairos, that crucial time in the past for what then must come after. (Rieff 1951:116)

The Freudian Kairos is not an event to be anticipated, for it belongs only to the past. Once the event has occurred, it determines the fate of an individual or a community with an inexorable logic of its own. Jung's concept of the Kairos is by contrast much closer to Chinese Daoism and the *I Ching*. Freud and Jung belong together as the two faces of a Janus head.

"The Moses of Michelangelo," an essay written in 1924, reveals that Moses was a numinous figure for Freud. In 1913, the year of the irrevocable break with Jung, he went to Rome and spent hours in a deserted church that housed Michelangelo's towering statue of Moses. Here, Freud regained his second naivete:

> For no piece of statuary has ever made a stronger impression on me than this. How often I mounted the steep steps from the unlovely Corso Cavour to the lonely plaza where the deserted church stands, and have essayed to support the angry scorn of the hero's glance! Sometimes I have crept cautiously out of the half gloom of the interior as though I myself belonged to the mob on which his eye is turned- the mob which can hold no conviction, which has neither faith nor patience, which rejoices when it has regained its illusory idols. (cited in Gay 1995: 524-5)

While Jung walked round the garden with a Gnostic magus called Philemon, Freud was engaged in an active imagination with the massively embodied Moses of Michelangelo!

In *Moses and Monotheism*, Freud treats the text of Exodus like the manifest content of a dream and works his way down to the latent content. The account of this work of interpretation that follows is selective. It does not do justice to the richness and complexity of his narrative—or the suspect methodology. Freud's scandalous argument that Moses was an Egyptian and that he was the creator of the Jewish faith rested entirely on psychological probability. Without some kind of external evidence, he was standing on thin ice, and he knew it. But he was fatefully entangled with this hypothesis, and he could not extricate himself. It was like a bronze statue with feet of clay, and yet it had a compelling explanatory power. Without it, Freud had no way of accounting for the origins of Jewish identity.

In the archetypical infancy myths of the hero, the child is born of royal or aristocratic parents but abandoned and then rescued by a humble family. He may remain in ignorance about his origins for some time. But with Moses, the situation is reversed: He is born into a humble Hebrew family, left in the reeds beside the Nile, and rescued by an Egyptian princess. This unusual twist seems to betray a need to make the Egyptian Moses a Jew. But if Moses was an Egyptian, would he have adhered to something as alien to Egyptian polytheism as ethical monotheism? Enter Akhenaten, the pharaoh who had attempted unsuccessfully to impose a monotheistic reformation on Egypt around 1375 BC. His reign lasted seventeen years, and when he died, everyone reverted to the old polytheistic faith. Freud conjectured that Moses was an official in the royal court and that he had been close to Akhenaten. When the pharaoh died and his reforms were undone, there was no future for Moses. Rather than quietly go into exile, he adopted the immigrant Hebrew community as his people, instructed them in the precepts of his austere monotheistic faith, and conferred a new identity on them by means of the Egyptian practice of circumcision. Eventually, he led his chosen people out of Egypt towards the Promised Land.

Relations between Moses and his chosen people were fraught. Thomas Mann captures the mood in his novella *The Book of the Law*:

> Just past the gate was an open square, free of tents, the assembly place. That's where they were carrying on, that's where they were writhing, that's where they were celebrating their miserable freedom. They all had stuffed themselves before singing and dancing—you could see that at a glance; everywhere the square bore the traces of slaughter and gluttony. And for whom had they sacrificed, slaughtered and stuffed their bellies? There it stood. In the middle of the bare space, on a stone, on an altar pedestal it stood: an image, a piece of junk, an idolatrous absurdity: a golden calf. (Mann 2010:96)

Moses brings this ecstatic rock concert to an abrupt halt and has the ring leaders executed.

Freud believed that Moses's subjects did not submit to his authority and that, eventually, they murdered their leader. He found support for his hypothesis in Ernst Sellin, a religious historian and archaeologist who published his study of Moses in 1922. Sellin thought the murder took place at Shittim, in the east of Jordan. Freud disagreed over the location, but that was peripheral. Sellin's research was indispensable:

> To my critical sense, this book, which takes its start from the man Moses, appears like a dancer balancing on the tip of one toe. If I could not find support in an analytic interpretation of the exposure myth and could not pass from there to Sellin's suspicion about the end of Moses, the whole thing would have to remain unwritten. (Freud 1985:299)

Freud also drew on a less controversial scholar Eduard Meyer. From Meyer's account of Moses's relation to Midian and the cult centres in the desert, Freud concluded that the Egyptian Moses and Moses, the son-in-law of Jethro, could not have been the same person. The first Moses led the Hebrews out of Egypt, and the second was instrumental in establishing a new cult at the oasis of Kadesh. It was at Kadesh that the migrants for Egypt joined forces with other Semitic tribes. These tribes worshiped a savage volcano god Yahweh, the seeming antithesis of the One God of Moses. The new tribal alliance required some concessions to those returning from Egypt. Somehow the identity of the founder had to be affirmed without being acknowledged:

> The man Moses was dealt with by shifting him to Midian and Kadesh, and by fusing him with the priest of Yahweh who founded the religion. Circumcision, the most suspicious indication of dependence on Egypt, had to be retained but no attempts were spared to detach the custom from Egypt—all evidence to the contrary. (Freud 1985:284)

The pillar of smoke that became a pillar of fire at night and the Sinai theophany are elements of the Midianite Yahweh that were incorporated into the Mosaic God image. From a Freudian perspective, Jung came face-to-face with the original Yahweh when he was writing *Answer to Job* but did not know the syncretistic background and the source of "God's shadow."

Sellin's account of the death of Moses enabled Freud to transpose his account of the murder of the primal father in *Totem and Taboo* to his narrative of the Egyptian Moses. The murder of the primal father was, according to Freud, repeated in the fate of Moses, and the guilt over the deed necessitated a massive repression. Only the biblical prophets preserved Moses's ethical monotheism as a religious tradition, but his memory lived on as a content of the mass unconscious. In times of collective crisis, the dormant primal father image was reactivated, and it gripped the community with an intensity that compelled total belief. In this way, Freud was able to account for the special character of the Jews, which has survived to this day in the face of every conceivable adversity. It was the Egyptian Moses who created the Jews and who gave them both their religious identity and the self-esteem of being God's chosen people.

Freud's transposition of the primal parricide in *Totem and Taboo* to his narrative of the Egyptian Moses is problematic. The murder of the primal father took place in primordial time and was repeated over and over in countless primal hordes. By contrast, the murder of Moses is a unique event that allegedly took place in chronological time, not long after the death of Akhenaten in 1358 BC. However, for Freud, this discrepancy makes no significant difference because both murders are Kairos events. Like the primal sons, the Jews repressed the memory of the deed, which then lived on in the mass unconscious to define their identity and shape their destiny.

Towards the end of his essay on the Freudian Kairos, Rieff points out an important weakness in Freud's reconstruction of the origins of the social contract in the murder of the primal father: "Freud has picked and chosen without regard to all the data. The father-murder is but one theme in myth literature." (Rieff 1951:127) What about the fratricide theme (Cain and Abel, Joseph and his brothers) or the sacrifice of the son by the father (Abraham and Isaac)? But this would be too close to Jung's collective unconscious for comfort. In *Moses and Monotheism*, Freud argued that nothing was to be gained in introducing the concept of the collective unconscious because "the content of the unconscious, indeed, is in any case, a collective universal property of mankind." (Freud 1985:381) I'm not so sure that Freud can distance himself from Jung himself as easily as this.

In Appendix G of *Moses and Monotheism*, Freud admits that his explanations have not done justice to "the element of grandeur about everything to do with the origin of a religion, certainly including the Jewish one." Even if his account of Moses and the Exodus could be proved to be correct, it would not adequately account for the phenomenon of monotheism, the belief in the existence of only one god and no other deities. It could be argued that monotheism arises from the universal human need to be protected by a higher power and that the greater the god, the more reliable is his protection. "But a god's power does not necessarily presuppose that he is the only one." (Freud 1985:376-7) His greatness is not diminished if there are other less-powerful gods beside him (henotheism). Freud is sympathetic to the argument advanced by the believer that the idea of an exclusive deity has produced such an overwhelming effect on men because it is the eternal truth. This argument is worthy of respect, and it has the merit of doing justice to the grandeur of the subject and its effect. Freud goes on to suggest that while the believer's argument may not be the *material* truth, it is the *historical* truth: "That is to say, we do not believe there is a single god today, but that in primeval times there was a single person who was bound to appear huge at that time and who afterwards returned in men's memories elevated to divinity":

> When Moses brought the people the idea of a single god, it was not a novelty but signified the revival of an experience in the primeval ages of the human family which has long vanished from men's conscious memory. But it had been important and had produced or paved the way for such deeply penetrating changes in men's life that we cannot avoid believing that it had left behind it in the human mind some permanent traces that can be compared to a tradition. (Freud 1985:378)

Freud's *imago Dei* consists of phylogenetic traces of the primal father in the mass unconscious. This father imago is not without an element of the *mysterium tremendum*, but it is too undifferentiated. Freud's God image does not evolve out of this primitive state. In Jung's *Answer to Job* Yahweh evolves to a higher level when he is challenged by Job's superior consciousness. To this end God has to become incarnate in fallen man.

*

Freud, S. (1985) *Moses and Monotheism*, trans. Strachey, J., Pelican Freud Library, Penguin Books, London.

Gay P. ed. (1995) The Freud Reader, Vintage / Random House, London.

Mann, T. (2010) *The Tables of the Law*, trans. Faber, M. and Lehmann, S., Haus Publishing Ltd., London.1970.

Ricoeur, P. (1970) Freud and Philosophy: An Essay in Interpretation," trans. Savage, D., Yale University Press, New Haven and London.

Rieff, P.: (1951) "The Meaning of Religion in Freud's Thought," *Journal of Religion* 31:2, pp. 114-31, University of Chicago, Illinois. (2007) *Charisma: The Gift of Grace and How It Has Been Taken Away from Us*, Pantheon Books, New York.

Yerusalmi, Y. H. (1991) *Freud's Moses: Judaism Terminable and Interminable*, Yale University Press, New Haven and London.

ABBREVIATIONS

CW C. G. Jung, Collected Works, ed. Herbert Read, Michael Fordham, and Gerhard Adler, trans. R. F. C. Hull. Routledge and Kegan Paul, London.

Citations from the Collected Works in the text will be given the volume number and the paragraph number. In the bibliography, the volume number and title are followed by the title of the essay when applicable, e.g., *CW11, Psychology and Religion: West and East: Transformation Symbolism in the Mass.*

DA C. G. Jung, The Seminars Vol. 1, Dream Analysis: Notes of the Seminar Given in 1928-30, ed. W. M. McGuire, Routledge and Kegan Paul, London 1984.

L1 C. G. Jung, Letters, 1906–1950, ed. Aniela Jaffe and Gerhard Adler, trans. R. F. C. Hull, Routledge and Kegan Paul, London 1973.

L2 C.G. Jung, Letters,1951–1961, ed. Aniela Jaffe and Gerhard Adler, trans. R.F.C. Hull, Routledge and Kegan Paul, London 1976.

MDR Memories, Dreams, Reflections, ed. Aniela Jaffe, trans. R. and C. Winstone, Fontana Press, London 1995.

V C. G. Jung, Visions, Notes of the Seminar Given in 1930-34, ed. Claire Douglas, Routledge, London, 1998.

Z C. G. Jung, The Seminars, Vol. 2 Parts 1 and 2: Nietzsche's Zarathustra, Notes of the Seminar Given in 1934-9, ed. James L. Jarrett, Routledge, London 1989.

BIBLIOGRAPHY

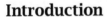

Introduction

Corbin, H. (1977) Spiritual Body and Celestial Earth, Princeton University Press, New Jersey.

Guenon, R.:

> (1962) The Crisis of the Modern World, trans. M. Pallis and R. Nicholson, Luzac and Company Ltd., London.

> (1972) The Reign of Quantity and the Signs of the Times, trans. Lord Northbourne, Penguin Books, Baltimore, Maryland.

Jung, C. G., Collected Works, eds. H. Read, M. Fordham, and G. Adler, trans. R. F. C. Hull, Routledge and Kegan Paul, London: CW9/2 (1968) Aion: Researches into the Phenomenology of the Self.

Jung, C. G., Letters Vol. 2 (1975): eds. A. Jaffe and G. Adler, trans. R. F. C. Hull, Routledge and Kegan Paul, London.

Jung, C. G. (2009) The Red Book/Liber Novus (Reader's Edition), ed. S. Shamdasani, trans. M. Kyburz, J. Peck, and S. Shamdasani. WWW Norton, New York, London.

Wilhelm, R. (1968) The I Ching or Book of Changes, trans. C.F. Baynes, Routledge and Kegan Paul, London.

Chapter 1

Clerc, O. (1997) Theories of Evolution: The Forgotten Work of Rene Quinton, The Scientific & Medical Network Review: 64.

Hirtenstein, S. (1999) The Unlimited Mercifier: The Spiritual Life and Thought of Ibn 'Arabi, Anqua Press, Oxford.

Jung, C. G. The Collected Works:

    CW4 (1961) Freud and Psychoanalysis: Some Crucial Points in Psychoanalysis.

    CW5 (1967) Symbols of Transformation

    CW6 (1971) Psychological Types: XI Definitions.

    CW8 (1969) The Structure and Dynamics of the Psyche: Analytical Psychology and Weltanschaung.

CW9/1 (1959) The Archetypes and the Collective Unconscious.

CW10 (1964/70) Civilization in Transition: The Undiscovered Self.

CW14 (1963) Mysterium Coniunctionis, An Enquiry into the Separation and Synthesis of the Opposites in Alchemy.

Jung, C. G. (1919) Psychology of the Unconscious, trans. B. M. Hinkle. Kegan Paul, Trench, Trubner and Co. Ltd., London.

Jung, C. G. Letters, Vol. 1 (1973) ed. G. Adler and A. Jaffe, trans. R. F. C. Hull, Routledge & Kegan Paul, London.

Jung, C. G. and Jaffe, A. (1995) Memories, Dreams, Reflections, trans. R. and C. Winstone, Fontana Press, London.

Neumann, E. (1954) The Origins and History of Consciousness, trans. R. F. C. Hull, Princeton University Press, New Jersey.

Noll, R:

(1995) The Jung Cult: Origins of a Charismatic Movement, Princeton University Press, New Jersey.
(1997) The Aryan Christ: The Secret Life of Carl Jung, Random House, New York.

Otto, R. (1958) The Idea of the Holy, trans. J. W. Harvey, Oxford University Press.

Chapter 2

Casey, E. (1991) Spirit and Soul: Essays in Philosophical Psychology, Spring Publications, Inc, Dallas Texas

Corbin, H.:

> (1966) The Visionary Dream in Islamic Spirituality; The Dream and Human Societies, eds. Von Grunebaum and Callais, University of California Press, Berkeley and Los Angeles.

> (1969) Creative Imagination in the Sufism of Ibn 'Arabi, trans. R. Manheim, Princeton University Press, New Jersey.

> (1977) Spiritual Body and Celestial Earth: From Mazdean Iran to Shi'ite Islam, trans. N. Pearson, Princeton University Press, New Jersey.

> (1978) The Man of Light in Iranian Sufism, trans. N. Pearson, Shambhala, Boulder and London.

> (1988) Avicenna and the Visionary Recital, trans. W. R. Trask, Princeton University Press, New Jersey.

> (1993) History of Islamic Philosophy, trans. L. Sherrard, Kegan Paul International, London and New York.

> (1995) Mundus Imaginalis in Swedenborg and Esoteric Islam, trans. L. Fox, Swedenborg Foundation, West Chester, Pennsylvania.

Dupre, L. (1993) Passage to Modernity: An Essay in the Hermeneutics of Nature and Culture, Yale University Press, New Haven and London.

Eliade, M.:

(1958) Patterns in Comparative Religion, trans. R. Sheed, Sheed and Ward, London and Sydney.

(1959) The Sacred and the Profane: The Nature of Religion, trans. W. R. Trask, Harcourt, Brace & World, New York.

(1961) Images and Symbols: Studies in Religious Symbolism, trans. P. Mairet, Sheed, Andrews and Mc Meel, Kansas.

(1962) The Two and the One, trans. J. M. Cohen, University of Chicago Press, Illinois.

(1963) Myth and Reality, trans. W. R. Trask, Harper and Row, New York.

(1969) The Quest: History and Meaning in Religion, University of Chicago Press, Illinois.

(1971) The Myth of the Eternal Return, trans. W. R. Trask, Princeton University Press, New Jersey.

Jung, C. G. The Collected Works:

CW 9/1(1968) The Archetypes and the Collective Unconscious: The Psychology of the Child Archetype.

CW 9/2 (1968) Aion: Researches into the Phenomenology of the Self.

CW16 (1966) The Practice of Psychotherapy: The Psychology of the Transference.

CW14 (1963) Mysterium Coniunctionis: An Enquiry into the Separation and Synthesis of Opposites.

CW18 (1977) The Symbolic Life, Miscellaneous Writings: On Resurrection.

Jung, C. G. and Jaffe, A. (1995) Memories, Dreams, Reflections, trans. R. and C. Winstone, Fontana Press, London.

Wasserstrom, S. (1999) Religion after Religion: Gershom Scholem, Henry Corbin, and Mircea Eliade at Eranos, Princeton University Press, New Jersey.

Chapter 3

Burckhardt, T. (1974) Cosmology and Modern Science— The Sword of Gnosis, ed. Needleman, J. (pp. 122-78), Penguin Metaphysical Library.

Coomaraswamy, A.:

(1956) Christian and Oriental Philosophy of Art, Dover Publications, New York.

(1977) Selected Papers 1, Traditional Art and Symbolism, ed. Roger Lipsey, Princeton/Bollingen.

(1977a) Athena and Hephaistos—Ananda Coomaraswamy on Traditional Art, Golgonooza Press, Ipswich.

Meister Eckhart (1979) Sermon 8, Sermons and Treatises, Vol. 1, trans. M. O' C. Walshe, Watkins Publications, Dulverton, Somerset.

Jung, C. G. Collected Works:

CW8 (1969) The Structure and Dynamics of the Psyche: Instinct and the Unconscious.

CW9/1(1968) The Archetypes and the Collective Unconscious: Concerning Mandala Symbolism.

CW10 (1970) Civilization in Transition: A Psychological View of Conscience.

CW13 (1967) Alchemical Studies: Commentary on the Secret of the Golden Flower, Paracelsus as a Spiritual Phenomenon.

CW14 (1963) Mysterium Coniunctionis, An Enquiry into the Separation and Synthesis of the Opposites in Alchemy.

Jung, C. G. and Pauli, W. (1955) The Interpretation of Nature and the Psyche, Routledge and Kegan Paul, London.

Philo of Alexandria:

(1929) De Opificio Mundi, trans. F. H. Colson and G. H. Whitaker, Loeb Classical Library.

(1981) Selections trans. D. Winstone, Classics of Western Spirituality, SPCK, London.

Schuon, F. (1982) From the Divine to the Human, trans. G. Polit and D. Lambert, World Wisdom Books, Bloomington, Indiana.

Von Franz, M. L. (1992) Psyche and Matter, trans. A. Dykes, Shambhala, Boston and London.

Chapter 4

Buber, M. (1953) Eclipse of God, Victor Gollanz Ltd., London.

Burckhardt, T. (1986) Cosmology and Modern Science in the Sword of Gnosis, ed. J. Needleman, pp. 122–178, Routledge & Kegan Paul, London.

Meister Eckhart. (1981) Sermons and Treatises Vol. 2, trans. M. O. C. Walshe, Watkins Publications, Dulverton.

Gaffney M.H. (2004) Gnostic Secrets of the Naassenes: The Initiatory Teachings of the Last Supper, Inner Traditions, Rochester, Vermont.

Guenon, R.:

(1972) The Reign of Quantity and the Signs of the Times, trans. Lord Northbourne, Penguin Metaphysical Library, Baltimore, Maryland.

(1986) Oriental Metaphysics in the Sword of Gnosis, pp. 40–56.

Jung, C. G., Collected Works:

CW7 (1966) Two Essays in Analytical Psychology.

CW8 (1969) The Structure and Dynamics of the Psyche: Basic Postulates of Analytical Psychology, Synchronicity: an Acausal Connecting Principle.

CW 9/1 (1968) The Archetypes and the Collective Unconscious: The Archetypes of the Collective Unconscious.

CW9/2 (1968) Aion: Researches into the Phenomenology of the Self.

CW11 (1969) Psychology and Religion West and East: Psychology and Religion, A Psychological Approach to the Trinity, The Holy Men of India.

CW13 (1967) Alchemical Studies: The Secret of the Golden Flower.

CW18 (1977) The Symbolic Life, Miscellaneous Writings: Religion and Psychology: A Reply to Martin Buber.

Jung, C. G. and Jaffe, A. (1995) Memories, Dreams, Reflections, trans. R and C Winstone, Fontana Press, London.

Schuon, F.

(1953) The Transcendent Unity of Religions, The Theosophical Publishing House, Wheaton, Illinois.

(1968) In Tracks of Buddhism, Allen and Unwin, London.

Upton, C. (2011) The Science of the Greater Jihad: Essays in Principial Psychology, Sophia Perennis, San Rafael, CA.

Chapter 5

Arberry, A. J. trans. (1964) The Koran, Oxford University Press.

Dorrien, G. (1997) The Word as True Myth: Interpreting Modern Theology, Westminster John Knox Press, Louisville, Kentucky.

Freud, S. (1964) Penguin Freud Library Volume 1, On Metapsychology: The Theory of Psychoanalysis, trans. J. Strachey, Penguin Books, London.

Guenon, R. The Reign of Quantity and the Signs of the Times, trans. L. Northbourne, Penguin Books, Baltimore, Maryland.

Jung, C. G. and Jaffe, A. (1995) Memories Dreams, Reflections, Fontana Press, London.

Lings, M.:

(1971) A Sufi Saint of the Twentieth Century, Shaikh Ahmad Al 'Alawi: His Spiritual Heritage and Legacy, George Allen and Unwin, London.

(1987) The Eleventh Hour: The Spiritual Crisis of the Modern World in the Light of Tradition and Prophecy Archetype, Cambridge.

Nasr, S. H. (1981) Knowledge and the Sacred, Edinburgh University Press.

Needleman, J. (1977) The Sword of Gnosis, Metaphysics, Cosmology, Tradition, Symbolism, Routledge and Kegan Paul, London.

Nietzsche, F. (2005) Thus Spake Zarathrustra, trans. G. Parkes, Oxford University Press.

Lord Northbourne (1963) Religion in the Modern World, J. M. Dent, London.

Rieff, P.:

(1966/87) The Triumph of the Therapeutic, Uses of Faith After Freud, University of Chicago Press, Illinois.

(1979) Freud, The Mind of the Moralist, University of Chicago Press, Illinois.

(1990) The Feeling Intellect, Selected Writings, ed. J. Imber, University of Chicago Press, Illinois.

(2007) Charisma, The Gift of Grace and How It Has Been Taken Away from Us, Pantheon Books, New York.

Schuon, F.:

(1968) In Tracks of Buddhism, Allen and Unwin, London.

(1998) Understanding Islam, World Wisdom Books, Bloomington, Indiana.

(1978) Stations of Wisdom, trans. G. E. H. Palmer, Perennial Books, Bedfont, Middlesex.

(1981) Esoterism as Principle and as Way, trans. W. Stoddart, Perennial Books, Bedfont, Middlesex.

(1982) From the Divine to the Human, trans. G. Polit and D. Lambert, World Wisdom Books, Bloomington, Indiana.

(1984) The Transcendent Unity of Religions, A Quest Book, Wheaton, Illinois.

(1984a) Logic and Transcendence, trans. P. N. Townsend, Perennial Books, Bedfont, Middlesex.

(1986) Survey of Metaphysics and Esoterism, trans. G. Polit, World Wisdom Books, Bloomington, Indiana.

(1999) The Language of the Self, revised translation, World Wisdom Books, Bloomington, Indiana.

Stevens, A. (1986) Withymede, A Jungian Therapeutic Community for the Healing Arts, Coventure, London.

Chapter 6

Burckhardt, T. (1986) Cosmology and Modern Science in Sword of Gnosis, ed. J. Needleman:122–178, Routledge & Kegan Paul, London.

Guenon, R.:

(1983) The Lord of the World, trans. C. Shaffer and O. de Nottbeck, Coombe Springs Press, Moorcote, Yorkshire.

(1986) Oriental Metaphysics in the Sword of Gnosis, ed. J. Needleman, Routledge & Kegan Paul, London.

(1995) The Sacred Heart and the Legend of the Grail in Fundamental Symbols: The Language of Sacred Science, compiled and edited by Michel Valsan, trans. A. Moore, Quinta Essentia, Cambridge.

Jung, C. G., Collected Works:

CW6 (1971) Psychological Types: V, The Type Problem in Poetry

CW7 (1966) Two Essays in Analytical Psychology: On the Psychology of the Unconscious 1: V, The Relations Between the Ego and the Unconscious 2:1.

CW9/1(1968), The Archetypes and the Collective Unconscious: The Psychology of the Child Archetype, Psychological Aspects of the Kore.

CW9/2 (1968) Aion: Researches into the Phenomenology of the Self.

CW 11 (1969) Psychology and Religion West and East: Answer to Job.

CW14 (1963) Mysterium Coniunctionis, An Enquiry into the Separation and Synthesis of the Opposites in Alchemy.

CW18 (1977) The Symbolic Life: On Resurrection.

Jung, C. G. (1984) Dream Analysis: Notes of the Seminar 1928-30, ed. W.M. McGuire, Bollingen Series, Princeton University Press, New Jersey.

Lings, M.:

(1971) A Sufi Saint of the 20th Century, Shaikh Ahmad Al 'Alawi, George Allen & Unwin, London.

(2001) Ancient Beliefs and Modern Superstitions, Archetype, Cambridge.

Nasr, S. H. (1981) Knowledge and the Sacred, The Gifford Lectures, Edinburgh University Press.

Osborne, A. (1970) Ramana Maharshi and the Path of Self Knowledge, Rider and Co., London.

Quispel, G. (1968) Gnostic Man: The Doctrine of Basilides, Papers from the Eranos Yearbooks 6, The Mystic Vision, trans. R. Manheim, ed. J. Campbell, Princeton University Press, New Jersey.

Schuon, F. (undated) A Note on Rene Guenon in Studies in Comparative Religion, 17:1-2, Bedfont, Middlesex.

Sedgwick, M. (2004) Against the Modern World: Traditionalism and the Secret Intellectual History of the Twentieth Century, Oxford University Press.

Chapter 7

Corbin, H. (1993) History of Islamic Philosophy, trans. L. Sherrard, Kegan Paul International, London.

Dodds, E. R. (1951) The Greeks and the Irrational, University of California Press, Berkeley and Los Angeles.

Hakl T.H. (2013) Eranos: An Alternative Intellectual History of the Twentieth Century (Trans. C. McIntosh) Equinox Publications, Sheffield and Bristol CT.

Hillman, J. (1978) The Myth of Analysis: Three Lectures, Harper and Row, New York.

Jung, C. G., Collected Works:

> CW8 (1969) The Structure and Dynamics of the Psyche: Synchronicity, An Acausal Connecting Principle.

CW12 (1968) Psychology and Alchemy.

Jung, C.G. (1988) The Seminars Volume 2, Nietzsche's Zarathrustra: notes on the Seminar given in 1934-9, ed. J. L. Jarrett, Routledge, London.

Jung, C. G. (1976) Letters Volume 2, eds. G. Adler and J. Jaffe, Routledge and Kegan Paul, London. Jung, C. G. and Jaffe, A. (1995) Memories, Dreams, Reflections, trans. R. and C. Winstone, Fontana Press, London.

Kerenyi, K.:

(1976) Dionysus: Archetypal Image of Indestructible Life, trans. R. Mannheim, Routledge and Kegan Paul, London.

(1986) Hermes, Guide of Souls, trans. M. Stein, Spring Publications, Dallas.

Meier, C. A. (1986) Body and Soul, The Lapis Press, San Francisco.

Nietzsche, F.:

(1962) Philosophy in the Tragic Age of the Greeks, trans. M. Cowan, Henry Regnery Co., Chicago, Illinois.

(1967) The Birth of Tragedy, trans. W. Kaufmann, Random House, New York.

(1968) The Will to Power, trans. W. Kaufmann and R. J. Hollingdale, Vintage Books, New York.

(1979) Ecce Homo, trans. R. J. Hollingdale, Penguin Books, London.

(2001) The Gay Science, ed. B. Williams, trans. J. Nauckhoff, Cambridge University Press.

(2005) Thus Spake Zarathrustra, trans. G. Parkes, Oxford University Press.

Otto, W.:

(1955/79) The Homeric Gods: The Spiritual Significance of Greek Religion, trans. M. Hadas, Thames and Hudson, London.

(1981) Dionysus Myth and Cult, trans. R. B. Palmer, Spring Publications, Dallas.

Pfeffer, R. (1972) Nietzsche Disciple of Dionysus, Associated Universities Press, New Jersey.

Stambaugh, J. (1972) Nietzsche's Thought of Eternal Return, John Hopkins University Press, Baltimore, Maryland.

Chapter 8

Baynes, H. G (1940) The Mythology of the Soul, Routledge & Kegan Paul, London.

Bloom, H. (1982) Agon: Towards a Theory of Revisionism, Oxford University Press, New York.

Coomaraswamy, A. (1977) Selected Papers 1: Traditional Art and Symbolism, ed. R. Lipsey, Princeton University Press, New Jersey.

Corbin, H.:

(1977) Spiritual Body and Celestial Earth, From Mazdean Iran to Shi'ite Iran, trans. N. Pearson, Princeton University Press, New Jersey.

(1978) *The Man of Light in Iranian Sufism*, trans. N. Pearson, Shambhala, Boulder and London.

(1983) Cyclical Time and Ishmaili Gnosis, Kegan Paul International and Islamic Publications, London.

Fagels, R. (1997) Homer - The Odyssey, Penguin, London.

Jung, C. G. Collected Works:

CW 9/1(1968) The Archetypes and the Collective Unconscious: On Rebirth.

CW9/2 (1968) Aion: Researches into the Phenomenology of the Self.

CW11 (1969) Psychology and Religion West and East: A Psychological Approach to the Dogma of the Trinity

Jung, C. G. (2009) The Red Book, Reader's Edition. ed. S. Shamdasani, trans. M. Kyburz, J. Peck, and S. Shamdasani, Norton, New York.

Jung, C. G. The Seminars:

(1989) Nietzsche's Zarathustra, Notes from the Seminars Given in 1934-9, ed. J. L. Jarrett, Routledge, London.

(1998) Visions, Notes of the Seminars Given in 1930-4, ed. C. Douglas, Routledge, London.

Lachmann, G. (2007) Rudolf Steiner: An Introduction to his Life and Work, Tarcher Penguin, New York.

Nasr, S. H. (1964) Three Muslim Sages, Caravan Books, New York.

Nietzsche, F.:

(1969) Thus Spake Zarathustra, trans. R. J. Hollingdale, Penguin, London.

(2001) The Gay Science, ed. B. Williams, trans. J. Nauckhoff. Poem trans. A. Del Caro, Cambridge University Press, Cambridge.

(2005) Thus Spake Zarathustra, trans. G. Parkes, Oxford University Press, Oxford.

(2005a) The Anti-Christ, Ecce Homo, and The Twilight of the Idols, eds. J. Norman, A. Ridley, trans. J. Norman, Cambridge University Press.

Prideaux, S. (2018) I Am Dynamite: A Life of Friedrich Nietzsche, Faber. And Faber, London.

Walbridge, J. (2005) Suhravardi and Illuminationism in the Cambridge Companion to Arabic Philosophy, eds. P. Adamson and R. Taylor, Cambridge University Press.

Yalom, I. D. (1992) When Nietzsche Wept, Harper Perennial, New York.

Chapter 9

Chittick, W. (1989) *The Sufi Path of Knowledge: Ibn al -'Arabi's Metaphysics of the Imagination*, State University of New York, Albany, New York.

Corbin, H. (1969) *Creative Imagination in the Sufism of Ibn 'Arabi*, Princeton University Press, New Jersey.

Jung, C. G: The Collected Works:

> CW4 (1961) Freud and Psychoanalysis: Introduction to Kransfeld's "Secret Ways of the Mind."

> CW8 (1969) The Structure and Dynamics of the Psyche: Instinct and the Unconscious, Synchronicity: an Acausal Connecting Principle.

> CW9/1(1968) The Archetypes and the Collective Unconscious: The Psychology of the Child Archetype.

> CW11 (1969) Psychology and Religion West and East: Psychology and Religion.

> CW13 (1967) Alchemical Studies: Paracelsus as a Spiritual Phenomenon.

CW18 (1977) The Symbolic Life: Miscellaneous Writings Foreword to Harding "Woman's Mysteries."

Jung, C. G. (1988) Nietzsche's Zarathustra, Notes on the Seminar Given in 1934-9 Part 1, ed. Jarrett, Routledge, London.

C. G. Jung (1973) C. G. Jung Letters Vol. 1, eds. G. Adler G and A. Jaffe, Routledge and Kegan Paul, London.

Jung, C. G. and Jaffe, A. (1995) *Memories, Dreams, Reflections*, trans. R. and C. Winston, Fontana Press, London.

Meier, C. A. (1986) *Soul and Body: Essays on the Theories of C. G. Jung*, The Lapis Press, Santa Monica.

Von Franz, M. L. (1977) *Individuation in Fairy Tales*, Spring Publications, Zurich.

Chapter 10

Izutsu, T. (1983) Sufism and Taoism: A Comparative Study of Key Philosophical Concepts, University of California Press, Berkeley, Los Angeles, London.

Jung, C. G. Collected Works:

CW7 (1966) Two Essays in Analytical Psychology: The Structure of the Unconscious, The Relations Between the Ego and the Unconscious.

CW9/2 (1968) Aion: Researches in the Phenomenology of the Self.

CW 11 (1969) Psychology and Religion West and East: Transformation Symbolism in the Mass.

CW12 (1968) Psychology and Alchemy.

Kerenyi, C. (1968) Prolegomena to Essays on a Science of Mythology, trans. R. F. C. Hull, Princeton/Bollingen, New Jersey.

Lauer, H. E. (2002) Riddles of the Soul: Depth Psychology and Anthroposophy, trans. H. E. Lauer, Appendix to Wehr G, Jung and Steiner: The Birth of a New Psychology, Anthroposophic Press, Great Barrington, Massachusetts.

Osborne, A. (1971) The Teachings of Ramana Maharshi, Rider, London.

Rawlinson, A. (1997) The Book of Enlightened Masters: Western Teachers of Eastern Traditions, Open Court, Chicago, Illinois.

Mouni Sadhu. (1957) In Days of Great Peace: The Highest Yoga as Lived, George Allen & Unwin, London.

Scholem, G. (1954) Major Trends in Jewish Mysticism, Schocken Books Inc. New York.

Chapter 11

Fowles, J. (1981) *The Aristos*, Jonathan Cape, London.

Jung, C. G. Collected Works:

CW6 (1971) Psychological Types.

CW11(1969) Psychology and Religion West and East: Psychological Commentary on the Tibetan Book of the Dead.

CW12 (1968) Psychology and Alchemy.

CW18 (1977) The Symbolic Life: The Tavistock Lectures.

Jung, C. G. (1989) Nietzsche's Zarathustra Notes of the Seminar given in 1934-9, ed. J. L. Jarrett, Routledge, London.

Jung, C. G. and Shamdasani, S. (2009) The Red Book/ Liber Novis, A Reader's Edition, ed. S. Shamdasani, trans. M. Kyburz, J. Peck, and S. Shamdasani, Philemon Series, W. W. Norton & Company, New York and London.

Lynn, R. J. (1994) The Classic of Changes: A New Translation of the I Ching as Interpreted by Wang Bi, Columbia University Press, New York.

Nietzsche, F.:

(1998) Beyond Good and Evil, trans. M. Faber, Oxford University Press.

(2001) The Gay Science, ed. B. Williams, trans. J. Nauckhoff, Cambridge University Press.

(2005) Thus Spake Zarathrustra, trans. G. Parkes, Oxford University Press.

(2005a) The Anti-Christ, Ecce Homo, Twilight of the Idols, trans. J. Norman, eds. A. Ridley and J. Norman, Cambridge University Press.

Ritsema R. and Sabbadini S. (trans.) (2005) The Original I Ching Oracle, Watkins Publishing, London.

Waley, A. (1934) The Way and Its Power: A Study of the Tao Te Ching and Its Place in Chinese Thought, George Allen and Unwin, London.

Wilhelm, R. (1967) I Ching or Book of Changes, trans. C. F. Baynes Bollingen Foundation, Princeton, New Jersey.

Zhang, D. (2002) Key Concepts in Chinese Philosophy, trans. E. Ryden, Yale University Press, New Haven and London.

Chapter 12

Addas, C. (1993) Quest for the Red Sulphur, The Life of Ibn 'Arabi, trans. P. Kingsley, Islamic Texts Society, Cambridge.

Bodeus, R. (1998) Aristotle: In the Pimlico *History of Western Philosophy*, ed. R. Popkin, Pimlico, London.

Buber, M. (1953) The Eclipse of God, Victor Gollancz, London.

Chittick, W. (1989) The Sufi Path of Knowledge, Ibn al 'Arabi's Metaphysics of the Imagination, State University of New York.

Chodkiewicz, M. (1993) An Ocean without Shore: Ibn 'Arabi's Book of the Law, trans. D. Streight, State University of New York.

Corbin, H. (1969) Creative Imagination in the Sufism of Ibn 'Arabi, trans. R Manheim, Princeton University Press, New Jersey.

Dagli, C. (trans.) (2004) The Ringstones of Wisdom (Fusus al Hikam), Great Books of the Islamic World/Kazi Publications, Chicago, Illinois.

Izutsu, T. (1983) Sufism and Taoism, A Comparative Study of Key Philosophical, University of California Press, Berkeley, Los Angeles and London.

Jung, C. G. Collected Works:

CW6 (1971) Psychological Types: The Relativity of the God Concept in Meister Eckhart.

CW7 (1966) Two Essays on Analytical Psychology: The Relations Between the Ego and the Unconscious.

CW 9/1 (1971) The Archetypes and the Collective Unconscious: The Psychology of the Child Archetype.

CW9/2 (1968) Aion: Researches into the Phenomenology of the Self.

CW11 (1969) Psychology and Religion West and East: Psychology and Religion, The Holy Men of India.

CW12 (1968) Psychology and Alchemy.

CW 14 (1963) Mysterium Coniunctionis, An Enquiry into the Separation and Synthesis of Psychic Opposites in Alchemy.

CW16 (1966) The Practice of Psychotherapy: The Psychology of the Transference.

CW18 (1977) The Symbolic Life: Religion and Psychology: A Reply to Martin Buber.

Jung, C. G. (1998) Visions, Notes on the Seminars Given in 1930-34, ed. C. Douglas, Vols. 1 and 2, Routledge, London.

Jung C. G (1973) Letters Volume 1 (1976) Letters Volume 2, eds. G. Adler and A. Jaffe) Routledge and Kegan Paul, London.

Jung, C. G. and Jaffe, A. (1995) Memories, Dreams, Reflections, trans. R. and C. Winstone, Fontana Press, London.

Murata, S. (1992) The Tao of Islam, A Sourcebook on Gender Relations in Islamic Thought, State University of New York.

Nettler, R. (2003) Sufi Metaphysics and Quranic Prophets, Ibn 'Arabi's Thought and Method in the Fusus al Hikam, Islamic Texts Society, Cambridge.

Osborne, A. (1970) Ramana Maharshi and the Path of Self Knowledge, Rider, London.

Otto, R.:

(1931) Religious Essays: A Supplement to the Idea of the Holy, trans. B. Lunn, Oxford University Press.

(1958) The Idea of the Holy, trans. J. W. Harvey, Oxford University Press.

Pilard, N. (2015) Jung and Intuition, On the Centrality and Variety of Forms of Intuition in Jung and Post-Jungians, Karnac, London.

Schleiermacher, F. (1996) On Religion, Speeches to its Cultured Despisers, trans. R. Crouter, Cambridge University Press.

Schuon, F. (1999) The Language of the Self, revised translation, World Wisdom Books, Bloomington, Indiana.

Shah Kazemi, R. (2006) Paths to Transcendence According to Shankara, Ibn Arabi and Meister Eckhart, World Wisdom Books, Bloomington, Indiana.

Chapter 13

Bair, D. (2003) Jung: A Biography, Little Brown & Co. New York and London.

Chodkiewicz, M. (1993) An Ocean without Shore: Ibn' Arabi and The Book of the Law, trans. D. Streight, State University of New York.

Corbin, H.:

> (1969) Creative Imagination in the Sufism of Ibn 'Arabi, trans. R. Manheim, Princeton University Press, New Jersey.

> (2019) Jung, Buddhism, and the Incarnation of Sophia, ed. M. Cazenave, trans. J. Cain, Inner Traditions, Rochester, Vermont.

Dagli, C. K. (trans.) (2004) Ibn 'Arabi: The Ringstones of Wisdom, Great Books of the Islamic World, Kazi Publications, Chicago, Illinois.

Edinger, E. F. (1992) Transformation of the God Image: An Elucidation of Jung's Answer to Job, Inner City Books, Toronto.

Izutsu, T. (1983) Sufism and Taoism: A Comparative Study of Key Concepts, University of California Press, Berkeley, Los Angeles, London.

Jung, C. G., Collected Works:

>CW6 (1971) Psychological Types.

>CW8 (1960) The Structure and Dynamics of the Psyche: On the Nature of the Psyche.

>CW9/1(1968) The Archetypes and the Collective Unconscious: The Psychology of the Trickster.

>CW11(1969) Psychology and Religion West and East: Answer to Job.

>CW12 (1968) *Psychology and Alchemy.*

>CW13(1967) Alchemical Studies: Paracelsus as a Spiritual Phenomenon.

Jung, C. G. (1998) The Visions Seminars. ed. C. Douglas, Routledge, London.

Jung, C. G. (1976) Letters Volume 2, eds. G. Adler and A. Jaffe. Routledge and Kegan Paul, London.

Jung, C. G. and Jaffe, A. (1995) Memories, Dreams, Reflections, trans. R. and C. Winston, Fontana Press, London.

Jung, C. G. and Neumann, E. (2015) Analytical Psychology in Exile: The Correspondence of C.G Jung and Erich Neumann (2015) ed. M. Liebscher, trans. H. McCartney, Philemon Series, Princeton University Press, New Jersey.

Neumann, E. (1989) The Place of Creation, trans. H. Nagel, Princeton University Press, New Jersey.

Otto, R. (1950) The Idea of the Holy, trans. J. W. Harvey, Oxford University Press.

Rieff, P. (1990) The Feeling Intellect, ed. J. Imber, University of Chicago Press, Illinois.

Schlamm, L. (2008) Active Imagination in Answer to Job, in Dreaming the Myth Onward: New Directions in Jungian Therapy and Thought, ed. L. Huskinson, Routledge, London.

Chapter 14

Burckhardt, T.:

> (1975) The Wisdom of the Prophets (Fusus al-Hikam), trans. A. Culme-Seymour, Beshara Publications, Aldsworth, Gloucestershire.

(1976) An Introduction to Sufi Doctrine, trans. D. M. Matheson, Aquarian Press, Wellingborough, Northhamptonshire.

(1977) Mystical Astrology According to Ibn 'Arabi, trans. B Rauf, Beshara Publications, Aldsworth, Gloucestershire.

(1983) Universal Man (Abd Al -Karim Al-Jili), trans. A. Culme-Seymour, Beshara Publication, Sherborne, Gloucestershire.

Corbin, H. (1986) Temple and Contemplation, trans. P. and L Sherrard, KPI, London, Boston and Henley/Islamic Publications, London.

Ferrer, J. N. (2002) Revisioning Transpersonal Theory, A Participatory Vision of Human Spirituality, State University Press of New York.

Hakl, T. H. (2013) *Eranos:* An Alternative Intellectual History of the Twentieth Century, Equinox Publishing, Sheffield and Bristol, Connecticut.

Hillman, J. (1977) Revisioning Psychology, Harper and Row, New York.

Izutsu, T.:

(1983) Sufism and Taoism: A Comparative Study of Key Philosophical Concepts, University of California Press, Berkeley and Los Angeles.

(2007) The Concept and Reality of Existence, Islamic Book Trust, Malaysia.

Jung, C. G., Collected Works:

CW 9/1 (1968) The Archetypes and the Collective Unconscious: The Phenomenology of the Spirit in Fairy Tales.

CW 9/2 (1968) Aion: Researches into the Phenomenology of the Self.

CW 10 (1970) Civilization in Transition: The Meaning of Psychology for Modern Man.

CW 13 (1967) Alchemical Studies: Commentary on The Secret of the Golden Flower.

CW 14 (1963) Mysterium Coniunctionis, An Enquiry into the Separation and Synthesis of the Opposites in Alchemy.

Jung, C. G. and Jaffe, A. (1995) Memories, Dreams, Reflections, Fontana Press, London.

Lindorff, D. (2004) Pauli and Jung: The Meeting of Two Great Minds, Quest Books, Wheaton, Illinois.

Lings, M. (1971) A Sufi Saint of the Twentieth Century: Shaikh Ahmad Al-Alawi His Spiritual Heritage and Legacy, George Allen & Unwin, London.

Lipton, G. (2018) Rethinking Ibn 'Arabi, Oxford University Press.

Osborne, A. (1971) The Teachings of Ramana Maharshi, Rider, London.

Schelling, F. W. J. (2007) Historical - Critical Introduction to the Philosophy of Mythology, trans. M. Richey and M. Zisselsberger, State University of New York.

Schuon, F. (2005) Understanding Islam, New Age Books, New Delhi.

Sells, M. (1994) Mystical Languages of Unsaying, University of Chicago Press, Illinois.

Stein, M (1985) Jung's Treatment of Christianity: The Psychotherapy of a Tradition, Chiron Publ., Wilmette, Illinois.

Versluis, A.:

(1994) *Theosophia:* Lindisfarne Press, New York.

(2000) *Wisdom's Book:* The Sophia Anthology: Hidden Dimensions of Christianity, Paragon House, St. Paul, Minnesota.

(2004) Wisdom's Children: A Christian Esoteric Tradition, State University Press of New York.

Wasserstrom S.M., (1999) Religion After Religion: Gershom Scholem, Mircea Eliade and Henry Corbin at Eranos, Princeton University Press, Princeton, New Jersey.

Printed and bound by CPI Group (UK) Ltd, Croydon, CR0 4YY